Copyright 2020 by Bert Moody -All rights reserved.

No part of this publication may be reproduced, distributed, or transmitted in any form or by any means, including photocopying, recording, or other electronic or mechanical methods, without the prior written permission of the publisher, except in the case of brief quotations embodied in reviews and certain other non-commercial uses permitted by copyright law.

This Book is provided with the sole purpose of providing relevant information on a specific topic for which every reasonable effort has been made to ensure that it is both accurate and reasonable. Nevertheless, by purchasing this Book you consent to the fact that the author, as well as the publisher, are in no way experts on the topics contained herein, regardless of any claims as such that may be made within. It is recommended that you always consult a professional prior to undertaking any of the advice or techniques discussed within.This is a legally binding declaration that is considered both valid and fair by both the Committee of Publishers Association and the American Bar Association and should be considered as legally binding within the United States.

CONTENTS

- Introduction 6
- Chapter 1: Instant Pot Air Fryer Lid Basics 7
  - Instant Pot Air Fryer Lid 7
  - The Proper Way to Use Instant Pot Air Fryer Lid 7
  - Functions and Buttons of Air Fryer Lid 7
  - Benefits of Using Air Fryer Lid 8
  - Care and Cleaning 9
- Chapter 2: Breakfast 10
  - Delicious Breakfast Potatoes 10
  - Breakfast French Toast Sticks 10
  - Classic Cheese Sandwich 10
  - Easy Breakfast Biscuits 10
  - Breakfast Potato Hash 11
  - Perfect Egg Bites 11
  - Breakfast Bagels 11
  - Cajun Sausage 12
  - Almond Flour Breakfast Biscuits 12
  - Tasty Tater Tots 12
  - Egg Stuffed Peppers 13
  - Healthy Egg Stuffed Avocado 13
  - Baked Oatmeal 13
  - Healthy Banana Muffins 13
  - Cheesy Egg Muffins 14
  - Healthy Quinoa Egg Muffins 14
  - Broccoli Breakfast Muffins 14
  - Jalapeno Cheese Biscuits 15
  - Breakfast Sausage Balls 15
  - Soft Sweet Potato Rolls 15
  - Cheddar Cheese Sausage Biscuits 15
  - Homemade Breakfast Sausage 16
  - Italian Egg Muffins 16
  - Spinach Ham Egg Muffins 16
  - Pizza Egg Muffins 17
  - Pumpkin Pie Muffins 17
  - Broccoli Bacon Egg Muffins 17
  - Delicious Frittata Muffins 18
  - Breakfast Sausage Patties 18
  - Turkey Patties 18
  - Tasty Breakfast Cookies 19
  - Zucchini Breakfast Cakes 19
  - Breakfast Sausage Balls 19
  - Tasty Pecan Pie Muffins 20
  - Oats Raspberry Muffins 20
  - Kale Egg Muffins 20
  - Cheddar Kale Egg Cups 20
  - Perfect Broccoli Tater Tots 21
  - Sweet Potato Chickpea Breakfast Hash 21
  - Cinnamon Sweet Potato Muffins 21
  - Vegetable Breakfast Hash 22
  - Healthy Oatmeal Cups 22
  - Roasted Sweet Potatoes 22
  - Oat Cinnamon Muffins 23
  - Breakfast Quiche Cups 23
  - Healthy Kale Muffins 23
  - Tomato Spinach Egg Muffins 24
  - Blueberry Breakfast Muffins 24
  - Delicious Banana Muffins 24
  - Tomato Pepper Egg Cups 25
- Chapter 3: Poultry 26
  - Cheese Garlic Chicken Wings 26
  - Tender & Juicy Chicken Tenders 26
  - Juicy Chicken Breasts 26
  - Easy & Tasty Parmesan Chicken 26
  - Delicious Lemon Chicken 27
  - Simple & Quick Chicken Tenders 27
  - Flavorful Chicken Breast 27
  - Perfect Air Fry Chicken Breast 28
  - Chicken with Vegetables 28
  - Tasty Chicken Fajitas 28
  - Perfect Chicken Thighs 28
  - Parmesan Chicken Tenders 29
  - Spicy Hassel Back Chicken 29
  - Delicious Bagel Chicken Tenders 29
  - Perfectly Tender Chicken Breast 30
  - Healthy Chicken Drumsticks 30
  - Easy BBQ Chicken Legs 30
  - Quick BBQ Chicken Breast 30
  - Crispy Chicken Drumsticks 31
  - Lemon Pepper Chicken Breasts 31
  - Mexican Chicken 31
  - Perfect Juicy Chicken Drumsticks 31
  - Asian Chicken Breast 32
  - Ranch Chicken Wings 32
  - Ginger Garlic Chicken Thighs 32
  - Air Fry Chicken Livers 33
  - Spicy & Easy Chicken Drumsticks 33
  - Delicious Lemon Pepper Chicken Thighs 33
  - Meatballs 34
  - Asian Chicken Thighs 34
  - Juicy Turkey Legs 34
  - Turkey Skewers 34
  - Turkey Patties 35
  - Best Baked Chicken Drumsticks 35
  - Tasty Cajun Chicken Thighs 35
  - Honey Dijon Chicken 35
  - Tasty Chicken Fritters 36
  - Healthy Chicken Vegetable Patties 36
  - Easy Ranch Chicken Wings 36
  - Easy Chicken Nuggets 37
  - Jerk Chicken 37
  - Flavors Chicken Wings 37
  - Spicy Chicken Wings 37
  - Rosemary Chicken Breasts 38
  - Delicious Sriracha Chicken Wings 38
  - Delicious Turkey Nuggets 38
  - Easy Turkey Patties 38
  - Ginger Garlic Chicken Thighs 39
  - Cajun Chicken Breasts 39
  - Flavorful Chicken & Potatoes 39
- Chapter 4: Beef, Pork & Lamb 40
  - Juicy & Tender Pork Chops 40
  - Dijon Maple Pork Chops 40
  - Mesquite Seasoned Pork Chops 40
  - Simple Spiced Pork Chops 40
  - Quick & Simple Pork Chops 41

Pork Sausage Balls 41	Quick Taco Shrimp 58
Pork Chops with Sauce 41	Delicious Crab Cakes 58
Perfect Air Fry Pork Chops 42	Perfect Air Fryer Salmon 58
Juicy Ranch Pork Chops 42	Healthy Coconut Shrimp 58
Herb Seasoned Pork Chops 42	Simple Garlic Butter Salmon 59
Cheese Mustard Pork Chops 42	Herbed Salmon 59
Crispy Crusted Pork Chops 43	Air Fryer Cod 59
Delicious & Moist Pork Chops 43	Healthy Salmon Patties 60
Asian Pork Ribs 43	Honey Glazed Fish Fillets 60
Marinated Pork Chops 44	Dijon Crab Cakes 60
Greek Ribeye Steak 44	Breaded Cod 60
Cripsy Pork Belly Bites 44	Shrimp Fajitas 61
Crunchy Pork Belly Crack 44	Delicious Lemon Pepper Shrimp 61
Baked Pork Chops 45	Shrimp with Pepper & Zucchini 61
Perfect Baked Pork Chops 45	Old Bay Shrimp 61
Delicious Mini Meatloaf 45	Shrimp with Sausage & Peppers 62
Steak & Mushrooms 45	Rosemary Garlic Shrimp 62
Tasty & Juicy Steak 46	Garlic Tomato Shrimp 62
Air Fry Steak Bites 46	Cajun Shrimp 62
Mexican Steak Fajitas 46	Spicy Lemon Pepper Shrimp 63
Meatballs 46	Lemon Pepper Tilapia 63
Steak Bites with Potatoes 47	Delicious Tuna Patties 63
Beef with Veggies 47	Chili Honey Salmon 64
Marinated Steak Fajitas 47	Flavorful Marinated Fish Fillets 64
Meatballs 48	Rosemary Basil Salmon 64
Beef Skewers 48	Baked Fish Fillet with Pepper 64
Easy Beef Patties 48	Greek Fish Fillets 65
Meatballs 49	Cheese Herb Cod 65
Tasty Pork Riblets 49	Delicious Air Fry Prawns 65
Meatballs 49	Cheese Garlic Shrimp 65
Healthy Pork Patties 49	Tasty Tuna Patties 66
Juicy & Tender Lamb Chops 50	Delicious Blackened Shrimp 66
Flavors Rosemary Thyme Lamb Chops 50	Cajun Fish Fillets 66
Herb Pork Chops 50	Air Fry Scallops 67
Classic Lamb Chops 50	White Fish Fillets 67
Onion Pork Chops 51	Spicy Scallops 67
Beef Zucchini Burgers 51	Shrimp with Vegetables 67
Meatballs 51	Miso White Fish Fillets 68
Cinnamon Lamb Chops 52	Air Fry Tilapia 68
Crispy Pork Chops 52	Tasty Crab Patties 68
Cheese Cracker Crust Pork Chops 52	Smoked Paprika Salmon 68
Meatballs 52	Pesto Fish Fillets 69
Cheesy Beef Patties 53	Easy Shrimp Scampi 69
Meatballs 53	Mediterranean Fish Fillet 69
Meatballs 53	Citrusy Salmon 69
Delicious Beef Kebabs 54	Easy Lemon Garlic Shrimp 70
Meatballs 54	Delicious Fish Sticks 70
Honey Garlic Pork Chops 54	Cheesy Baked Tilapia 70
Pork Tenderloin 54	Pecan Crust Halibut Fillets 71
Basil Pork Loin 55	Bagel Seasoned Fish Fillets 71
Pork Belly Strips 55	Tasty Pesto Scallops 71
Cajun Pork Chops 55	Cheese Crust Salmon 71
Honey Ginger Pork Shoulder 55	Baked Halibut Fillets 72
Flavors Beef Strips 56	Basil Mahi Mahi 72
Easy Mustard Pork Chops 56	Cheese Paprika Cod 72
Chapter 5: Fish & Seafood 57	Blackened Fish Fillets 72
Parmesan Shrimp 57	Chapter 6: Vegetables & Side Dishes 74
Quick & Healthy Salmon 57	Herb Mushrooms 74
Easy Tuna Cakes 57	Lemon Garlic Brussels Sprouts 74
Crispy White Fish Fillets 57	Cheesy Veggie Fritters 74

Potato Patties	74
Air Fry Corn	75
Simple Crisp Tofu	75
Spicy Sweet Potato Fries	75
Zucchini Cheese Burger	76
Roasted Cauliflower	76
Roasted Potatoes	76
Roasted Asparagus	76
Roasted Carrots & Potatoes	77
Spicy Brussels Sprouts	77
Flavorful Ranch Potatoes	77
Broccoli Fritters	78
Roasted Mushrooms & Cauliflower	78
Cauliflower Tomato Roast	78
Healthy Roasted Asparagus	78
Roasted Cauliflower & Pepper	79
Easy Roasted Broccoli	79
Air Fry Bell Peppers	79
Tasty Eggplant Cubes	80
Air Fry Green Beans	80
Air Fried Okra	80
Garlicky Baby Potatoes	80
Spicy Cauliflower Florets	81
Sweet Potatoes & Brussels Sprouts	81
Spicy Brussels Sprouts	81
Crispy Green Beans	81
Chili Lime Sweet Potatoes	82
Healthy Air Fry Mushrooms	82
Tasty Butternut Squash	82
Zucchini Cheese Patties	83
Rosemary Potatoes	83
Tofu Bites	83
Chickpea Zucchini Patties	83
Roasted Brussels Sprouts	84
Old Bay Seasoned Cauliflower Florets	84
Tasty Herb Mushrooms	84
Green Beans & Potatoes	85
Simple Air Fry Cabbage	85
Zucchini & Squash	85
Bagel Seasoned Brussels Sprouts	85
Air Fry Mix Vegetables	86
Simple & Healthy Asparagus	86
Easy Green Beans	86
Flavorful Okra	86
Broccoli & Brussels Sprouts	87
Stuffed Peppers	87
Roasted Carrots	87
Potato Beans & Mushrooms	88
Cheesy Zucchini Eggplant	88
Roasted Squash	88
Healthy Ratatouille	89
Healthy Artichoke Hearts	89
Tasty Green Beans	89
Cinnamon Butternut Squash	89
Balsamic Vegetables	90
Healthy Root Vegetables	90
Roasted Vegetables	90
Chapter 7: Snacks & Appetizers	**91**
Spicy Cashew Nuts	91
Tasty Hassel Back Potatoes	91
Crunchy Chickpeas	91
Cauliflower Hummus	91
Crispy Tofu	92
Honey Cinnamon Potato Bites	92
Air Fry Nuts	92
Spicy Walnuts	92
Tasty Roasted Olives	93
Sweet Potato Quinoa Patties	93
Tasty Carrot Fries	93
Delicious Jalapeno Poppers	94
Maple Chickpeas	94
Spicy Potato Fries	94
Tasty Potato Wedges	94
Vegetable Skewers	95
Flavorful Green Beans	95
Cheesy Cauliflower and Broccoli	95
Broccoli Patties	96
Tasty Jalapeno Poppers	96
Healthy Roasted Nuts	96
Zucchini Chips	96
Cream Cheese Stuff Mushrooms	97
Savory Pecans	97
Meatballs	97
Roasted Olives	97
Ranch Potato Wedges	98
Easy Apple Chips	98
Beef Burger Patties	98
Cheesy Zucchini Fries	98
Delicious Zucchini Chips	99
Turkey Stuffed Poblanos	99
Easy Ranch Zucchini Chips	99
Healthy Beetroot Chips	100
Meatballs	100
Air Fry Vegetables	100
Meatballs	100
Meatballs	101
Eggplant Fries	101
Radish Chips	101
Cajun Zucchini Chips	102
Spicy Okra	102
Tasty Cajun Potato Wedges	102
Spicy Baby Potatoes	102
Tasty Potato Chips	103
Roasted Nuts	103
Healthy Kale Chips	103
Crispy Onion Rings	103
Tasty BBQ Chickpeas	104
Vegetable Fritters	104
Cheesy Carrot Fries	104
Stuffed Mushrooms	105
Stuffed Sweet Peppers	105
Easy Cauliflower Popcorn	105
Cheesy Cauliflower Bites	105
Easy Cinnamon Cashews	106
Simple Crisp Bacon Slices	106
Flavors Jalapeno Poppers	106
Paprika Eggplant Chips	106
Blue Cheese Jalapeno Poppers	107
Chapter 8: Dehydrate	**108**
Dehydrated Brussels Sprouts	108

Dehydrated Zucchini Chips	108
Dehydrated Eggplant Slices	108
Dehydrated Zucchini Chips	108
Dehydrated Carrots	109
Dehydrated Cauliflower Popcorn	109
Dehydrated Broccoli Chips	109
Dehydrated Squash Chips	109
Dehydrated Sweet Potato Chips	110
Dehydrated Bell Peppers	110
Dehydrated Kale Chips	110
Dehydrated Kiwi	110
Dehydrated Pecans	110
Dehydrated Raspberries	111
Dehydrated Almonds	111
Dehydrated Strawberries	111
Dehydrated Pineapple Slices	111
Dehydrated Green Apple Slices	112
Dehydrated Mango	112
Dehydrated Apple Chips	112
Dehydrated Spicy Almonds	112
Dehydrated Peach	113
Dehydrated Bananas	113
Dehydrated Mango	113
Dehydrated Pork Jerky	113
Dehydrated Eggplant	114
Dehydrated Turkey Jerky	114
Dehydrated Cucumber Slices	114
Dehydrated Beet	114
Dehydrated Tomato	114
Dehydrated Beef Jerky	115
Dehydrated Flank Steak Jerky	115
Dehydrated Green Beans	115
Dehydrated Parsnips	115
Dehydrated Salmon Jerky	116
Dehydrated Carrot	116
Dehydrated Chicken Jerky	116
Dehydrated Dragon Fruit	116
Dehydrated Asian Salmon Jerky	117
Dehydrated Orange	117
Dehydrated Mexican Pork Jerky	117
Dehydrated Lamb Jerky	117
Dehydrated Teriyaki Beef Jerky	118
Dehydrated Spicy Beef Jerky	118
Dehydrated Tofu Jerky	118
Dehydrated Kiwi	118
Dehydrated Asian Beef Jerky	119
Dehydrated Chickpeas	119
Dehydrated Pineapple Pieces	119
Dehydrated Summer Squash	119
Dehydrated Eggplant Bacon	119
Dehydrated Shredded Carrots	120
Dehydrated Tomatoes	120
Dehydrated Okra	120
Dehydrated Pear	120
Dehydrated Lemon	120
Dehydrated Mushroom	121
Dehydrated Snap Peas	121
Dehydrated Avocado	121
Dehydrated Parsnips Chips	121
Chapter 9: Desserts	122
Greek Blueberry Muffins	122
Delicious Lemon Cupcake	122
Choco Peanut Butter Muffins	122
Baked Apple Slices	122
Chocolate Brownies Muffins	123
Low-Carb Chocolate Muffins	123
Moist Lemon Muffins	123
Healthy Carrot Muffins	124
Baked Peaches	124
Delicious Banana Walnut Muffins	124
Chocolate Lava Cake	125
Yummy Nutella Sandwich	125
Sweet Pineapple Wedges	125
Quick Choco Mug Cake	125
Cinnamon Pineapple Slices	126
Coconut Sunbutter Brownie Bites	126
Zucchini Coconut Muffins	126
Easy Chocolate Cookies	127
Healthy Nut Cookies	127
Peanut Butter Cookies	127
Pumpkin Cookies	127
Hazelnut Cookies	128
Delicious Gingersnap Cookies	128
Almond Cookies	128
Cranberry Orange Cupcakes	129
Vanilla Butter Cupcakes	129
Choco Chip Pumpkin Muffins	129
Brownies Cupcake	130
Chocolate Banana Muffins	130
Lemon Cinnamon Apple Slices	130
Strawberry Muffins	130
Cream Cheese Muffins	131
Easy Lemon Cheese Muffins	131
Chocolate Walnut Cupcakes	131
Cinnamon Cranberry Cupcakes	132
Simple Blueberry Cupcakes	132
Chocolate Chip Cookies	132
Cinnamon Pumpkin Pie	133
Easy Nutella Cupcakes	133
Flour-Less Banana Muffins	133
Fudgy Brownie Bites	133
Butter Cookies	134
Blonde Brownie Bites	134
Choco Chip Brownie Bites	135
Chocolate Almond Butter Muffins	135
Coffee Cupcakes	135
Zucchini Muffins	135
Walnut Cookies	136
Cappuccino Muffins	136
Chocolate Macaroon	136
Chapter 10: 30-Day Meal Plan	138
Appendix : Recipes Index	139

Introduction

The instant pot air fryer lid is one of the members that come from the instant pot family. It is a versatile cooking appliance that makes your daily cooking process a fast and convenient way. Using an air fryer lid you can easily convert your instant pot into a mini convection oven. The air fryer lid is one of the multifunctional cooking appliances available in the market. It converts your instant pot into an advanced air fryer machine that not only air fry your food but also roast, bake, dehydrate, reheat and broil food. It performs 6 different cooking functions in single appliances. You never need to buy a separate appliance for each function.

The air fryer lid is used instant hot air ventilation mechanism to cook your food fast and gives you even cooking results. It blows 400°F hot air with the help of a convection fan to gives you food even and faster-cooking results. It's even crisp techniques give your food nice crispy and golden texture. It's like a portable cooking appliance suitable for most of the instant pot pressure cooker models. It easily converts your instant pot into an advanced air fryer machine by just changing the instant pot lid with air fryer lid.

The Book contains healthy instant pot air fryer recipes range from breakfast to desserts. The recipes are written into easily understandable form and the ingredients used in recipes are easily available in your kitchen. All the recipes written in this cookbook are unique and written with its actual preparation and cooking. Each and every recipe is written along with their nutritional calories and other nutritional values. The calorie and nutritional information help you to keep track of daily calorie consumption.

My purpose to write this cookbook is to give you detailed information about instant pot air fryer lid with unique, healthy, and delicious recipes. There are various books that are available in the market on this topic thanks for choosing my book. I hope you love all the recipes written in this cookbook

Chapter 1: Instant Pot Air Fryer Lid Basics

Instant Pot Air Fryer Lid

The instant pot air fryer lid is one of the advanced lid shape cooking appliances which easily converts your instant pot into an advanced air fryer machine. It transforms your instant pot into a mini convection oven by just changing the instant pot lid with air fryer lid. The air fryer lid comes with separate controls and a digital display which is situated at the top surface of the lid. The instant pot air fryer lid is not only used for air frying purposes but also loaded with additional cooking functions like roasting, baking, broiling, reheating and even you can dehydrating your favourite fruits, meats, and veggies.

The instant pot air fryer lid can easily fit with most of the instant pot 6-quart pressure cooker models. It works on an advanced hot air ventilation mechanism to cook your food fast and evenly from all the sides. It blows hot air with the help of a convection fan fixed at the inner top side of the lid behind the heating elements. The instant pot air fryer lid is easy to use and anyone can easily operate it to make a healthy and delicious meal. If you like fried food but worried about extra calories consumption then this kitchen gadget is the perfect choice for you. It cooks your food with very low oil and fats sometimes with no oil. If you fry a bowl of French fries then you have to add just a tablespoon of oil to make your French fries tender from inside and nicely crisp and brown from outside. If you have an instant pot already then you just need to buy an instant pot air fryer lid only to add additional functions into your instant pot.

The instant pot air fryer lid is loaded with 6 preset settings, these settings are pre-programmed. It's even crisp technology makes this a unique cooking appliance. The even crisp technology makes your chicken tender and juicy from inside and makes a crispy, crunchy, and golden finish from outside. It not only improves the taste but also gives a nice texture to your food. It takes 95% less oil to compare to the traditional deep frying method and the perfect choice for Crispy French fries, onion rings, chicken wings, golden batter vegetables, and more. It not only saves your cooking time but also saves your money. You never need to buy a separate appliance for single operations like air fry, bake, roast, broil, dehydrate, and reheat purpose.

The Proper Way to Use Instant Pot Air Fryer Lid

The instant pot air fryer lid is easy to operate you just need to follow the step by step guide given below

Step#1: After finishing your instant pot cooking make sure your instant pot is completely depressurized. Then unplug the instant pot and remove the lid.

Step#2: Place your air fryer lid over the instant pot. Then plug the power cord of the air fryer lid into the socket. If the lid is set in its right position then you will hear the jingle sound and the display will be turned on. If the lid is not its correct position then the display remains off.

Step#3: Always remember that the instant air fryer lid only works with stainless steel inner pot. It is not recommended to use a non-stick ceramic inner pot while using an air fryer lid.

Step#4: Select the proper settings from 6 preset functions or you may select your manual settings as per recipe needs. To set time and temperature you can toggle between + and – keys to increase or decrease settings.

Step#5: To start the actual cooking process press the Start button. When the cooking process is completed half then display shows Turn Food message. It indicates that you need to turn your food. If you ignore this message then the cooking process.

Step#6: When the actual cooking process is finished the display reads End message. Then unplug your air fryer lid from the socket. Place the hot lid on protective pads which are provided into accessories.

Following these simple steps, you can cook health, tasty and delicious meal easily at home.

Functions and Buttons of Air Fryer Lid

The instant pot air fryer lid is equipped with 6 preset functions and buttons. Using these functions you can make your cooking fast and easy. These functions are mention below:

1. Air Fry

If you want to cook your food with very little oil then use these functions to air fry your food. It takes very little oil to air fry your food like French fries, crispy onion rings, chicken wings, and more. You can also use this function to make your frozen and pressure cooked food crisp and gives a golden finish over it. While using this function the inner temperature of the cooking basket goes to 400°F. The default time for Air fryer is preset for 20 minutes but you can adjust it in the range between (1 minute to 45 minutes) as per your recipe needs. The temperature settings are also adjustable in the range of (300°F to 400°F).

2. Broil

Broiling is the process in which food is placed near the heating elements. Using this function you can easily melt cheese, toppings spread over the pizza burger pasta and more. You can use a dehydrating tray or air fryer basket while using this function. The default time for broiling is preset for 10 minutes and you can adjust it in the range between (1 minute to 20 minutes) as per your recipe needs. The temperature range is not adjustable while using the broil function.

3. Bake

Using this function you can cook your favorite delicious cakes, brownies, and pastries. You can use an appropriate utensil, oven-safe baking dish, or air fryer basket for baking purposes. The default temperature is 365°F and the default baking time is set at 30 minutes. You can also adjust the temperature range in between (180°F to 380°F) and time settings in between (1 minute to 60 minutes) as per your recipe needs.

4. Roast

Using this function you can roast your favorite chicken, pork, lamb, and beef. It also roasts your favorite vegetables into the air fryer basket. The default time is set for 40 minutes. You can adjust the time range in between (1 minute to 45 minutes) and temperature range in between (250°F to 380°F) as per your recipe needs.

5. Reheat

This function allows you to reheat your frozen food or leftover food without overcooking and enhance the taste of food. Adjust the time and temperature setting by just pressing the + and – key. Normally the 15 minutes is sufficient to reheat your food at the temperature settings 138°F or 280°F.

6. Dehydrate

Using this function you can dehydrate your favorite meat, vegetables, and fruits. Dehydrating is one of the longer processes so the average time set for dehydrating purpose is 6 hours and the ideal temperature for these settings is 125°F. It dries out your food slices so you can preserve it for a long period of time.

7. Time / Temp (+ / -)

Using these functions you can adjust the time and temperature settings manually by just pressing the + and – buttons.

8. Start

This function is used to start the actual cooking process.

9. Cancel

Using this function you can stop the current running smart program and the air fryer lid returns to standby mode.

Benefits of Using Air Fryer Lid

The instant pot air fryer lid is one of the versatile cooking appliances having various kinds of benefits some of the important benefits are given as below:

1. It's an economical appliance

The air fryer lid is one of the economical appliances that save your money. While using air fryer lid you never need to purchase an extra cooking appliance. It fits over your instant pot and works as an air fryer, roast, broil bake reheat and dehydrate. You never need to purchase a separate appliance for these single functions. It also consumes fewer oils and fats to cook your food. Compare to a deep fryer air fryer lid requires very little power to cook your food faster.

2. Requires very less oil to cook food

If you like fried food but worried about extra fats then an air fryer lid is one of the best choices for you. It cooks your food into very little oil or no oil, depending on your recipe needs. Less oil means fewer calories consumption it is one of the healthier choices for your daily cooking. The air fryer lid cooking is an economical and cheap way to cook your food. It saves your money on purchasing the cooking oils and fats.

3. Saves Time and energy

Due to the hot air ventilation mechanism, the air fryer lid cooks your food in very little time. Compare to the traditional deep frying method your air fryer needs very less energy to cook healthy and delicious food. When the air fryer lid finishes the cooking process it automatically goes into standby mode.

4. One-touch preset programs

The air fryer lid loaded with 6 preset programs like Air Fry, Roast, Bake, Broil, Dehydrate and Reheat. While using this preset functions you never worry about the time and temperature settings all things are preset. You just select the appropriate preset function and forgot.

5. Safe to use

Your air fryer lid is one of the safe cooking appliances comes with a various safety feature. It provides overheat protection, comes with an automatic shutoff feature, and more safety features.

Care and Cleaning

- First, unplug the power cable and allow it to cool down at room temperature before starting the cleaning process.
- Remove the air fryer lid from the instant pot base and put the lid over the protective pad.
- Clean inner pot, accessories like dehydrating tray, air fryer basket, air fryer basket base, protective pad, and storage covers. Clean all the accessories with hot water and dish soap. All the accessories are dishwasher safe so you can also clean it into the dishwasher.
- Once the air fryer lid is cool down then clean the heating elements and its surrounding area for any residues or food particles stuck over it. Clean it with the help of a soft damp cloth or sponge. While cleaning does not remove the element cover.
- Do not use metal scouring pads to clean the air fryer lid base because any piece of scouring pad breaks down and touch with electrical components having the risk of electric shock
- Clean and wipe the exterior of the air fryer lid with a soft damp cloth.
- Wipe the power cord if any food particle or residues stuck over it. Do not fold the power cable when store.

Chapter 2: Breakfast

Delicious Breakfast Potatoes

Preparation Time: 10 minutes
Cooking Time: 14 minutes
Serve: 4
Ingredients:
- 2 lbs potatoes, diced
- 1/2 tsp onion powder
- 1/4 tsp garlic powder
- 2 tsp olive oil
- 1/4 tsp chili powder
- 1/4 tsp pepper
- 1 tsp salt

Directions:
1. Add diced potatoes into the large bowl, cover potatoes with water, and let it sit for 30 minutes. Drain well and pat dry.
2. Add potatoes into the mixing bowl and toss with oil, onion powder, garlic powder, chili powder, pepper, and salt.
3. Line multi-level air fryer basket with parchment paper.
4. Add half potatoes into the multi-level air fryer basket and spread evenly.
5. Place the dehydrating tray in the air fryer basket and spread the remaining potatoes on the dehydrating tray.
6. Place multi-level air fryer basket into the inner pot of the instant pot.
7. Secure pot with air fryer lid, select air fry mode then cook at 370 F for 10-14 minutes. Stir potatoes half-way through.
8. Serve and enjoy.

Nutritional Value (Amount per Serving):
- Calories 179
- Fat 2.6 g
- Carbohydrates 36.2 g
- Sugar 2.8 g
- Protein 3.9 g
- Cholesterol 0 mg

Breakfast French Toast Sticks

Preparation Time: 10 minutes
Cooking Time: 8 minutes
Serve: 2
Ingredients:
- 2 large eggs
- 4 bread slices, cut each bread slice into 3 pieces vertically
- 1/4 tsp ground cinnamon
- 1 tsp vanilla
- 2/3 cup milk

Directions:
1. In a bowl, whisk eggs with cinnamon, vanilla, and milk.
2. Line multi-level air fryer basket with parchment paper.
3. Dip each bread piece into the egg mixture and coat well.
4. Place coated bread pieces into the multi-level air fryer basket.
5. Place multi-level air fryer basket into the inner pot of the instant pot.
6. Secure pot with air fryer lid, select air fry mode then cook at 370 F for 5 minutes. Flip bread pieces and air fry for 3 minutes more.
7. Serve and enjoy.

Nutritional Value (Amount per Serving):
- Calories 167
- Fat 7.2 g
- Carbohydrates 14 g
- Sugar 5.1 g
- Protein 10.4 g
- Cholesterol 193 mg

Classic Cheese Sandwich

Preparation Time: 10 minutes
Cooking Time: 12 minutes
Serve: 1
Ingredients:
- 2 bread slices
- 2 cheese slices
- 2 tsp butter

Directions:
1. Place cheese slices on top of one bread slice and cover cheese with another bread slice.
2. Spread butter on top of both the bread slices.
3. Line multi-level air fryer basket with parchment paper.
4. Place the prepared sandwich into the multi-level air fryer basket.
5. Place multi-level air fryer basket into the inner pot of the instant pot.
6. Secure pot with air fryer lid, select air fry mode then cook at 350 F for 8 minutes. Flip the sandwich and air fry for 4 minutes more.
7. Serve and enjoy.

Nutritional Value (Amount per Serving):
- Calories 341
- Fat 26.8 g
- Carbohydrates 9.8 g
- Sugar 1.1 g
- Protein 15.4 g
- Cholesterol 79 mg

Easy Breakfast Biscuits

Preparation Time: 10 minutes
Cooking Time: 17 minutes
Serve: 6
Ingredients:

- 1 cup all-purpose flour
- 1 tsp vanilla
- 2 tbsp heavy cream
- 1/4 cup pumpkin puree
- 1/4 cup butter, unsalted & cubed
- 3/4 tsp pumpkin pie spice
- 1 tsp baking powder
- 1/4 cup brown sugar
- 1/4 tsp salt

Directions:
1. Add flour, butter, pumpkin pie spice, baking powder, brown sugar, and salt into the food processor and process until just mix.
2. Add vanilla, heavy cream, and pumpkin puree and process until dough is formed.
3. Roll out dough onto a clean & flour surface. Cut the biscuits using a round cookie cutter and brush with milk.
4. Line multi-level air fryer basket with parchment paper.
5. Place biscuits into the multi-level air fryer basket.
6. Place multi-level air fryer basket into the inner pot of the instant pot.
7. Secure pot with air fryer lid, select air fry mode then cook at 400 F for 17 minutes.
8. Serve and enjoy.

Nutritional Value (Amount per Serving):
- Calories 191
- Fat 9.8 g
- Carbohydrates 23.4 g
- Sugar 6.4 g
- Protein 2.5 g
- Cholesterol 27 mg

Breakfast Potato Hash

Preparation Time: 10 minutes
Cooking Time: 12 minutes
Serve: 4

Ingredients:
- 2 sweet potatoes, peeled & diced
- 3/4 tsp Italian seasoning
- 1 tsp paprika
- 2 tbsp olive oil
- 2 bacon slices, cut into 1-inch pieces
- Pepper
- Salt

Directions:
1. In a mixing bowl, add sweet potatoes, Italian seasoning, paprika, oil, bacon, pepper, and salt and toss well.
2. Line multi-level air fryer basket with parchment paper.
3. Add sweet potato mixture into the multi-level air fryer basket and spread well.
4. Place multi-level air fryer basket into the inner pot of the instant pot.
5. Secure pot with air fryer lid, select air fry mode then cook at 400 F for 12 minutes. Stir sweet potato mixture halfway through.
6. Serve and enjoy.

Nutritional Value (Amount per Serving):
- Calories 172
- Fat 11.4 g
- Carbohydrates 13.8 g
- Sugar 0.4 g
- Protein 4.3 g
- Cholesterol 11 mg

Perfect Egg Bites

Preparation Time: 10 minutes
Cooking Time: 10 minutes
Serve: 6

Ingredients:
- 4 eggs
- 1/4 cup cheddar cheese, shredded
- 1 tbsp milk
- Pepper
- Salt

Directions:
1. In a bowl, whisk eggs with milk, pepper, and salt until frothy.
2. Add cheese and stir well.
3. Pour egg mixture into the 6 greased silicone muffin molds.
4. Place the dehydrating tray in the air fryer basket. Place silicone muffin molds onto the dehydrating tray.
5. Place multi-level air fryer basket into the inner pot of the instant pot.
6. Secure pot with air fryer lid, select air fry mode then cook at 330 F for 10 minutes.
7. Serve and enjoy.

Nutritional Value (Amount per Serving):
- Calories 62
- Fat 4.5 g
- Carbohydrates 0.4 g
- Sugar 0.4 g
- Protein 4.9 g
- Cholesterol 114 mg

Breakfast Bagels

Preparation Time: 10 minutes
Cooking Time: 15 minutes
Serve: 4

Ingredients:
- 1 egg, lightly beaten
- 1 cup all-purpose flour
- 2 tbsp everything bagel seasoning
- 1 cup Greek yogurt
- 2 tsp baking powder
- 2 tsp kosher salt

Directions:
1. In a mixing bowl, mix together flour, baking powder, and 1 tsp kosher salt.

2. Add yogurt and mix until dough forms.
3. Knead dough onto the floured surface for 2-3 minutes. Divide dough into four equal portions.
4. Roll each dough ball into a 1-inch thick rope and join the ends to make a bagel.
5. Brush bagel with egg and sprinkle with remaining salt and bagel seasoning.
6. Line multi-level air fryer basket with parchment paper.
7. Place bagels into the multi-level air fryer basket and spread well.
8. Place multi-level air fryer basket into the inner pot of the instant pot.
9. Secure pot with air fryer lid, select air fry mode then cook at 300 F for 15 minutes.
10. Serve and enjoy.

Nutritional Value (Amount per Serving):
- Calories 170
- Fat 2.4 g
- Carbohydrates 27.1 g
- Sugar 2.2 g
- Protein 9.7 g
- Cholesterol 43 mg

Cajun Sausage

Preparation Time: 10 minutes
Cooking Time: 20 minutes
Serve: 6

Ingredients:
- 3/4 lb ground sausage
- 1 1/2 tsp garlic, minced
- 1 tsp brown sugar
- 1/4 tsp paprika
- 1/2 tsp onion powder
- 1/4 tsp dried thyme
- 1/2 tsp red chili flakes
- Salt

Directions:
1. Add ground sausage and remaining ingredients into the mixing bowl and mix until well combined.
2. Make 6 equal shapes of patties from the mixture.
3. Line multi-level air fryer basket with parchment paper.
4. Place sausage patties into the multi-level air fryer basket and spread well.
5. Place multi-level air fryer basket into the inner pot of the instant pot.
6. Secure pot with air fryer lid, select air fry mode then cook at 370 F for 20 minutes.
7. Serve and enjoy.

Nutritional Value (Amount per Serving):
- Calories 196
- Fat 16.1 g
- Carbohydrates 1 g
- Sugar 0.6 g
- Protein 11.1 g
- Cholesterol 48 mg

Almond Flour Breakfast Biscuits

Preparation Time: 10 minutes
Cooking Time: 6 minutes
Serve: 8

Ingredients:
- 2 eggs
- 1 cup almond flour
- 2 tbsp sour cream
- 2 tbsp butter, melted
- 1 cup cheddar cheese, shredded
- 1/2 tsp baking powder
- 1/2 tsp salt

Directions:
1. In a bowl, mix almond flour, cheddar cheese, baking powder, and salt until well combined.
2. Add sour cream, butter, and eggs and mix until sticky mixture forms.
3. Line multi-level air fryer basket with parchment paper.
4. Drop about 1/4 cup batter onto the parchment paper for 1 biscuit. Make 4 biscuits.
5. Place multi-level air fryer basket into the inner pot of the instant pot.
6. Secure pot with air fryer lid, select air fry mode then cook at 400 F for 6 minutes.
7. Repeat with the remaining mixture.
8. Serve and enjoy.

Nutritional Value (Amount per Serving):
- Calories 125
- Fat 11 g
- Carbohydrates 1.3 g
- Sugar 0.3 g
- Protein 5.8 g
- Cholesterol 65 mg

Tasty Tater Tots

Preparation Time: 10 minutes
Cooking Time: 15 minutes
Serve: 4

Ingredients:
- 16 oz frozen tater tots
- 1 tbsp olive oil
- Salt

Directions:
1. Add tater tots into the mixing bowl, drizzle with oil, and season with salt. Toss well.
2. Add tater tots into the multi-level air fryer basket and spread well.
3. Place multi-level air fryer basket into the inner pot of the instant pot.
4. Secure pot with air fryer lid, select air fry mode then cook at 400 F for 15 minutes. Stir halfway through.
5. Serve and enjoy.

Nutritional Value (Amount per Serving):
- Calories 246
- Fat 14.3 g
- Carbohydrates 27 g

- Sugar 0.7 g
- Protein 2.7 g
- Cholesterol 0 mg

Egg Stuffed Peppers

Preparation Time: 10 minutes
Cooking Time: 13 minutes
Serve: 2
Ingredients:
- 4 eggs
- 1 bell pepper, cut in half & remove seeds
- 1/4 tsp red chili flakes
- Pepper
- Salt

Directions:
1. Break 2 eggs into each bell pepper half. Season with pepper and salt.
2. Sprinkle red chili flakes on top of each bell pepper half.
3. Place stuff bell pepper halves into the multi-level air fryer basket and spread well.
4. Place multi-level air fryer basket into the inner pot of the instant pot.
5. Secure pot with air fryer lid, select air fry mode then cook at 390 F for 13 minutes.
6. Serve and enjoy.

Nutritional Value (Amount per Serving):
- Calories 145
- Fat 8.9 g
- Carbohydrates 5.2 g
- Sugar 3.7 g
- Protein 11.7 g
- Cholesterol 327 mg

Healthy Egg Stuffed Avocado

Preparation Time: 10 minutes
Cooking Time: 9 minutes
Serve: 2
Ingredients:
- 2 eggs
- 1 avocado, cut in half and remove the seed
- 1/4 tsp red chili flakes
- Pepper
- Salt

Directions:
1. Break each egg into the hole on the avocado half. Season with pepper and salt.
2. Sprinkle red chili flakes on top of each avocado half.
3. Place stuff avocado halves into the multi-level air fryer basket and spread well.
4. Place multi-level air fryer basket into the inner pot of the instant pot.
5. Secure pot with air fryer lid, select air fry mode then cook at 400 F for 9 minutes.
6. Serve and enjoy.

Nutritional Value (Amount per Serving):
- Calories 268
- Fat 24 g
- Carbohydrates 9 g
- Sugar 0.8 g
- Protein 7.5 g
- Cholesterol 164 mg

Baked Oatmeal

Preparation Time: 10 minutes
Cooking Time: 15 minutes
Serve: 12
Ingredients:
- 1 egg
- 2 bananas
- 1 apple, pee & diced
- 1 tsp ground cinnamon
- 1 tsp baking powder
- 1/2 cup milk
- 2 cups rolled oats
- Pinch of salt

Directions:
1. In a bowl, add bananas and mash using a fork.
2. Add egg, cinnamon, baking powder, milk, oats, and salt and mix until well combined.
3. Add apple and mix well.
4. Pour batter into the 12 greased silicone muffin molds.
5. Place the dehydrating tray in the air fryer basket.
6. Place 6 silicone muffin molds onto the dehydrating tray.
7. Place multi-level air fryer basket into the inner pot of the instant pot.
8. Secure pot with air fryer lid, select bake mode then cook at 375 F for 15 minutes.
9. Serve and enjoy.

Nutritional Value (Amount per Serving):
- Calories 90
- Fat 1.6 g
- Carbohydrates 17.2 g
- Sugar 5 g
- Protein 2.9 g
- Cholesterol 14 mg

Healthy Banana Muffins

Preparation Time: 10 minutes
Cooking Time: 12 minutes
Serve: 6
Ingredients:
- 1 egg
- 1/2 cup walnuts, chopped
- 1/4 cup butter, melted
- 1 cup yogurt
- 2 bananas
- 1 tsp ground cinnamon
- 1/4 tsp ground nutmeg
- 2 tsp baking powder
- 1 1/3 cup all-purpose flour
- 1/2 cup sugar

- 1/2 tsp salt

Directions:
1. In a bowl, mix flour, cinnamon, nutmeg, baking powder, sugar, and salt.
2. In a mixing bowl, add bananas and mash using a fork. Add egg, butter, and yogurt and beat until well blended.
3. Add flour mixture and mix until well combined.
4. Add walnuts and stir well.
5. Pour batter into the 6 greased silicone muffin molds.
6. Place the dehydrating tray in the air fryer basket.
7. Place silicone muffin molds onto the dehydrating tray.
8. Place multi-level air fryer basket into the inner pot of the instant pot.
9. Secure pot with air fryer lid, select air fry mode then cook at 320 F for 12 minutes.
10. Serve and enjoy.

Nutritional Value (Amount per Serving):
- Calories 363
- Fat 15 g
- Carbohydrates 52.3 g
- Sugar 24.1 g
- Protein 7.7 g
- Cholesterol 48 mg

Cheesy Egg Muffins

Preparation Time: 10 minutes
Cooking Time: 5 minutes
Serve: 4

Ingredients:
- 4 eggs
- 1/4 cup cheddar cheese
- 1/4 cup heavy cream
- 4 tbsp tomato, chopped
- Pepper
- Salt

Directions:
1. In a bowl, whisk eggs with cheese, heavy cream, pepper, and salt.
2. Add tomato and mix well.
3. Pour egg mixture into the 4 greased silicone muffin molds.
4. Place the dehydrating tray in the air fryer basket.
5. Place silicone muffin molds onto the dehydrating tray.
6. Place multi-level air fryer basket into the inner pot of the instant pot.
7. Secure pot with air fryer lid, select air fry mode then cook at 350 F for 5 minutes.
8. Serve and enjoy.

Nutritional Value (Amount per Serving):
- Calories 119
- Fat 9.5 g
- Carbohydrates 1.1 g
- Sugar 0.7 g
- Protein 7.6 g
- Cholesterol 148 mg

Healthy Quinoa Egg Muffins

Preparation Time: 10 minutes
Cooking Time: 20 minutes
Serve: 6

Ingredients:
- 4 eggs
- 3 cups cooked quinoa
- 1 1/2 cups fresh spinach, chopped
- 1 tsp garlic, minced
- 1 1/2 cups cheddar cheese, shredded
- Pepper
- Salt

Directions:
1. In a mixing bowl, whisk eggs with pepper and salt.
2. Add quinoa, spinach, garlic, and cheese and mix well.
3. Pour batter into the 6 greased silicone muffin molds.
4. Place the dehydrating tray in the air fryer basket.
5. Place silicone muffin molds onto the dehydrating tray.
6. Place multi-level air fryer basket into the inner pot of the instant pot.
7. Secure pot with air fryer lid, select bake mode then cook at 350 F for 20 minutes.
8. Serve and enjoy.

Nutritional Value (Amount per Serving):
- Calories 471
- Fat 17.5 g
- Carbohydrates 55.6 g
- Sugar 0.4 g
- Protein 23 g
- Cholesterol 139 mg

Broccoli Breakfast Muffins

Preparation Time: 10 minutes
Cooking Time: 15 minutes
Serve: 6

Ingredients:
- 4 eggs
- 1/2 cup cheddar cheese, shredded
- 1 cup broccoli, steamed & chopped
- 1/2 tsp pepper
- 1/2 tsp sea salt

Directions:
1. In a bowl, whisk eggs with pepper, and salt.
2. Add cheese and broccoli and stir well.
3. Pour egg mixture into the 6 silicone muffin molds.
4. Place the dehydrating tray in the air fryer basket.
5. Place silicone muffin molds onto the dehydrating tray.

6. Place multi-level air fryer basket into the inner pot of the instant pot.
7. Secure pot with air fryer lid, select bake mode then cook at 375 F for 15 minutes.
8. Serve and enjoy.

Nutritional Value (Amount per Serving):
- Calories 86
- Fat 6.1 g
- Carbohydrates 1.5 g
- Sugar 0.5 g
- Protein 6.5 g
- Cholesterol 119 mg

Jalapeno Cheese Biscuits

Preparation Time: 10 minutes
Cooking Time: 17 minutes
Serve: 6
Ingredients:
- 1 egg
- 1 1/2 cups almond flour
- 1 1/2 tsp dried parsley
- 4 tsp jalapeno, diced
- 3 tbsp butter, cubed
- 1/4 cup heavy cream
- 1/2 cup cheddar cheese, shredded
- 1 1/2 tsp baking powder
- Pepper
- Salt

Directions:
1. In a mixing bowl, mix together almond flour, parsley, butter, baking powder, pepper, and salt.
2. Add egg, heavy cream, cheese, and jalapeno and mix until well combined.
3. Line multi-level air fryer basket with parchment paper.
4. Make 6 balls from the mixture and place it into the multi-level air fryer basket.
5. Place multi-level air fryer basket into the inner pot of the instant pot.
6. Secure pot with air fryer lid, select bake mode then cook at 350 F for 17 minutes.
7. Serve and enjoy.

Nutritional Value (Amount per Serving):
- Calories 161
- Fat 15 g
- Carbohydrates 3 g
- Sugar 0.7 g
- Protein 5.1 g
- Cholesterol 59 mg

Breakfast Sausage Balls

Preparation Time: 10 minutes
Cooking Time: 20 minutes
Serve: 4
Ingredients:
- 1/2 lb sausage, uncooked
- 2 cups frozen shredded hash brown potatoes
- 3/4 cup cheddar cheese, shredded
- 3/4 cup Bisquick
- 4 oz cream cheese, softened

Directions:
1. Add all ingredients into the mixing bowl and mix until well combined.
2. Make 1 1/2-inch ball from the mixture.
3. Line multi-level air fryer basket with parchment paper.
4. Place prepared balls into the multi-level air fryer basket.
5. Place multi-level air fryer basket into the inner pot of the instant pot.
6. Secure pot with air fryer lid, select bake mode then cook at 380 F for 20-22 minutes.
7. Serve and enjoy.

Nutritional Value (Amount per Serving):
- Calories 533
- Fat 39.8 g
- Carbohydrates 22.1 g
- Sugar 2.7 g
- Protein 20.7 g
- Cholesterol 102 mg

Soft Sweet Potato Rolls

Preparation Time: 10 minutes
Cooking Time: 14 minutes
Serve: 6
Ingredients:
- 1 cup self-rising flour
- 1 cup sweet potato, cooked & mashed

Directions:
1. Mix together flour and mashed sweet potato until well combined.
2. Transfer dough onto the floured surface and knead for 1 minute or until smooth.
3. Divide dough into the 6 equal portions and roll into the balls.
4. Let rest dough balls for a half-hour.
5. Line multi-level air fryer basket with parchment paper.
6. Brush dough balls with oil and place them into the multi-level air fryer basket.
7. Place multi-level air fryer basket into the inner pot of the instant pot.
8. Secure pot with air fryer lid, select air fry mode then cook at 330 F for 10-14 minutes.
9. Serve and enjoy.

Nutritional Value (Amount per Serving):
- Calories 106
- Fat 0.3 g
- Carbohydrates 22.8 g
- Sugar 2.2 g
- Protein 2.8 g
- Cholesterol 0 mg

Cheddar Cheese Sausage Biscuits

Preparation Time: 10 minutes
Cooking Time: 12 minutes

Serve: 6
Ingredients:
- 2 eggs
- 1 1/2 cups almond flour
- 2 tbsp fresh chives, chopped
- 1/2 cup cheddar cheese, shredded
- 1/2 lb breakfast sausage, cooked & drained
- 1/4 cup butter, melted
- 1/3 cup sour cream
- 1 tbsp baking powder
- 1/4 tsp salt

Directions:
1. In a large bowl, mix together almond flour, baking powder, and salt.
2. In a separate bowl, whisk eggs with butter, and sour cream.
3. Pour egg mixture into the almond flour mixture and mix until well combined.
4. Add chives, cheese, and sausage and fold well. Let sit the mixture for 10 minutes.
5. Line multi-level air fryer basket with parchment paper.
6. Drop 1/4 cup dough for 1 biscuit onto the parchment paper in the multi-level air fryer basket. Make four biscuits.
7. Place multi-level air fryer basket into the inner pot of the instant pot.
8. Secure pot with air fryer lid, select bake mode then cook at 380 F for 12-15 minutes.
9. Serve and enjoy.

Nutritional Value (Amount per Serving):
- Calories 285
- Fat 29.2 g
- Carbohydrates 3.5 g
- Sugar 0.5 g
- Protein 13.6 g
- Cholesterol 122 mg

Homemade Breakfast Sausage

Preparation Time: 10 minutes
Cooking Time: 30 minutes
Serve: 8

Ingredients:
- 1 lb ground chicken
- 1/4 tsp onion powder
- 1/4 tsp garlic powder
- 1 tsp dried thyme
- 1 apple, grated
- 1/2 tsp sea salt

Directions:
1. Add all ingredients into the mixing bowl and mix until well combined.
2. Make 8 patties from the mixture and set aside.
3. Line multi-level air fryer basket with parchment paper.
4. Place four patties into the multi-level air fryer basket.
5. Place multi-level air fryer basket into the inner pot of the instant pot.
6. Secure pot with air fryer lid, select bake mode then cook at 380 F for 30 minutes. Turn patties halfway through.
7. Cook remaining patties.
8. Serve and enjoy.

Nutritional Value (Amount per Serving):
- Calories 123
- Fat 4.3 g
- Carbohydrates 4.1 g
- Sugar 3 g
- Protein 16.5 g
- Cholesterol 50 mg

Italian Egg Muffins

Preparation Time: 10 minutes
Cooking Time: 20 minutes
Serve: 6

Ingredients:
- 3 eggs
- 1 tbsp basil, chopped
- 1/4 cup feta cheese, crumbled
- 1 spring onion, chopped
- 2 cherry tomatoes, chopped
- 3 sun-dried tomatoes, chopped
- Pepper
- Salt

Directions:
1. In a bowl, whisk eggs with pepper and salt.
2. Add remaining ingredients and stir until well combined.
3. Pour egg mixture into the 6 greased silicone muffin molds.
4. Place the dehydrating tray in the air fryer basket.
5. Place silicone muffin molds onto the dehydrating tray.
6. Place multi-level air fryer basket into the inner pot of the instant pot.
7. Secure pot with air fryer lid, select bake mode then cook at 380 F for 20 minutes.
8. Serve and enjoy.

Nutritional Value (Amount per Serving):
- Calories 67
- Fat 3.7 g
- Carbohydrates 4.6 g
- Sugar 3.2 g
- Protein 4.6 g
- Cholesterol 87 mg

Spinach Ham Egg Muffins

Preparation Time: 10 minutes
Cooking Time: 16 minutes
Serve: 6

Ingredients:
- 6 eggs
- 1/3 cup ham, diced

- 1/3 cup mozzarella cheese, shredded
- 1/4 cup fresh spinach, chopped
- 1/4 tsp garlic powder
- Pepper
- Salt

Directions:
1. In a bowl, whisk eggs with garlic powder, pepper, and salt.
2. Add ham, cheese, and spinach and stir to mix.
3. Pour egg mixture into the 6 greased silicone muffin molds.
4. Place the dehydrating tray in the air fryer basket.
5. Place silicone muffin molds onto the dehydrating tray.
6. Place multi-level air fryer basket into the inner pot of the instant pot.
7. Secure pot with air fryer lid, select bake mode then cook at 375 F for 16-20 minutes.
8. Serve and enjoy.

Nutritional Value (Amount per Serving):
- Calories 80
- Fat 5.3 g
- Carbohydrates 0.8 g
- Sugar 0.4 g
- Protein 7.3 g
- Cholesterol 169 mg

Pizza Egg Muffins

Preparation Time: 10 minutes
Cooking Time: 12 minutes
Serve: 6

Ingredients:
- 5 eggs
- 1 tsp garlic, minced
- 2 oz mozzarella cheese, shredded
- 2 tbsp onion, chopped
- 2 tbsp pizza sauce
- 1.5 oz turkey pepperoni
- 1.5 oz ham
- 1/2 tsp sea salt

Directions:
1. In a mixing bowl, whisk eggs with garlic, pizza sauce, and salt.
2. Add remaining ingredients and stir well.
3. Pour egg mixture into the 6 greased silicone muffin molds.
4. Place the dehydrating tray in the air fryer basket.
5. Place silicone muffin molds onto the dehydrating tray.
6. Place multi-level air fryer basket into the inner pot of the instant pot.
7. Secure pot with air fryer lid, select bake mode then cook at 380 F for 12-15 minutes.
8. Serve and enjoy.

Nutritional Value (Amount per Serving):
- Calories 112
- Fat 6.9 g
- Carbohydrates 1.9 g
- Sugar 0.6 g
- Protein 10.7 g
- Cholesterol 155 mg

Pumpkin Pie Muffins

Preparation Time: 10 minutes
Cooking Time: 18 minutes
Serve: 6

Ingredients:
- 3 eggs
- 1/8 tsp baking powder
- 1/2 tsp vanilla
- 1/2 tsp pumpkin pie spice
- 1 1/2 tbsp maple syrup
- 1/2 cup pumpkin puree

Directions:
1. In a bowl, whisk eggs with vanilla, baking powder, pumpkin pie spice, maple syrup, and pumpkin puree.
2. Pour egg mixture into the 6 greased silicone muffin molds.
3. Place the dehydrating tray in the air fryer basket.
4. Place silicone muffin molds onto the dehydrating tray.
5. Place multi-level air fryer basket into the inner pot of the instant pot.
6. Secure pot with air fryer lid, select bake mode then cook at 375 F for 18-20 minutes.
7. Serve and enjoy.

Nutritional Value (Amount per Serving):
- Calories 53
- Fat 2.3 g
- Carbohydrates 5.4 g
- Sugar 3.9 g
- Protein 3 g
- Cholesterol 82 mg

Broccoli Bacon Egg Muffins

Preparation Time: 10 minutes
Cooking Time: 20 minutes
Serve: 6

Ingredients:
- 4 eggs
- 1/4 cup cheddar cheese, shredded
- 1/4 tsp black pepper
- 2 tbsp milk
- 2 bacon slices, cooked & crumbled
- 1 cup broccoli florets, cooked and chopped
- 1/4 tsp salt

Directions:
1. In a bowl, whisk eggs with milk, pepper, and salt.
2. Add cheese, bacon, and broccoli and stir well.

3. Pour egg mixture into the 6 greased silicone muffin molds.
4. Place the dehydrating tray in the air fryer basket.
5. Place silicone muffin molds onto the dehydrating tray.
6. Place multi-level air fryer basket into the inner pot of the instant pot.
7. Secure pot with air fryer lid, select bake mode then cook at 350 F for 18-20 minutes.
8. Serve and enjoy.

Nutritional Value (Amount per Serving):
- Calories 103
- Fat 7.3 g
- Carbohydrates 1.7 g
- Sugar 0.7 g
- Protein 7.8 g
- Cholesterol 121 mg

Delicious Frittata Muffins

Preparation Time: 10 minutes
Cooking Time: 20 minutes
Serve: 6

Ingredients:
- 4 eggs
- 2 tbsp mozzarella cheese, shredded
- 1/4 cup cheddar cheese, shredded
- 1 cup broccoli florets, chopped
- 1/4 onion, grated
- 3/4 cup cooked quinoa
- Pepper
- Salt

Directions:
1. In a bowl, whisk eggs with pepper and salt until fluffy.
2. Add remaining ingredients and stir well.
3. Pour egg mixture into the 6 greased silicone muffin molds.
4. Place the dehydrating tray in the air fryer basket.
5. Place silicone muffin molds onto the dehydrating tray.
6. Place multi-level air fryer basket into the inner pot of the instant pot.
7. Secure pot with air fryer lid, select bake mode then cook at 380 F for 20 minutes.
8. Serve and enjoy.

Nutritional Value (Amount per Serving):
- Calories 173
- Fat 7.5 g
- Carbohydrates 15.7 g
- Sugar 0.7 g
- Protein 11 g
- Cholesterol 119 mg

Breakfast Sausage Patties

Preparation Time: 10 minutes
Cooking Time: 20 minutes
Serve: 12

Ingredients:
- 1 egg
- 1 cup frozen hash browns
- 2 cup kale, chopped
- 1 small onion, diced & sauteed
- 1 lb ground pork sausage

Directions:
1. Add all ingredients into the mixing bowl and mix until well combined.
2. Make 12 even shapes of patties from the mixture and set aside.
3. Line multi-level air fryer basket with parchment paper.
4. Place 6 patties into the multi-level air fryer basket.
5. Place multi-level air fryer basket into the inner pot of the instant pot.
6. Secure pot with air fryer lid, select bake mode then cook at 380 F for 20 minutes. Turn patties halfway through.
7. Cook remaining patties.
8. Serve and enjoy.

Nutritional Value (Amount per Serving):
- Calories 168
- Fat 12 g
- Carbohydrates 6.3 g
- Sugar 0.5 g
- Protein 7.9 g
- Cholesterol 47 mg

Turkey Patties

Preparation Time: 10 minutes
Cooking Time: 20 minutes
Serve: 8

Ingredients:
- 1 lb ground turkey
- 1/2 tsp red chili flakes
- 1 tbsp dried sage
- 1/2 tsp pepper
- 1/2 tsp sea salt

Directions:
1. Add all ingredients into the bowl and mix until well combined.
2. Make 8 even shapes of patties from the mixture and set aside.
3. Line multi-level air fryer basket with parchment paper.
4. Place 6 patties into the multi-level air fryer basket.
5. Place multi-level air fryer basket into the inner pot of the instant pot.
6. Secure pot with air fryer lid, select bake mode then cook at 380 F for 15-20 minutes. Turn patties halfway through.
7. Cook remaining patties.
8. Serve and enjoy.

Nutritional Value (Amount per Serving):
- Calories 112
- Fat 6.3 g

- Carbohydrates 0.2 g
- Sugar 0 g
- Protein 15.6 g
- Cholesterol 58 mg

Tasty Breakfast Cookies

Preparation Time: 10 minutes
Cooking Time: 10 minutes
Serve: 12
Ingredients:
- 3 eggs
- 1 cup cheddar cheese, shredded
- 1 tsp baking powder
- 3/4 cup almond flour
- 1/2 cup bell peppers, chopped
- 1/2 cup onion, chopped
- 4 oz pork sausage
- 1/2 tsp pepper
- 1/2 tsp salt

Directions:
1. In a pan, add sausage, onion, and bell pepper and sauté over medium-high heat until sausage is browned and onion is softened. Remove from heat and let it cool completely.
2. Transfer sausage mixture into the mixing bowl.
3. Add remaining ingredients and mix until well combined.
4. Line multi-level air fryer basket with parchment paper.
5. Drop a spoonful of mixture for 1 cookie onto the parchment paper in the multi-level air fryer basket. Make six cookies
6. Place multi-level air fryer basket into the inner pot of the instant pot.
7. Secure pot with air fryer lid, select bake mode then cook at 375 F for 10 minutes.
8. Make the remaining mixture cookies.
9. Serve and enjoy.

Nutritional Value (Amount per Serving):
- Calories 100
- Fat 7.8 g
- Carbohydrates 1.7 g
- Sugar 0.6 g
- Protein 6.1 g
- Cholesterol 59 mg

Zucchini Breakfast Cakes

Preparation Time: 10 minutes
Cooking Time: 30 minutes
Serve: 8
Ingredients:
- 2 eggs
- 1/4 cup parmesan cheese, grated
- 1 cup breadcrumbs
- 1 tsp basil
- 1 tsp garlic, minced
- 1 small onion, chopped
- 2 small zucchini, grated & squeeze out all liquid
- Pepper
- Salt

Directions:
1. Add all ingredients into the mixing bowl and mix until well combined.
2. Make 8 equal shapes of patties from the mixture and set aside.
3. Line multi-level air fryer basket with parchment paper.
4. Place 4 patties into the multi-level air fryer basket.
5. Place multi-level air fryer basket into the inner pot of the instant pot.
6. Secure pot with air fryer lid, select bake mode then cook at 380 F for 30 minutes. Turn patties halfway through.
7. Cook remaining patties.
8. Serve and enjoy.

Nutritional Value (Amount per Serving):
- Calories 87
- Fat 2.5 g
- Carbohydrates 11.8 g
- Sugar 1.8 g
- Protein 4.6 g
- Cholesterol 43 mg

Breakfast Sausage Balls

Preparation Time: 10 minutes
Cooking Time: 18 minutes
Serve: 4
Ingredients:
- 1/2 lb sausage, uncooked
- 6 oz pimento cheese
- 3/4 cup Bisquick
- 4 oz cream cheese, softened

Directions:
1. Add all ingredients into the bowl and mix until well combined.
2. Make 1-inch balls from the mixture and set aside.
3. Line multi-level air fryer basket with parchment paper.
4. Place sausage balls into the multi-level air fryer basket.
5. Place multi-level air fryer basket into the inner pot of the instant pot.
6. Secure pot with air fryer lid, select bake mode then cook at 380 F for 18-20 minutes.
7. Serve and enjoy.

Nutritional Value (Amount per Serving):
- Calories 383
- Fat 42.5 g
- Carbohydrates 15 g
- Sugar 2.8 g
- Protein 24.3 g
- Cholesterol 119 mg

Tasty Pecan Pie Muffins

Preparation Time: 10 minutes
Cooking Time: 12 minutes
Serve: 6
Ingredients:
- 1 egg
- 5 1/2 tbsp butter, melted
- 1/2 cup brown sugar
- 1/2 tsp vanilla
- 6 tbsp flour
- 1/2 cup pecans, chopped

Directions:
1. In a bowl, mix together egg, butter, sugar, vanilla, and flour until well combined.
2. Add pecans and stir well.
3. Pour mixture into the 6 greased silicone muffin molds.
4. Place the dehydrating tray in the air fryer basket.
5. Place silicone muffin molds onto the dehydrating tray.
6. Place multi-level air fryer basket into the inner pot of the instant pot.
7. Secure pot with air fryer lid, select bake mode then cook at 350 F for 12-15 minutes.
8. Serve and enjoy.

Nutritional Value (Amount per Serving):
- Calories 214
- Fat 14.9 g
- Carbohydrates 18.6 g
- Sugar 12 g
- Protein 2.4 g
- Cholesterol 55 mg

Oats Raspberry Muffins

Preparation Time: 10 minutes
Cooking Time: 30 minutes
Serve: 6
Ingredients:
- 1 egg
- 1 tsp vanilla
- 1 tbsp Swerve
- 1.75 oz raspberries
- 6.2 oz yogurt
- 1 1/4 cups rolled oats

Directions:
1. In a mixing bowl, mix together all ingredients until combined.
2. Pour mixture into the 6 greased silicone muffin molds.
3. Place the dehydrating tray in the air fryer basket.
4. Place silicone muffin molds onto the dehydrating tray.
5. Place multi-level air fryer basket into the inner pot of the instant pot.
6. Secure pot with air fryer lid, select bake mode then cook at 350 F for 30 minutes.
7. Serve and enjoy.

Nutritional Value (Amount per Serving):
- Calories 103
- Fat 2.3 g
- Carbohydrates 15.1 g
- Sugar 2.8 g
- Protein 4.9 g
- Cholesterol 29 mg

Kale Egg Muffins

Preparation Time: 10 minutes
Cooking Time: 20 minutes
Serve: 6
Ingredients:
- 5 eggs
- 1 tbsp spring onion, chopped
- 1/2 cup kale, shredded
- 3 tomatoes, chopped
- 2/3 cup milk
- 1/8 tsp pepper
- 1/4 tsp salt

Directions:
1. In a bowl, whisk eggs with, milk, pepper, and salt.
2. Add onion, kale, and tomatoes and stir well.
3. Pour egg mixture into the 6 greased silicone muffin molds.
4. Place the dehydrating tray in the air fryer basket.
5. Place silicone muffin molds onto the dehydrating tray.
6. Place multi-level air fryer basket into the inner pot of the instant pot.
7. Secure pot with air fryer lid, select bake mode then cook at 350 F for 20 minutes.
8. Serve and enjoy.

Nutritional Value (Amount per Serving):
- Calories 80
- Fat 4.3 g
- Carbohydrates 4.7 g
- Sugar 3.1 g
- Protein 6.2 g
- Cholesterol 139 mg

Cheddar Kale Egg Cups

Preparation Time: 10 minutes
Cooking Time: 15 minutes
Serve: 6
Ingredients:
- 5 eggs
- 3 oz cheddar cheese, shredded
- 1 cup kale, chopped
- Pepper
- Salt

Directions:
1. In a bowl, whisk eggs with pepper and salt. Add cheese and kale and stir well.

2. Pour egg mixture into the 6 greased silicone muffin molds.
3. Place the dehydrating tray in the air fryer basket.
4. Place silicone muffin molds onto the dehydrating tray.
5. Place multi-level air fryer basket into the inner pot of the instant pot.
6. Secure pot with air fryer lid, select bake mode then cook at 380 F for 15 minutes.
7. Serve and enjoy.

Nutritional Value (Amount per Serving):
- Calories 115
- Fat 8.3 g
- Carbohydrates 1.6 g
- Sugar 0.4 g
- Protein 8.5 g
- Cholesterol 151 mg

Perfect Broccoli Tater Tots

Preparation Time: 10 minutes
Cooking Time: 20 minutes
Serve: 12

Ingredients:
- 1 egg
- 2 cups broccoli florets
- 2 medium potatoes, peel & dice
- 1/2 tsp garlic powder
- 1/4 cup onion, minced
- 1/2 tsp pepper
- 1/2 tsp salt

Directions:
1. Boil broccoli and potatoes until tender. Drain well.
2. Chop cooked broccoli and mash the potatoes.
3. In a mixing bowl, mix together broccoli, mashed potatoes, egg, garlic powder, onion, pepper, and salt until well combined.
4. Make small balls from the mixture and set aside.
5. Line multi-level air fryer basket with parchment paper.
6. Place prepared balls into the multi-level air fryer basket.
7. Place multi-level air fryer basket into the inner pot of the instant pot.
8. Secure pot with air fryer lid, select bake mode then cook at 380 F for 15-20 minutes.
9. Serve and enjoy.

Nutritional Value (Amount per Serving):
- Calories 37
- Fat 0.5 g
- Carbohydrates 7 g
- Sugar 0.8 g
- Protein 1.5 g
- Cholesterol 14 mg

Sweet Potato Chickpea Breakfast Hash

Preparation Time: 10 minutes
Cooking Time: 30 minutes
Serve: 4

Ingredients:
- 14 oz can chickpeas, drained
- 1 sweet potato, peeled and cubed
- 1 tbsp olive oil
- 1 bell pepper, chopped
- 1 onion, diced
- 1 tsp paprika
- 1 tsp garlic powder
- 1/2 tsp pepper
- 1 tsp salt

Directions:
1. Add chickpeas, sweet potatoes, oil, bell pepper, onion, paprika, garlic powder, pepper, and salt into the mixing bowl and toss well.
2. Line multi-level air fryer basket with parchment paper.
3. Add chickpea sweet potato mixture into the multi-level air fryer basket.
4. Place multi-level air fryer basket into the inner pot of the instant pot.
5. Secure pot with air fryer lid, select roast then cook at 380 F for 35-40 minutes. Stir halfway through.
6. Serve and enjoy.

Nutritional Value (Amount per Serving):
- Calories 199
- Fat 4.9 g
- Carbohydrates 34.1 g
- Sugar 4.7 g
- Protein 6.3 g
- Cholesterol 0 mg

Cinnamon Sweet Potato Muffins

Preparation Time: 10 minutes
Cooking Time: 25 minutes
Serve: 12

Ingredients:
- 2 1/2 cups sweet potatoes, cooked and mashed
- 3/4 cup milk
- 1 tsp ground cinnamon
- 3 tsp baking powder
- 1/2 cup coconut sugar
- 1 1/2 cups whole wheat flour
- 1/2 tsp vanilla
- Pinch of salt

Directions:
1. Add sweet potatoes, vanilla, and milk into the blender and blend until smooth.
2. In a mixing bowl, mix flour, cinnamon, baking powder, coconut sugar, and salt.
3. Add blended sweet potato mixture and mix until well combined.

4. Pour batter into the 12 greased silicone muffin molds.
5. Place the dehydrating tray in the air fryer basket.
6. Place 6 silicone muffin molds onto the dehydrating tray.
7. Place multi-level air fryer basket into the inner pot of the instant pot.
8. Secure pot with air fryer lid, select bake mode then cook at 350 F for 25-30 minutes.
9. Cook remaining muffins.
10. Serve and enjoy.

Nutritional Value (Amount per Serving):
- Calories 134
- Fat 3.8 g
- Carbohydrates 23 g
- Sugar 0.7 g
- Protein 2.5 g
- Cholesterol 0 mg

Vegetable Breakfast Hash

Preparation Time: 10 minutes
Cooking Time: 35 minutes
Serve: 4

Ingredients:
- 1 cup zucchini, chopped
- 4 cups potatoes, peeled and cubed
- 1 red bell pepper, chopped
- 1 cup squash, chopped
- 1/2 cup mushrooms, sliced
- 14 oz can pinto beans, drained and rinsed
- 1 tsp onion powder
- 1 tsp garlic powder
- 1/2 tsp paprika
- Pepper
- Salt

Directions:
1. Line multi-level air fryer basket with parchment paper.
2. In a bowl, toss potatoes with pepper and salt.
3. Add potatoes into the multi-level air fryer basket.
4. Place multi-level air fryer basket into the inner pot of the instant pot.
5. Secure pot with air fryer lid, select bake than cook at 380 F for 25 minutes. Stir halfway through.
6. In a mixing bowl, mix remaining vegetables, beans, and spices.
7. Add vegetable mixture into the multi-level air fryer basket.
8. Secure pot with air fryer lid, select bake than cook at 380 F for 15 minutes. Stir halfway through.
9. In a large bowl, mix together potatoes, vegetable and bean mixture.
10. Serve and enjoy.

Nutritional Value (Amount per Serving):
- Calories 190
- Fat 0.8 g
- Carbohydrates 39.4 g
- Sugar 5.4 g
- Protein 7.4 g
- Cholesterol 0 mg

Healthy Oatmeal Cups

Preparation Time: 10 minutes
Cooking Time: 30 minutes
Serve: 12

Ingredients:
- 3 cups old fashioned oats
- 1 1/2 cups almond milk
- 1/2 tsp vanilla
- 1 1/2 tsp cinnamon
- 1 cup apples, chopped
- 1/4 cup maple syrup
- 1 1/4 cups applesauce
- 1 tsp baking powder
- 1/4 tsp salt

Directions:
1. Add all ingredients in a large mixing bowl and mix until well combined.
2. Pour batter into the 12 greased silicone muffin molds.
3. Place the dehydrating tray in the air fryer basket.
4. Place 6 silicone muffin molds onto the dehydrating tray.
5. Place multi-level air fryer basket into the inner pot of the instant pot.
6. Secure pot with air fryer lid, select bake mode then cook at 350 F for 25-30 minutes.
7. Cook remaining muffins.
8. Serve and enjoy.

Nutritional Value (Amount per Serving):
- Calories 264
- Fat 9.8 g
- Carbohydrates 38.8 g
- Sugar 10.5 g
- Protein 5.8 g
- Cholesterol 0 mg

Roasted Sweet Potatoes

Preparation Time: 10 minutes
Cooking Time: 40 minutes
Serve: 6

Ingredients:
- 2 lbs sweet potatoes, peel and cut into 1/2-inch cubes
- 1/2 tsp chili powder
- 1/4 tsp cinnamon
- 2 tbsp olive oil
- 1/2 tsp onion powder
- 1/2 tsp garlic powder
- Pepper
- Salt

Directions:
1. Add sweet potatoes and remaining ingredients into the mixing bowl and toss well.
2. Line multi-level air fryer basket with parchment paper.
3. Add sweet potatoes into the multi-level air fryer basket.
4. Place multi-level air fryer basket into the inner pot of the instant pot.
5. Secure pot with air fryer lid, select roast then cook at 380 F for 35-40 minutes. Stir halfway through.
6. Serve and enjoy.

Nutritional Value (Amount per Serving):
- Calories 221
- Fat 5 g
- Carbohydrates 42.7 g
- Sugar 0.9 g
- Protein 2.4 g
- Cholesterol 0 mg

Oat Cinnamon Muffins

Preparation Time: 10 minutes
Cooking Time: 30 minutes
Serve: 12

Ingredients:
- 2 cups oat flour
- 1/3 cup coconut oil, melted
- 1/2 cup maple syrup
- 1 cup applesauce
- 1 tsp cinnamon
- 2 tsp baking powder
- 1 tsp vanilla
- 1/4 tsp salt

Directions:
1. In a bowl, mix together applesauce, cinnamon, vanilla, oil, maple syrup, and salt.
2. Add baking powder and oat flour and stir well. Let the sit mixture for 10 minutes.
3. Pour batter into the 12 greased silicone muffin molds.
4. Place the dehydrating tray in the air fryer basket.
5. Place 6 silicone muffin molds onto the dehydrating tray.
6. Place multi-level air fryer basket into the inner pot of the instant pot.
7. Secure pot with air fryer lid, select bake mode then cook at 350 F for 30 minutes.
8. Cook remaining muffins.
9. Serve and enjoy.

Nutritional Value (Amount per Serving):
- Calories 158
- Fat 7.1 g
- Carbohydrates 22.2 g
- Sugar 9.9 g
- Protein 2 g
- Cholesterol 0 mg

Breakfast Quiche Cups

Preparation Time: 10 minutes
Cooking Time: 20 minutes
Serve: 12

Ingredients:
- 8 eggs
- 1/4 cup bell pepper, diced
- 3/4 cup cheddar cheese, shredded
- 10 oz frozen spinach, chopped
- 1/4 cup onion, chopped
- 1/4 cup mushroom, diced

Directions:
1. Add all ingredients into the mixing bowl and mix until well combined.
2. Pour egg mixture into the 12 greased silicone muffin molds.
3. Place the dehydrating tray in the air fryer basket.
4. Place 6 silicone muffin molds onto the dehydrating tray.
5. Place multi-level air fryer basket into the inner pot of the instant pot.
6. Secure pot with air fryer lid, select bake mode then cook at 375 F for 20 minutes.
7. Cook remaining muffins.
8. Serve and enjoy.

Nutritional Value (Amount per Serving):
- Calories 78
- Fat 5.4 g
- Carbohydrates 1.6 g
- Sugar 0.6 g
- Protein 6.2 g
- Cholesterol 117 mg

Healthy Kale Muffins

Preparation Time: 10 minutes
Cooking Time: 30 minutes
Serve: 8

Ingredients:
- 6 eggs
- 1/4 cup chives, chopped
- 1 cup kale, chopped
- 1/2 cup milk
- Pepper
- Salt

Directions:
1. Add all ingredients into the mixing bowl and mix well.
2. Pour egg mixture into the 8 greased silicone muffin molds.
3. Place the dehydrating tray in the air fryer basket.
4. Place 6 silicone muffin molds onto the dehydrating tray.
5. Place multi-level air fryer basket into the inner pot of the instant pot.
6. Secure pot with air fryer lid, select bake mode then cook at 350 F for 30 minutes.

7. Cook remaining muffins.
8. Serve and enjoy.

Nutritional Value (Amount per Serving):
- Calories 59
- Fat 3.6 g
- Carbohydrates 2 g
- Sugar 1 g
- Protein 5 g
- Cholesterol 124 mg

Tomato Spinach Egg Muffins

Preparation Time: 10 minutes
Cooking Time: 20 minutes
Serve: 12

Ingredients:
- 6 eggs
- 1 1/2 tsp dried oregano
- 1 1/2 tsp dried basil
- 2 tbsp olives, diced
- 1/2 cup sun-dried tomatoes, diced
- 1/4 cup spinach, cooked
- 1/2 cup egg whites
- 2 tbsp feta cheese, crumbled

Directions:
1. In a bowl, whisk eggs, egg whites, pepper, and salt.
2. Add remaining ingredients and stir well.
3. Pour egg mixture into the 12 greased silicone muffin molds.
4. Place the dehydrating tray in the air fryer basket.
5. Place 6 silicone muffin molds onto the dehydrating tray.
6. Place multi-level air fryer basket into the inner pot of the instant pot.
7. Secure pot with air fryer lid, select bake mode then cook at 350 F for 20 minutes.
8. Cook remaining muffins.
9. Serve and enjoy.

Nutritional Value (Amount per Serving):
- Calories 45
- Fat 2.7 g
- Carbohydrates 0.8 g
- Sugar 0.5 g
- Protein 4.2 g
- Cholesterol 83 mg

Blueberry Breakfast Muffins

Preparation Time: 10 minutes
Cooking Time: 30 minutes
Serve: 12

Ingredients:
- 2 cups all-purpose flour
- 2 eggs, lightly beaten
- 2 tsp baking powder
- 1/3 cup sugar
- 1 cup almond flour
- 1 1/2 cups blueberry
- 1/4 cup butter, melted
- 1/4 cup maple syrup
- 1 cup milk
- Pinch of salt

Directions:
1. In a bowl, mix together all dry ingredients.
2. In a separate bowl, whisk together wet ingredients.
3. Slowly stir wet mixture into the dry mixture. Add blueberries and fold well.
4. Pour batter into the 12 greased silicone muffin molds.
5. Place the dehydrating tray in the air fryer basket.
6. Place 6 silicone muffin molds onto the dehydrating tray.
7. Place multi-level air fryer basket into the inner pot of the instant pot.
8. Secure pot with air fryer lid, select bake mode then cook at 375 F for 25-30 minutes.
9. Cook remaining muffins.
10. Serve and enjoy.

Nutritional Value (Amount per Serving):
- Calories 180
- Fat 6.4 g
- Carbohydrates 30.4 g
- Sugar 12.4 g
- Protein 4.4 g
- Cholesterol 39 mg

Delicious Banana Muffins

Preparation Time: 10 minutes
Cooking Time: 25 minutes
Serve: 12

Ingredients:
- 2 large eggs, lightly beaten
- 1/4 tsp ground cardamom
- 1/4 tsp ground cloves
- 1/2 tsp ground ginger
- 1 tsp baking powder
- 1 tsp ground cinnamon
- 1/4 cup butter, melted
- 1/4 cup brown sugar
- 1/3 cup granulated sugar
- 1 cup bananas, mashed
- 1 3/4 cup flour
- 1/2 tsp salt

Directions:
1. In a bowl, mix together flour, spices, baking powder, and salt.
2. In a separate bowl, mix together bananas, eggs, brown sugar, sugar, and butter.
3. Add flour mixture to the banana mixture and stir until well combined.
4. Pour batter into the 12 greased silicone muffin molds.
5. Place the dehydrating tray in the air fryer basket.

6. Place 6 silicone muffin molds onto the dehydrating tray.
7. Place multi-level air fryer basket into the inner pot of the instant pot.
8. Secure pot with air fryer lid, select bake mode then cook at 350 F for 20-25 minutes.
9. Cook remaining muffins.
10. Serve and enjoy.

Nutritional Value (Amount per Serving):
- Calories 157
- Fat 4.9 g
- Carbohydrates 25.8 g
- Sugar 10.1 g
- Protein 3.1 g
- Cholesterol 41 mg

Tomato Pepper Egg Cups

Preparation Time: 10 minutes
Cooking Time: 30 minutes
Serve: 12
Ingredients:
- 6 eggs
- 2 tsp dried oregano
- 1/3 cup milk
- 1 bell pepper, chopped
- 1 tomato, chopped
- 3/4 cup feta cheese, crumbled
- 1/4 tsp pepper
- 1/8 tsp salt

Directions:
1. In a bowl, whisk eggs with milk, oregano, pepper, and salt.
2. Add bell pepper, tomato, and cheese and stir well.
3. Pour egg mixture into the 12 greased silicone muffin molds.
4. Place the dehydrating tray in the air fryer basket.
5. Place 6 silicone muffin molds onto the dehydrating tray.
6. Place multi-level air fryer basket into the inner pot of the instant pot.
7. Secure pot with air fryer lid, select bake mode then cook at 350 F for 25-30 minutes.
8. Cook remaining muffins.
9. Serve and enjoy.

Nutritional Value (Amount per Serving):
- Calories 65
- Fat 4.4 g
- Carbohydrates 2 g
- Sugar 1.5 g
- Protein 4.5 g
- Cholesterol 91 mg

Chapter 3: Poultry

Cheese Garlic Chicken Wings

Preparation Time: 10 minutes
Cooking Time: 30 minutes
Serve: 4
Ingredients:
- 1 lb chicken wings, pat dry
- 1 tbsp baking powder
- 1/2 tsp onion powder
- 1/2 tsp paprika
- 1/2 tsp garlic powder
- Pepper
- Salt

For Sauce:
- 1/2 cup parmesan cheese, grated
- 1/4 cup butter, melted
- 1 tsp dried parsley
- 1/2 tsp garlic powder
- 1/2 tsp onion powder
- 1/4 tsp pepper

Directions:
1. Toss chicken wings with baking powder, onion powder, paprika, garlic powder, pepper, and salt.
2. Add chicken wings into the multi-level air fryer basket.
3. Place multi-level air fryer basket into the inner pot of the instant pot.
4. Secure pot with air fryer lid, select air fry mode then cook at 400 F for 25-30 minutes. Flip chicken wings halfway through.
5. Transfer chicken wings into the large bowl.
6. In a small bowl, mix together all sauce ingredients and pour over chicken wings.
7. Toss chicken wings well and serve.

Nutritional Value (Amount per Serving):
- Calories 363
- Fat 22.4 g
- Carbohydrates 3.4 g
- Sugar 0.4 g
- Protein 36.8 g
- Cholesterol 139 mg

Tender & Juicy Chicken Tenders

Preparation Time: 10 minutes
Cooking Time: 12 minutes
Serve: 4
Ingredients:
- 3 eggs, lightly beaten
- 1 lb chicken tenderloin
- 1/2 cup all-purpose flour
- 1/3 cup breadcrumbs
- Pepper
- Salt

Directions:
1. In a small bowl, add eggs and whisk well.
2. In a separate bowl, add flour.
3. In a shallow dish, mix breadcrumbs, pepper, and salt.
4. Dip chicken in flour, then in egg and coat with breadcrumbs.
5. Line multi-level air fryer basket with parchment paper.
6. Place coated chicken tenderloins into the multi-level air fryer basket.
7. Place multi-level air fryer basket into the inner pot of the instant pot.
8. Secure pot with air fryer lid, select air fry mode then cook at 330 F for 12 minutes.
9. Serve and enjoy.

Nutritional Value (Amount per Serving):
- Calories 236
- Fat 4.5 g
- Carbohydrates 18.7 g
- Sugar 0.9 g
- Protein 29.9 g
- Cholesterol 171 mg

Juicy Chicken Breasts

Preparation Time: 10 minutes
Cooking Time: 16 minutes
Serve: 4
Ingredients:
- 4 chicken breasts, skinless & boneless
- 1/2 tsp paprika
- 1/2 tsp garlic powder
- 1 tbsp olive oil
- Pepper
- Salt

Directions:
1. Mix together oil, garlic powder, paprika, pepper, and salt and rub all over chicken breasts.
2. Place chicken breasts into the multi-level air fryer basket.
3. Place multi-level air fryer basket into the inner pot of the instant pot.
4. Secure pot with air fryer lid, select air fry mode then cook at 360 F for 16 minutes. Turn chicken halfway through.
5. Slice and serve.

Nutritional Value (Amount per Serving):
- Calories 309
- Fat 14.4 g
- Carbohydrates 0.4 g
- Sugar 0.1 g
- Protein 42.3 g
- Cholesterol 130 mg

Easy & Tasty Parmesan Chicken

Preparation Time: 10 minutes
Cooking Time: 15 minutes
Serve: 4
Ingredients:
- 2 chicken breasts split in half

- 1 cup mayonnaise
- 1 cup breadcrumbs
- 1 cup parmesan cheese, shredded
- Pepper
- Salt

Directions:
1. In a shallow dish, mix together parmesan cheese, breadcrumbs, pepper, and salt.
2. Spread mayonnaise on both sides of chicken breasts and coat chicken breasts with cheese mixture.
3. Place coated chicken breasts into the multi-level air fryer basket.
4. Place multi-level air fryer basket into the inner pot of the instant pot.
5. Secure pot with air fryer lid, select air fry mode then cook at 390 F for 15 minutes. Turn chicken after 10 minutes.
6. Serve and enjoy.

Nutritional Value (Amount per Serving):
- Calories 547
- Fat 31.3 g
- Carbohydrates 34.3 g
- Sugar 5.4 g
- Protein 32.5 g
- Cholesterol 96 mg

Delicious Lemon Chicken

Preparation Time: 10 minutes
Cooking Time: 16 minutes
Serve: 4
Ingredients:
- 2 eggs, lightly beaten
- 1 lb chicken breasts, skinless & boneless
- 1/2 cup parmesan cheese, grated
- 1/2 cup breadcrumbs
- 1/2 tsp dried parsley
- 1 tbsp garlic, minced
- 1/4 cup fresh lemon juice
- Pepper
- Salt

Directions:
1. In a bowl, whisk together eggs, parsley, garlic, lemon juice, pepper, and salt.
2. Add chicken into the egg mixture, cover, and place in the refrigerator for 1 hour.
3. In a shallow dish mix, parmesan cheese, and breadcrumbs.
4. Remove chicken from marinade and coat with parmesan cheese mixture.
5. Place coated chicken breasts into the multi-level air fryer basket.
6. Place multi-level air fryer basket into the inner pot of the instant pot.
7. Secure pot with air fryer lid, select air fry mode then cook at 390 F for 16 minutes. Turn chicken halfway through.
8. Serve and enjoy.

Nutritional Value (Amount per Serving):
- Calories 343
- Fat 13.9 g
- Carbohydrates 11.3 g
- Sugar 1.4 g
- Protein 41.3 g
- Cholesterol 191 mg

Simple & Quick Chicken Tenders

Preparation Time: 10 minutes
Cooking Time: 10 minutes
Serve: 4
Ingredients:
- 1 lb chicken tenders
- 1 tbsp olive oil
- 1 tbsp poultry seasoning

Directions:
1. Add chicken tender tenders, oil, and poultry seasoning into the mixing bowl and toss well.
2. Place chicken tenders into the multi-level air fryer basket.
3. Place multi-level air fryer basket into the inner pot of the instant pot.
4. Secure pot with air fryer lid, select air fry mode then cook at 400 F for 10 minutes. Turn chicken tenders halfway through.
5. Serve and enjoy.

Nutritional Value (Amount per Serving):
- Calories 248
- Fat 12 g
- Carbohydrates 0.6 g
- Sugar 0 g
- Protein 32.9 g
- Cholesterol 101 mg

Flavorful Chicken Breast

Preparation Time: 10 minutes
Cooking Time: 20 minutes
Serve: 4
Ingredients:
- 2 chicken breasts
- 1 tsp onion powder
- 1/2 tsp dried rosemary
- 1 tsp oregano
- 1 tsp ground thyme
- 1/2 tsp pepper
- 1/2 tsp salt

Directions:
1. Mix together onion powder, rosemary, oregano, thyme, pepper, and salt and rub all over chicken breasts.
2. Place chicken breasts into the multi-level air fryer basket.
3. Place multi-level air fryer basket into the inner pot of the instant pot.
4. Secure pot with air fryer lid, select air fry mode then cook at 350 F for 20 minutes. Turn chicken halfway through.
5. Serve and enjoy.

Nutritional Value (Amount per Serving):

- Calories 144
- Fat 5.5 g
- Carbohydrates 1.2 g
- Sugar 0.2 g
- Protein 21.3 g
- Cholesterol 65 mg

Perfect Air Fry Chicken Breast

Preparation Time: 10 minutes
Cooking Time: 18 minutes
Serve: 2
Ingredients:
- 2 chicken breasts, skinless
- 1/2 tsp onion powder
- 1/2 tsp garlic powder
- 1 tsp dried rosemary, crushed
- 1 1/2 tsp pepper
- 2 tbsp brown sugar
- 1 tsp fresh lemon juice
- 2 tbsp soy sauce
- 3 tbsp vinegar
- 3 tbsp olive oil
- 1 tsp salt

Directions:
1. Add all ingredients except chicken into the bowl and mix well.
2. Add chicken and coat well with the marinade, cover bowl, and place in the refrigerator overnight.
3. Place marinated chicken into the multi-level air fryer basket.
4. Place multi-level air fryer basket into the inner pot of the instant pot.
5. Secure pot with air fryer lid, select air fry mode then cook at 360 F for 18 minutes. Turn chicken halfway through.
6. Serve and enjoy.

Nutritional Value (Amount per Serving):
- Calories 516
- Fat 32 g
- Carbohydrates 12.7 g
- Sugar 9.5 g
- Protein 43.7 g
- Cholesterol 130 mg

Chicken with Vegetables

Preparation Time: 10 minutes
Cooking Time: 15 minutes
Serve: 4
Ingredients:
- 1 lb chicken breast, cut into bite-size pieces
- 1 tbsp Italian seasoning
- 1/2 tsp garlic powder
- 1/2 tsp chili powder
- 2 tbsp olive oil
- 1 tsp garlic, minced
- 1/2 onion, chopped
- 1 cup bell pepper, chopped
- 1 zucchini, chopped
- 1 cup broccoli florets
- Pepper
- Salt

Directions:
1. Add chicken and remaining ingredients into the mixing bowl and mix well.
2. Add chicken and vegetable mixture into the multi-level air fryer basket.
3. Place multi-level air fryer basket into the inner pot of the instant pot.
4. Secure pot with air fryer lid, select air fry mode then cook at 400 F for 15 minutes. Stir the chicken mixture after 10 minutes.
5. Serve and enjoy.

Nutritional Value (Amount per Serving):
- Calories 234
- Fat 11.2 g
- Carbohydrates 7.7 g
- Sugar 3.8 g
- Protein 25.9 g
- Cholesterol 75 mg

Tasty Chicken Fajitas

Preparation Time: 10 minutes
Cooking Time: 15 minutes
Serve: 8
Ingredients:
- 1 lb chicken, cut into strips
- 1 tbsp olive oil
- 3 tbsp fajita seasoning
- 1 onion, sliced
- 1 green bell pepper, sliced
- 1 yellow bell pepper, sliced
- 1 red bell pepper, sliced

Directions:
1. Add chicken and remaining ingredients into the mixing bowl and toss well.
2. Add chicken mixture into the multi-level air fryer basket.
3. Place multi-level air fryer basket into the inner pot of the instant pot.
4. Secure pot with air fryer lid, select air fry mode then cook at 390 F for 15 minutes. Stir the chicken mixture after 10 minutes.
5. Serve and enjoy.

Nutritional Value (Amount per Serving):
- Calories 131
- Fat 3.6 g
- Carbohydrates 6.4 g
- Sugar 2.5 g
- Protein 16.9 g
- Cholesterol 44 mg

Perfect Chicken Thighs

Preparation Time: 10 minutes
Cooking Time: 22 minutes
Serve: 4

Ingredients:
- 4 chicken thighs, bone-in & skin-on
- 1/2 tsp onion powder
- 1/2 tsp oregano
- 1 tsp garlic powder
- 1 tsp paprika
- 1/2 tsp kosher salt

Directions:
1. Mix together onion powder, oregano, garlic powder, paprika, and salt and rub all over chicken thighs.
2. Place chicken thighs into the multi-level air fryer basket.
3. Place multi-level air fryer basket into the inner pot of the instant pot.
4. Secure pot with air fryer lid, select air fry mode then cook at 380 F for 22 minutes. Flip chicken thighs after 12 minutes.
5. Serve and enjoy.

Nutritional Value (Amount per Serving):
- Calories 283
- Fat 10.9 g
- Carbohydrates 1.2 g
- Sugar 0.3 g
- Protein 42.5 g
- Cholesterol 130 mg

Parmesan Chicken Tenders

Preparation Time: 10 minutes
Cooking Time: 16 minutes
Serve: 4

Ingredients:
- 1 lb chicken breasts, skinless & cut into strips
- 1 tsp Italian seasoning
- 1/4 cup flour
- 1 egg, lightly beaten
- 1/3 cup breadcrumbs
- 1/3 cup parmesan cheese, grated
- Pepper
- Salt

Directions:
1. In a small bowl, add egg and whisk well.
2. In a separate bowl, add flour.
3. In a shallow dish, mix breadcrumbs, parmesan cheese, Italian seasoning, pepper, and salt.
4. Dip chicken in flour, then in egg and coat with breadcrumbs.
5. Line multi-level air fryer basket with parchment paper.
6. Place coated chicken breasts into the multi-level air fryer basket.
7. Place multi-level air fryer basket into the inner pot of the instant pot.
8. Secure pot with air fryer lid, select air fry mode then cook at 400 F for 16 minutes. Flip chicken halfway through.
9. Serve and enjoy.

Nutritional Value (Amount per Serving):
- Calories 323
- Fat 12 g
- Carbohydrates 12.9 g
- Sugar 0.8 g
- Protein 38.6 g
- Cholesterol 148 mg

Spicy Hassel Back Chicken

Preparation Time: 10 minutes
Cooking Time: 15 minutes
Serve: 2

Ingredients:
- 2 chicken breasts, skinless, boneless, Cut 6 slits across the top
- 1/2 cup cheddar cheese, shredded
- 1/4 cup pickled jalapenos, chopped
- 2 oz cream cheese, softened
- 4 bacon slices, cooked & crumbled

Directions:
1. In a bowl, mix together half cheddar cheese, jalapenos, cream cheese, and bacon.
2. Stuff cheese mixture into the chicken breasts slits.
3. Line multi-level air fryer basket with parchment paper.
4. Place chicken breasts into the multi-level air fryer basket.
5. Place multi-level air fryer basket into the inner pot of the instant pot.
6. Secure pot with air fryer lid, select air fry mode then cook at 350 F for 14 minutes.
7. Add remaining cheese on top of chicken breasts, cover, and cook for 1 minute more.
8. Serve and enjoy.

Nutritional Value (Amount per Serving):
- Calories 755
- Fat 49.5 g
- Carbohydrates 6 g
- Sugar 3.3 g
- Protein 67.9 g
- Cholesterol 239 mg

Delicious Bagel Chicken Tenders

Preparation Time: 10 minutes
Cooking Time: 14 minutes
Serve: 6

Ingredients:
- 6 chicken breast tenderloins
- 2 tbsp everything bagel seasoning
- 2 tbsp flour
- 3/4 cup breadcrumbs
- 1 cup buttermilk
- Pepper
- Salt

Directions:
1. Add chicken tenderloins and buttermilk into the large bowl, cover bowl, and place in the refrigerator for 1 hour.

2. In a shallow dish, mix together flour, breadcrumbs, bagel seasoning, pepper, and salt.
3. Dip each chicken tender into the flour mixture and coat well.
4. Place chicken tenders into the multi-level air fryer basket.
5. Place multi-level air fryer basket into the inner pot of the instant pot.
6. Secure pot with air fryer lid, select air fry mode then cook at 350 F for 14 minutes. Turn chicken tenders halfway through.
7. Serve and enjoy.

Nutritional Value (Amount per Serving):
- Calories 187
- Fat 1.7 g
- Carbohydrates 15.4 g
- Sugar 3 g
- Protein 25.7 g
- Cholesterol 72 mg

Perfectly Tender Chicken Breast

Preparation Time: 10 minutes
Cooking Time: 14 minutes
Serve: 4

Ingredients:
- 4 chicken breasts, boneless
- 1/4 tsp garlic powder
- 2 tbsp butter, melted
- 1/4 tsp pepper
- 1/2 tsp salt

Directions:
1. In a small bowl, mix together butter, garlic powder, pepper, and salt.
2. Brush chicken breasts with melted butter.
3. Place chicken breasts into the multi-level air fryer basket.
4. Place multi-level air fryer basket into the inner pot of the instant pot.
5. Secure pot with air fryer lid, select air fry mode then cook at 380 F for 14 minutes. Turn chicken halfway through.
6. Serve and enjoy.

Nutritional Value (Amount per Serving):
- Calories 329
- Fat 16.6 g
- Carbohydrates 0.2 g
- Sugar 0 g
- Protein 42.3 g
- Cholesterol 145 mg

Healthy Chicken Drumsticks

Preparation Time: 10 minutes
Cooking Time: 20 minutes
Serve: 2

Ingredients:
- 4 chicken drumsticks
- 1/2 tsp onion powder
- 1/4 tsp chili powder
- 3/4 tsp paprika
- 1/2 tsp garlic powder
- 1 tbsp olive oil
- 1/4 tsp pepper
- 1/2 tsp sea salt

Directions:
1. In a small bowl, mix together oil, garlic powder, paprika, chili powder, onion powder, pepper, and salt and rub all over chicken drumsticks.
2. Place chicken drumsticks into the multi-level air fryer basket.
3. Place multi-level air fryer basket into the inner pot of the instant pot.
4. Secure pot with air fryer lid, select air fry mode then cook at 400 F for 20 minutes. Turn chicken drumsticks halfway through.
5. Serve and enjoy.

Nutritional Value (Amount per Serving):
- Calories 224
- Fat 12.4 g
- Carbohydrates 1.8 g
- Sugar 0.5 g
- Protein 25.7 g
- Cholesterol 81 mg

Easy BBQ Chicken Legs

Preparation Time: 10 minutes
Cooking Time: 30 minutes
Serve: 4

Ingredients:
- 1 1/2 lbs chicken legs
- 1/2 cup BBQ sauce
- 1 1/2 tbsp BBQ rub

Directions:
1. Rub chicken legs with BBQ rub.
2. Place chicken legs into the multi-level air fryer basket.
3. Place multi-level air fryer basket into the inner pot of the instant pot.
4. Secure pot with air fryer lid, select air fry mode then cook at 400 F for 25 minutes.
5. Brush chicken legs with BBQ sauce and air fry for 5 minutes more.
6. Serve and enjoy.

Nutritional Value (Amount per Serving):
- Calories 370
- Fat 12.7 g
- Carbohydrates 11.3 g
- Sugar 8.1 g
- Protein 49.2 g
- Cholesterol 151 mg

Quick BBQ Chicken Breast

Preparation Time: 10 minutes
Cooking Time: 14 minutes
Serve: 4

Ingredients:
- 4 chicken breasts, skinless & boneless
- 1 tbsp BBQ seasoning

Directions:

1. Rub chicken with BBQ seasoning, cover, and place in the refrigerator for 1 hour.
2. Place chicken into the multi-level air fryer basket.
3. Place multi-level air fryer basket into the inner pot of the instant pot.
4. Secure pot with air fryer lid, select air fry mode then cook at 400 F for 14 minutes. Turn chicken halfway through.
5. Serve and enjoy.

Nutritional Value (Amount per Serving):
- Calories 280
- Fat 10.9 g
- Carbohydrates 0.3 g
- Sugar 0.1 g
- Protein 42.4 g
- Cholesterol 130 mg

Crispy Chicken Drumsticks

Preparation Time: 10 minutes
Cooking Time: 20 minutes
Serve: 2

Ingredients:
- 4 chicken drumsticks
- 1/2 tsp garlic powder
- 1/2 tsp onion powder
- 1/2 tsp paprika
- 1/2 tbsp baking powder
- 1/2 tbsp olive oil
- 1/4 tsp pepper
- Salt

Directions:
1. Toss chicken drumsticks with oil.
2. In a small bowl, mix together garlic powder, onion powder, paprika, baking powder, pepper, and salt and sprinkle over chicken.
3. Place chicken drumsticks into the multi-level air fryer basket.
4. Place multi-level air fryer basket into the inner pot of the instant pot.
5. Secure pot with air fryer lid, select air fry mode then cook at 400 F for 20 minutes. Flip chicken drumsticks halfway through.
6. Serve and enjoy.

Nutritional Value (Amount per Serving):
- Calories 196
- Fat 8.9 g
- Carbohydrates 3.2 g
- Sugar 0.4 g
- Protein 25.6 g
- Cholesterol 81 mg

Lemon Pepper Chicken Breasts

Preparation Time: 10 minutes
Cooking Time: 30 minutes
Serve: 4

Ingredients:
- 4 chicken breasts, boneless & skinless
- 1 tsp granulated garlic
- 1 tbsp lemon pepper
- 1 tsp salt

Directions:
1. Season chicken with garlic, lemon pepper, and salt.
2. Place chicken into the multi-level air fryer basket.
3. Place multi-level air fryer basket into the inner pot of the instant pot.
4. Secure pot with air fryer lid, select air fry mode then cook at 360 F for 30 minutes. Flip chicken halfway through.
5. Serve and enjoy.

Nutritional Value (Amount per Serving):
- Calories 284
- Fat 10.9 g
- Carbohydrates 1.6 g
- Sugar 0.2 g
- Protein 42.5 g
- Cholesterol 130 mg

Mexican Chicken

Preparation Time: 10 minutes
Cooking Time: 25 minutes
Serve: 4

Ingredients:
- 1 lb chicken breasts, skinless & boneless
- 1/4 tsp garlic powder
- 1/4 tsp onion powder
- 1/2 tsp cumin
- 1/2 tsp chili powder
- 1 tbsp olive oil
- 2 tbsp fresh lime juice
- 1/4 tsp salt

Directions:
1. Add chicken and remaining ingredients into the zip-lock bag, seal bag and shake well and place in the refrigerator for 1 hour.
2. Place marinated chicken into the multi-level air fryer basket.
3. Place multi-level air fryer basket into the inner pot of the instant pot.
4. Secure pot with air fryer lid, select air fry mode then cook at 400 F for 25 minutes. Flip chicken halfway through.
5. Serve and enjoy.

Nutritional Value (Amount per Serving):
- Calories 254
- Fat 12 g
- Carbohydrates 2.4 g
- Sugar 0.5 g
- Protein 33 g
- Cholesterol 101 mg

Perfect Juicy Chicken Drumsticks

Preparation Time: 10 minutes
Cooking Time: 20 minutes
Serve: 4

Ingredients:

- 6 chicken drumsticks
- 1 tsp dried parsley
- 1 tsp garlic powder
- 1 tsp paprika
- 2 tbsp olive oil
- 1 tsp pepper
- 1 tsp salt

Directions:
1. Brush chicken drumsticks with oil.
2. Mix together parsley, garlic powder, paprika, pepper, and salt and sprinkle over chicken drumsticks.
3. Place chicken drumsticks into the multi-level air fryer basket.
4. Place multi-level air fryer basket into the inner pot of the instant pot.
5. Secure pot with air fryer lid, select air fry mode then cook at 400 F for 20 minutes. Flip chicken halfway through.
6. Serve and enjoy.

Nutritional Value (Amount per Serving):
- Calories 182
- Fat 11 g
- Carbohydrates 1.2 g
- Sugar 0.2 g
- Protein 19.3 g
- Cholesterol 61 mg

Asian Chicken Breast

Preparation Time: 10 minutes
Cooking Time: 30 minutes
Serve: 2

Ingredients:
- 2 chicken breasts, skin-on & bone-in
- 1 tsp garlic powder
- 1 tsp onion powder
- 1/4 tsp cayenne pepper
- 1 tbsp sweet paprika
- 1/2 tsp pepper
- 2 tbsp sesame oil
- 1 tsp kosher salt

Directions:
1. Mix together oil, paprika, cayenne, onion powder, garlic powder, pepper, and salt and rub all over chicken breasts.
2. Place chicken breasts into the multi-level air fryer basket.
3. Place multi-level air fryer basket into the inner pot of the instant pot.
4. Secure pot with air fryer lid, select air fry mode then cook at 380 F for 20 minutes.
5. Flip chicken and cook for 10 minutes more.
6. Serve and enjoy.

Nutritional Value (Amount per Serving):
- Calories 418
- Fat 25 g
- Carbohydrates 4.4 g
- Sugar 1.2 g
- Protein 43.2 g

- Cholesterol 130 mg

Ranch Chicken Wings

Preparation Time: 10 minutes
Cooking Time: 25 minutes
Serve: 2

Ingredients:
- 1 lb chicken wings
- 3 garlic cloves, minced
- 2 tbsp butter, melted
- 1 1/2 tbsp ranch seasoning mix

Directions:
1. Add chicken wings into the mixing bowl. Add garlic, butter, and ranch seasoning over chicken wings and toss well.
2. Place chicken wings into the multi-level air fryer basket.
3. Place multi-level air fryer basket into the inner pot of the instant pot.
4. Secure pot with air fryer lid, select air fry mode then cook at 360 F for 20 minutes.
5. Flip chicken wings turn temperature to 390 F and cook for 5 minutes more.
6. Serve and enjoy.

Nutritional Value (Amount per Serving):
- Calories 553
- Fat 28.4 g
- Carbohydrates 1.5 g
- Sugar 0.1 g
- Protein 66 g
- Cholesterol 232 mg

Ginger Garlic Chicken Thighs

Preparation Time: 10 minutes
Cooking Time: 10 minutes
Serve: 6

Ingredients:
- 6 chicken thighs, skinless & boneless
- 1 tbsp garlic, minced
- 1 tbsp ginger, grated
- 2 tbsp brown sugar
- 1/2 tbsp Worcestershire sauce
- 2 tbsp soy sauce

Directions:
1. Add chicken and remaining ingredients into the zip-lock bag, seal bag shake well and place in the refrigerator for 3 hours.
2. Place marinated chicken thighs into the multi-level air fryer basket.
3. Place multi-level air fryer basket into the inner pot of the instant pot.
4. Secure pot with air fryer lid, select air fry mode then cook at 390 F for 10 minutes. Flip chicken halfway through.
5. Serve and enjoy.

Nutritional Value (Amount per Serving):
- Calories 297
- Fat 10.8 g
- Carbohydrates 4.5 g

- Sugar 3.7 g
- Protein 42.7 g
- Cholesterol 130 mg

Air Fry Chicken Livers

Preparation Time: 10 minutes
Cooking Time: 15 minutes
Serve: 2
Ingredients:
- 8 oz chicken livers
- 1 egg, lightly beaten
- 1/2 cup milk
- 2 tbsp cornstarch
- 1/4 cup flour
- 1/4 tsp garlic powder
- 1/4 tsp onion powder
- Pepper
- Salt

Directions:
1. In a small bowl, whisk the egg with milk.
2. In a shallow dish, mix together flour, cornstarch, garlic powder, onion powder, pepper, and salt.
3. Dip chicken livers into the egg mixture then coat with flour mixture.
4. Place chicken livers into the multi-level air fryer basket.
5. Place multi-level air fryer basket into the inner pot of the instant pot.
6. Secure pot with air fryer lid, select air fry mode then cook at 390 F for 10 minutes.
7. Flip chicken liver and cook for 5 minutes more.
8. Serve and enjoy.

Nutritional Value (Amount per Serving):
- Calories 341
- Fat 11 g
- Carbohydrates 23.9 g
- Sugar 3.2 g
- Protein 34.2 g
- Cholesterol 725 mg

Spicy & Easy Chicken Drumsticks

Preparation Time: 10 minutes
Cooking Time: 35 minutes
Serve: 3
Ingredients:
- 6 chicken drumsticks
- 6 tbsp hot sauce
- 2 tbsp Worcestershire sauce
- 1 cup Italian dressing

Directions:
1. Add chicken drumsticks and remaining ingredients into the zip-lock bag, seal bag, and place in the refrigerator overnight.
2. Place marinated chicken drumsticks into the multi-level air fryer basket.
3. Place multi-level air fryer basket into the inner pot of the instant pot.
4. Secure pot with air fryer lid, select air fry mode then cook at 400 F for 20 minutes.
5. Flip chicken drumsticks and cook at 325 F for 15 minutes more.
6. Serve and enjoy.

Nutritional Value (Amount per Serving):
- Calories 397
- Fat 27.6 g
- Carbohydrates 10.7 g
- Sugar 8.9 g
- Protein 25.8 g
- Cholesterol 133 mg

Delicious Lemon Pepper Chicken Thighs

Preparation Time: 10 minutes
Cooking Time: 15 minutes
Serve: 6
Ingredients:
- 6 chicken thighs, skinless & boneless
- 1/2 tsp garlic powder
- 1/2 tsp Italian seasoning
- 1/2 tsp paprika
- 1/2 tbsp lemon pepper seasoning
- 1 1/2 tbsp fresh lemon juice
- 1/4 tsp pepper

Directions:
1. In a small bowl, mix together garlic powder, Italian seasoning, paprika, lemon pepper seasoning, lemon juice, and pepper and rub all over chicken thighs.
2. Place chicken thighs into the multi-level air fryer basket.
3. Place multi-level air fryer basket into the inner pot of the instant pot.
4. Secure pot with air fryer lid, select air fry mode then cook at 360 F for 15 minutes. Turn chicken halfway through.
5. Serve and enjoy.

Nutritional Value (Amount per Serving):
- Calories 282
- Fat 11 g
- Carbohydrates 0.8 g
- Sugar 0.2 g
- Protein 42.4 g
- Cholesterol 130 mg

Meatballs

Preparation Time: 10 minutes
Cooking Time: 10 minutes
Serve: 4
Ingredients:
- 1 egg
- 1 lb ground turkey
- 1 tbsp soy sauce
- 1/4 cup fresh parsley, chopped
- 1/2 cup breadcrumbs
- Pepper
- Salt

Directions:
1. Add all ingredients into the bowl and mix until well combined.
2. Make small balls from the meat mixture and set aside.
3. Place meatballs into the multi-level air fryer basket.
4. Place multi-level air fryer basket into the inner pot of the instant pot.
5. Secure pot with air fryer lid, select air fry mode then cook at 400 F for 10 minutes. Turn meatballs halfway through.
6. Serve and enjoy.

Nutritional Value (Amount per Serving):
- Calories 294
- Fat 14.3 g
- Carbohydrates 10.4 g
- Sugar 1 g
- Protein 34.6 g
- Cholesterol 157 mg

Asian Chicken Thighs

Preparation Time: 10 minutes
Cooking Time: 25 minutes
Serve: 6
Ingredients:
- 6 chicken thighs
- 1 tbsp onion powder
- 1 tbsp garlic powder
- 3 tbsp honey
- 2 tbsp lime juice
- 1 tbsp Worcestershire sauce
- 1/4 cup soy sauce
- 1 tbsp sesame oil
- 2 tbsp olive oil
- 1/2 tsp kosher salt

Directions:
1. Add chicken into the large bowl.
2. Pour remaining ingredients over chicken and coat well.
3. Place chicken into the multi-level air fryer basket.
4. Place multi-level air fryer basket into the inner pot of the instant pot.
5. Secure pot with air fryer lid, select air fry mode then cook at 400 F for 25 minutes. Turn chicken after 15 minutes.
6. Serve and enjoy.

Nutritional Value (Amount per Serving):
- Calories 390
- Fat 17.8 g
- Carbohydrates 13.1 g
- Sugar 10.3 g
- Protein 43.4 g
- Cholesterol 130 mg

Juicy Turkey Legs

Preparation Time: 10 minutes
Cooking Time: 40 minutes
Serve: 2
Ingredients:
- 2 turkey legs
- 1/2 tsp garlic powder
- 1 tsp brown sugar
- 1 1/2 tsp paprika
- 1 tsp garlic salt

Directions:
1. Mix together garlic powder, brown sugar, paprika, and salt and rub all over turkey legs.
2. Place turkey legs into the multi-level air fryer basket.
3. Place multi-level air fryer basket into the inner pot of the instant pot.
4. Secure pot with air fryer lid, select air fry mode then cook at 400 F for 40 minutes. Turn turkey legs halfway through.
5. Serve and enjoy.

Nutritional Value (Amount per Serving):
- Calories 165
- Fat 7.2 g
- Carbohydrates 3.9 g
- Sugar 2.1 g
- Protein 20.4 g
- Cholesterol 60 mg

Turkey Skewers

Preparation Time: 10 minutes
Cooking Time: 14 minutes
Serve: 4
Ingredients:
- 1 1/2 lbs turkey tenderloin, cut into 1-inch pieces
- 2 tbsp olive oil
- 1 tbsp Italian seasoning
- 2 tsp garlic, minced
- Pepper
- Salt

Directions:
1. Add turkey pieces, oil, Italian seasoning, garlic, pepper, and salt into the zip-lock bag, seal bag, and place in the refrigerator overnight.

2. Thread marinated turkey pieces onto the skewers.
3. Place turkey skewers into the multi-level air fryer basket.
4. Place multi-level air fryer basket into the inner pot of the instant pot.
5. Secure pot with air fryer lid, select air fry mode then cook at 350 F for 14 minutes.
6. Serve and enjoy.

Nutritional Value (Amount per Serving):
- Calories 254
- Fat 10.3 g
- Carbohydrates 0.9 g
- Sugar 0.3 g
- Protein 42.3 g
- Cholesterol 70 mg

Turkey Patties

Preparation Time: 10 minutes
Cooking Time: 10 minutes
Serve: 4
Ingredients:
- 1 lb ground turkey
- 1 tsp garlic, minced
- 1 shallot, diced
- 1 jalapeno pepper, diced
- Pepper
- Salt

Directions:
1. Add all ingredients into the mixing bowl and mix until well combined.
2. Make four equal shapes of patties from the mixture.
3. Line multi-level air fryer basket with parchment paper.
4. Place turkey patties into the multi-level air fryer basket.
5. Place multi-level air fryer basket into the inner pot of the instant pot.
6. Secure pot with air fryer lid, select air fry mode then cook at 380 F for 10 minutes.
7. Serve and enjoy.

Nutritional Value (Amount per Serving):
- Calories 225
- Fat 12.5 g
- Carbohydrates 0.9 g
- Sugar 0.1 g
- Protein 31.2 g
- Cholesterol 116 mg

Best Baked Chicken Drumsticks

Preparation Time: 10 minutes
Cooking Time: 45 minutes
Serve: 6
Ingredients:
- 6 chicken legs
- 1/4 cup soy sauce
- 2 tbsp olive oil
- 1/2 tsp paprika
- 1/2 tsp oregano
- 1 1/2 tsp onion powder
- 1 1/2 tsp garlic powder
- 1/2 tsp pepper
- 1/2 tsp salt

Directions:
1. Add chicken legs and remaining ingredients into the zip-lock bag, seal bag, and place in the refrigerator for 1 hour.
2. Place marinated chicken legs into the multi-level air fryer basket.
3. Place multi-level air fryer basket into the inner pot of the instant pot.
4. Secure pot with air fryer lid, select bake mode then cook at 375 F for 45 minutes. Turn chicken halfway through.
5. Serve and enjoy.

Nutritional Value (Amount per Serving):
- Calories 329
- Fat 15.6 g
- Carbohydrates 2.1 g
- Sugar 0.5 g
- Protein 43.2 g
- Cholesterol 130 mg

Tasty Cajun Chicken Thighs

Preparation Time: 10 minutes
Cooking Time: 25 minutes
Serve: 4
Ingredients:
- 1 egg, lightly beaten
- 4 chicken thighs
- 1/2 cup flour
- 2 tbsp Cajun seasoning
- Salt

Directions:
1. In a small bowl, add egg and whisk well.
2. In a dish, mix together cajun seasoning, flour, and salt.
3. Coat chicken thighs with flour mixture then dip in egg and finally coat with flour mixture.
4. Place coated chicken thighs into the multi-level air fryer basket.
5. Place multi-level air fryer basket into the inner pot of the instant pot.
6. Secure pot with air fryer lid, select air fry mode then cook at 390 F for 25 minutes. Turn chicken thighs halfway through.
7. Serve and enjoy.

Nutritional Value (Amount per Serving):
- Calories 350
- Fat 12.1 g
- Carbohydrates 12 g
- Sugar 0.1 g
- Protein 45.3 g
- Cholesterol 171 mg

Honey Dijon Chicken

Preparation Time: 10 minutes

Cooking Time: 16 minutes
Serve: 4
Ingredients:
- 4 chicken thighs
- 1/2 tbsp garlic powder
- 1 1/2 Dijon mustard
- 2 tbsp honey
- Pepper
- Salt

Directions:
1. In a mixing bowl, mix Dijon mustard, honey, garlic powder, pepper, and salt.
2. Add chicken thighs and toss well.
3. Place chicken thighs into the multi-level air fryer basket.
4. Place multi-level air fryer basket into the inner pot of the instant pot.
5. Secure pot with air fryer lid, select air fry mode then cook at 400 F for 16 minutes. Turn chicken thighs halfway through.
6. Serve and enjoy.

Nutritional Value (Amount per Serving):
- Calories 376
- Fat 14.6 g
- Carbohydrates 14.4 g
- Sugar 9.7 g
- Protein 46.6 g
- Cholesterol 130 mg

Tasty Chicken Fritters

Preparation Time: 10 minutes
Cooking Time: 10 minutes
Serve: 4
Ingredients:
- 1 lb ground chicken
- 1/2 tsp garlic powder
- 1/2 cup parmesan cheese, shredded
- 1/2 cup breadcrumbs
- 2 tbsp green onions, chopped
- 1/2 tsp onion powder
- Pepper
- Salt

Directions:
1. In a large bowl, add all ingredients and mix until well combined.
2. Make four equal shapes of patties from the mixture.
3. Place patties into the multi-level air fryer basket.
4. Place multi-level air fryer basket into the inner pot of the instant pot.
5. Secure pot with air fryer lid, select air fry mode then cook at 350 F for 10 minutes. Turn patties halfway through.
6. Serve and enjoy.

Nutritional Value (Amount per Serving):
- Calories 308
- Fat 11.5 g
- Carbohydrates 10.9 g
- Sugar 1.1 g
- Protein 38.4 g
- Cholesterol 109 mg

Healthy Chicken Vegetable Patties

Preparation Time: 10 minutes
Cooking Time: 28 minutes
Serve: 4
Ingredients:
- 1 lb ground chicken
- 1 egg, lightly beaten
- 1 cup Monterey jack cheese, grated
- 1 cup carrot, grated
- 1 cup cauliflower, grated
- 1/8 tsp red chili flakes
- 1 tsp garlic, minced
- 1 onion, minced
- 3/4 cup breadcrumbs
- Pepper
- Salt

Directions:
1. In a large bowl, add all ingredients and mix until well combined.
2. Make four equal shapes of patties from the mixture.
3. Place patties into the multi-level air fryer basket.
4. Place multi-level air fryer basket into the inner pot of the instant pot.
5. Secure pot with air fryer lid, select bake mode then cook at 380 F for 28 minutes. Turn patties halfway through.
6. Serve and enjoy.

Nutritional Value (Amount per Serving):
- Calories 446
- Fat 19.2 g
- Carbohydrates 21.7 g
- Sugar 4.6 g
- Protein 44.9 g
- Cholesterol 167 mg

Easy Ranch Chicken Wings

Preparation Time: 10 minutes
Cooking Time: 20 minutes
Serve: 2
Ingredients:
- 1 lb chicken wings
- 2 tbsp butter, melted
- 1 tbsp ranch seasoning
- 1 tsp garlic, minced

Directions:
1. In a mixing bowl, mix butter, ranch seasoning, and garlic,
2. Add chicken wings and toss well.
3. Place chicken wings into the multi-level air fryer basket.
4. Place multi-level air fryer basket into the inner pot of the instant pot.

5. Secure pot with air fryer lid, select air fry mode then cook at 360 F for 20 minutes. Turn chicken wings halfway through.
6. Serve and enjoy.

Nutritional Value (Amount per Serving):
- Calories 550
- Fat 28.3 g
- Carbohydrates 0.5 g
- Sugar 0 g
- Protein 65.8 g
- Cholesterol 232 mg

Easy Chicken Nuggets

Preparation Time: 10 minutes
Cooking Time: 25 minutes
Serve: 4

Ingredients:
- 1 1/2 lbs chicken breast, boneless & cut into chunks
- 1/4 cup parmesan cheese, shredded
- 1/4 cup mayonnaise
- 1/2 tsp garlic powder
- 1/4 tsp onion powder
- 1/4 tsp salt

Directions:
1. In a large bowl, mix mayonnaise, garlic powder, onion powder, parmesan cheese, and salt.
2. Add chicken pieces and toss well.
3. Place chicken pieces into the multi-level air fryer basket.
4. Place multi-level air fryer basket into the inner pot of the instant pot.
5. Secure pot with air fryer lid, select air fry mode then cook at 400 F for 25 minutes. Turn chicken pieces halfway through.
6. Serve and enjoy.

Nutritional Value (Amount per Serving):
- Calories 271
- Fat 10.4 g
- Carbohydrates 4.1 g
- Sugar 1.1 g
- Protein 38.1 g
- Cholesterol 117 mg

Jerk Chicken

Preparation Time: 10 minutes
Cooking Time: 20 minutes
Serve: 2

Ingredients:
- 1 lb chicken wings
- 1 tbsp jerk seasoning
- 1 tsp olive oil
- 1 tbsp cornstarch

Directions:
1. In a bowl, add chicken wings, jerk seasoning, oil, and cornstarch and toss well.
2. Place chicken wings into the multi-level air fryer basket.

3. Place multi-level air fryer basket into the inner pot of the instant pot.
4. Secure pot with air fryer lid, select air fry mode then cook at 380 F for 20 minutes. Turn chicken wings halfway through.
5. Serve and enjoy.

Nutritional Value (Amount per Serving):
- Calories 466
- Fat 19.1 g
- Carbohydrates 3.7 g
- Sugar 0 g
- Protein 65.6 g
- Cholesterol 202 mg

Flavors Chicken Wings

Preparation Time: 10 minutes
Cooking Time: 30 minutes
Serve: 2

Ingredients:
- 1 lb chicken wings
- 2 tbsp vinegar
- 1/4 tsp onion powder
- 1/4 tsp garlic powder
- 1 tbsp olive oil
- 1 tsp salt

Directions:
1. In a bowl, toss chicken wings with garlic powder, oil, onion powder, and salt.
2. Place chicken wings into the multi-level air fryer basket.
3. Place multi-level air fryer basket into the inner pot of the instant pot.
4. Secure pot with air fryer lid, select air fry mode then cook at 360 F for 25 minutes.
5. Turn chicken wings and air fry for 5 minutes more.
6. Toss chicken wings with vinegar and serve.

Nutritional Value (Amount per Serving):
- Calories 496
- Fat 23.8 g
- Carbohydrates 0.6 g
- Sugar 0.3 g
- Protein 65.7 g
- Cholesterol 202 mg

Spicy Chicken Wings

Preparation Time: 10 minutes
Cooking Time: 25 minutes
Serve: 2

Ingredients:
- 10 chicken wings
- 1/2 tbsp fresh lemon juice
- 1/2 tbsp honey
- 2 tbsp hot sauce
- Pepper
- Salt

Directions:

1. Add chicken wings and remaining ingredients into the mixing bowl and toss well.
2. Place chicken wings into the multi-level air fryer basket.
3. Place multi-level air fryer basket into the inner pot of the instant pot.
4. Secure pot with air fryer lid, select air fry mode then cook at 350 F for 25 minutes.
5. Serve and enjoy.

Nutritional Value (Amount per Serving):
- Calories 961
- Fat 36.8 g
- Carbohydrates 4.7 g
- Sugar 4.6 g
- Protein 143 g
- Cholesterol 442 mg

Rosemary Chicken Breasts

Preparation Time: 10 minutes
Cooking Time: 25 minutes
Serve: 4

Ingredients:
- 1 lb chicken breasts, boneless and cubed
- 1 tbsp rosemary, chopped
- 1 tbsp garlic, minced
- 2 tbsp olive oil
- 1 tbsp fresh lime juice
- 1 tsp garlic powder
- Pepper
- Salt

Directions:
1. Add chicken and remaining ingredients into the large bowl and mix well.
2. Place chicken breasts into the multi-level air fryer basket.
3. Place multi-level air fryer basket into the inner pot of the instant pot.
4. Secure pot with air fryer lid, select air fry mode then cook at 370 F for 25 minutes.
5. Serve and enjoy.

Nutritional Value (Amount per Serving):
- Calories 286
- Fat 15.6 g
- Carbohydrates 2.7 g
- Sugar 0.4 g
- Protein 33.1 g
- Cholesterol 101 mg

Delicious Sriracha Chicken Wings

Preparation Time: 10 minutes
Cooking Time: 30 minutes
Serve: 4

Ingredients:
- 1 lb chicken wings
- 2 tbsp sriracha sauce
- 1/4 cup honey
- 1/2 lemon juice
- 1 tbsp butter
- 1 1/2 tbsp soy sauce
- Pepper
- Salt

Directions:
1. Season chicken wings with pepper and salt.
2. Place chicken wings into the multi-level air fryer basket.
3. Place multi-level air fryer basket into the inner pot of the instant pot.
4. Secure pot with air fryer lid, select air fry mode then cook at 360 F for 30 minutes. Flip chicken wings halfway through.
5. In a small saucepan, add butter, soy sauce, lemon juice, honey, and sriracha sauce and cook over medium heat for 3-5 minutes.
6. Add chicken wings into the sauce. Toss well and serve.

Nutritional Value (Amount per Serving):
- Calories 360
- Fat 16.3 g
- Carbohydrates 18.6 g
- Sugar 18.1 g
- Protein 33.3 g
- Cholesterol 114 mg

Delicious Turkey Nuggets

Preparation Time: 10 minutes
Cooking Time: 10 minutes
Serve: 2

Ingredients:
- 8 oz ground turkey
- 1 cup breadcrumbs
- 1 egg, lightly beaten
- 1/4 tsp garlic powder
- 1/4 tsp onion powder
- Pepper
- Salt

Directions:
1. In a bowl, mix together ground turkey, garlic powder, onion powder, pepper, and salt.
2. Make nuggets of turkey mixture, then dip in egg and coat with breadcrumbs.
3. Place nuggets into the multi-level air fryer basket.
4. Place multi-level air fryer basket into the inner pot of the instant pot.
5. Secure pot with air fryer lid, select air fry mode then cook at 350 F for 10 minutes.
6. Serve and enjoy.

Nutritional Value (Amount per Serving):
- Calories 468
- Fat 17.5 g
- Carbohydrates 39.6 g
- Sugar 3.7 g
- Protein 41.1 g
- Cholesterol 198 mg

Easy Turkey Patties

Preparation Time: 10 minutes

Cooking Time: 25 minutes
Serve: 8
Ingredients:
- 1 egg, lightly beaten
- 1 lb ground turkey
- 1/3 cup breadcrumbs
- 1/2 tsp garlic, minced
- 1 tsp creole seasoning
- 2 tbsp lemon juice
- 2 tbsp fresh parsley, chopped
- Pepper
- Salt

Directions:
1. Add all ingredients into the large bowl and mix until well combined.
2. Make eight equal shapes of patties from the mixture.
3. Place patties into the multi-level air fryer basket.
4. Place multi-level air fryer basket into the inner pot of the instant pot.
5. Secure pot with air fryer lid, select bake mode then cook at 380 F for 25 minutes. Flip patties halfway through.
6. Serve and enjoy.

Nutritional Value (Amount per Serving):
- Calories 138
- Fat 7.1 g
- Carbohydrates 3.5 g
- Sugar 0.4 g
- Protein 16.9 g
- Cholesterol 78 mg

Ginger Garlic Chicken Thighs

Preparation Time: 10 minutes
Cooking Time: 20 minutes
Serve: 4
Ingredients:
- 1 lb chicken thighs, boneless
- 1/2 tbsp ground coriander
- 1 tbsp olive oil
- 1 tbsp fresh lemon juice
- 1 tbsp ginger garlic paste
- Pepper
- Salt

Directions:
1. Add chicken thighs into the large bowl. Add remaining ingredients over chicken and coat well
2. Place chicken thighs into the multi-level air fryer basket.
3. Place multi-level air fryer basket into the inner pot of the instant pot.
4. Secure pot with air fryer lid, select air fry mode then cook at 370 F for 20 minutes. Flip chicken thighs halfway through.
5. Serve and enjoy.

Nutritional Value (Amount per Serving):
- Calories 253
- Fat 12.2 g
- Carbohydrates 0.9 g
- Sugar 0.1 g
- Protein 33.1 g
- Cholesterol 101 mg

Cajun Chicken Breasts

Preparation Time: 10 minutes
Cooking Time: 10 minutes
Serve: 2
Ingredients:
- 2 chicken breasts, boneless
- 2 tbsp cajun seasoning

Directions:
1. Rub chicken breasts with cajun seasoning.
2. Place chicken breasts into the multi-level air fryer basket.
3. Place multi-level air fryer basket into the inner pot of the instant pot.
4. Secure pot with air fryer lid, select air fry mode then cook at 350 F for 10 minutes. Flip chicken breasts halfway through.
5. Serve and enjoy.

Nutritional Value (Amount per Serving):
- Calories 277
- Fat 10.8 g
- Carbohydrates 0 g
- Sugar 0 g
- Protein 42.4 g
- Cholesterol 130 mg

Flavorful Chicken & Potatoes

Preparation Time: 10 minutes
Cooking Time: 40 minutes
Serve: 4
Ingredients:
- 1 lb chicken breasts, boneless & cut into cubes
- 1/2 lb potatoes, cut into chunks
- 1 tbsp olive oil
- 1/4 tsp onion powder
- 1/4 tsp chili powder
- 1/2 tsp garlic powder
- Pepper
- Salt

Directions:
1. Add chicken, oil, garlic powder, potatoes, onion powder, chili powder, pepper, and salt into the mixing bowl and toss well.
2. Add chicken potato mixture into the multi-level air fryer basket.
3. Place multi-level air fryer basket into the inner pot of the instant pot.
4. Secure pot with air fryer lid, select bake mode then cook at 380 F for 40 minutes. Stir chicken potato halfway through.
5. Serve and enjoy.

Nutritional Value (Amount per Serving):
- Calories 287
- Fat 12 g
- Carbohydrates 9.4 g
- Sugar 0.8 g
- Protein 33.9 g
- Cholesterol 101 mg

Chapter 4: Beef, Pork & Lamb

Juicy & Tender Pork Chops

Preparation Time: 10 minutes
Cooking Time: 16 minutes
Serve: 4
Ingredients:
- 4 pork chops, boneless
- 1 tsp dried parsley
- 1/4 tsp paprika
- 2 tbsp breadcrumbs
- 1/4 cup parmesan cheese, grated
- 2 tbsp olive oil
- 1/4 tsp pepper
- 1/4 tsp garlic powder
- Salt

Directions:
1. In a shallow dish, mix parmesan cheese, garlic powder, pepper, breadcrumbs, paprika, parsley, and salt.
2. Brush pork chops with oil and coat with parmesan cheese mixture.
3. Place pork chops into the multi-level air fryer basket.
4. Place multi-level air fryer basket into the inner pot of the instant pot.
5. Secure pot with air fryer lid, select air fry mode then cook at 360 F for 16 minutes. Flip pork chops halfway through.
6. Serve and enjoy.

Nutritional Value (Amount per Serving):
- Calories 367
- Fat 29.5 g
- Carbohydrates 3.1 g
- Sugar 0.3 g
- Protein 22.1 g
- Cholesterol 77 mg

Dijon Maple Pork Chops

Preparation Time: 10 minutes
Cooking Time: 12 minutes
Serve: 4
Ingredients:
- 4 pork chops, boneless
- 2 tsp fresh lemon juice
- 2 tbsp Dijon mustard
- 1/4 cup maple syrup
- 1 tbsp Montreal chicken seasoning
- 1 tbsp olive oil
- 1/2 tsp salt

Directions:
1. Brush pork chops with oil and season with Montreal chicken seasoning.
2. Place pork chops into the multi-level air fryer basket.
3. Place multi-level air fryer basket into the inner pot of the instant pot.
4. Secure pot with air fryer lid, select air fry mode then cook at 375 F for 12-15 minutes. Flip pork chops halfway through.
5. In a small bowl, mix together lemon juice, mustard, maple syrup, and salt.
6. Pour lemon juice mixture over pork chops and serve.

Nutritional Value (Amount per Serving):
- Calories 343
- Fat 23.8 g
- Carbohydrates 13.7 g
- Sugar 11.8 g
- Protein 18.3 g
- Cholesterol 69 mg

Mesquite Seasoned Pork Chops

Preparation Time: 10 minutes
Cooking Time: 14 minutes
Serve: 2
Ingredients:
- 2 pork chops, bone-in
- 1 tbsp olive oil
- 2 tbsp honey
- 1 1/2 tbsp mesquite seasoning

Directions:
1. Mix together oil, honey, and mesquite seasoning and rub all over pork chops.
2. Place pork chops in the dish, cover dish, and place in the refrigerator for 1 hour.
3. Place marinated pork chops into the multi-level air fryer basket.
4. Place multi-level air fryer basket into the inner pot of the instant pot.
5. Secure pot with air fryer lid, select air fry mode then cook at 380 F for 14 minutes. Flip pork chops halfway through.
6. Serve and enjoy.

Nutritional Value (Amount per Serving):
- Calories 390
- Fat 27.1 g
- Carbohydrates 19 g
- Sugar 17.3 g
- Protein 18.4 g
- Cholesterol 69 mg

Simple Spiced Pork Chops

Preparation Time: 10 minutes
Cooking Time: 12 minutes
Serve: 4
Ingredients:
- 4 pork chops, bone-in
- 1 tsp onion powder
- 1 tsp olive oil
- 1 tsp smoked paprika
- 1/4 tsp pepper
- 1 tsp salt

Directions:

1. Brush pork chops with olive oil.
2. Mix together onion powder, paprika, pepper, and salt and rub all over pork chops.
3. Place pork chops into the multi-level air fryer basket.
4. Place multi-level air fryer basket into the inner pot of the instant pot.
5. Secure pot with air fryer lid, select air fry mode then cook at 380 F for 12 minutes. Flip pork chops halfway through.
6. Serve and enjoy.

Nutritional Value (Amount per Serving):
- Calories 270
- Fat 21.1 g
- Carbohydrates 0.9 g
- Sugar 0.3 g
- Protein 18.1 g
- Cholesterol 69 mg

Quick & Simple Pork Chops

Preparation Time: 10 minutes
Cooking Time: 12 minutes
Serve: 4

Ingredients:
- 4 pork chops
- 2 tbsp brown sugar
- 1 tsp olive oil
- Pepper
- Salt

Directions:
1. Brush pork chops with olive oil.
2. Mix together brown sugar, pepper, and salt and rub all over pork chops.
3. Place pork chops into the multi-level air fryer basket.
4. Place multi-level air fryer basket into the inner pot of the instant pot.
5. Secure pot with air fryer lid, select air fry mode then cook at 400 F for 12 minutes. Flip pork chops halfway through.
6. Serve and enjoy.

Nutritional Value (Amount per Serving):
- Calories 283
- Fat 21.1 g
- Carbohydrates 4.4 g
- Sugar 4.4 g
- Protein 18 g
- Cholesterol 69 mg

Pork Sausage Balls

Preparation Time: 10 minutes
Cooking Time: 18 minutes
Serve: 4

Ingredients:
- 1 lb ground pork sausage
- 1 cup cheddar cheese, shredded
- 1 cup almond flour
- Pepper
- Salt

Directions:
1. Add all ingredients into the mixing bowl and mix until well combined.
2. Make 1-inch balls from mixture and place into the multi-level air fryer basket.
3. Place multi-level air fryer basket into the inner pot of the instant pot.
4. Secure pot with air fryer lid, select air fry mode then cook at 375 F for 16-18 minutes.
5. Serve and enjoy.

Nutritional Value (Amount per Serving):
- Calories 514
- Fat 42.9 g
- Carbohydrates 1.9 g
- Sugar 0.4 g
- Protein 28.5 g
- Cholesterol 130 mg

Pork Chops with Sauce

Preparation Time: 10 minutes
Cooking Time: 20 minutes
Serve: 2

Ingredients:
- 2 pork chops, bone-in
- 1 tbsp olive oil
- Pepper
- Salt

For sauce:
- 1 garlic clove, minced
- 1 tbsp onion, chopped
- 1 tbsp cilantro, chopped
- 1 tbsp parsley, chopped
- 1 tsp honey
- 1 tsp Dijon mustard
- 1 tbsp fresh lime juice
- 1/2 cup olive oil
- 1/4 tsp pepper
- 1/2 tsp kosher salt

Directions:
1. In a small bowl, mix together all sauce ingredients and place them in the refrigerator.
2. Brush pork chops with oil and season with pepper and salt.
3. Place pork chops into the multi-level air fryer basket.
4. Place multi-level air fryer basket into the inner pot of the instant pot.
5. Secure pot with air fryer lid, select air fry mode then cook at 400 F for 20 minutes.
6. Serve pork chops with sauce.

Nutritional Value (Amount per Serving):
- Calories 772
- Fat 77.4 g
- Carbohydrates 6.2 g
- Sugar 3.5 g
- Protein 18.5 g
- Cholesterol 69 mg

Perfect Air Fry Pork Chops

Preparation Time: 10 minutes
Cooking Time: 9 minutes
Serve: 4
Ingredients:
- 4 pork chops, boneless
- 2 tsp paprika
- 2 tsp onion powder
- 1 1/2 tsp garlic powder
- 1 tbsp olive oil
- 1/2 tsp pepper
- 1 tsp salt

Directions:
1. Brush pork chops with olive oil.
2. In a small bowl, mix paprika, onion powder, garlic powder, pepper, and salt and rub all over pork chops.
3. Place pork chops into the multi-level air fryer basket.
4. Place multi-level air fryer basket into the inner pot of the instant pot.
5. Secure pot with air fryer lid, select air fry mode then cook at 375 F for 9 minutes.
6. Serve and enjoy.

Nutritional Value (Amount per Serving):
- Calories 297
- Fat 23.6 g
- Carbohydrates 2.5 g
- Sugar 0.8 g
- Protein 18.5 g
- Cholesterol 69 mg

Juicy Ranch Pork Chops

Preparation Time: 10 minutes
Cooking Time: 10 minutes
Serve: 4
Ingredients:
- 4 pork chops, boneless
- 2 tbsp olive oil
- 2 tsp ranch seasoning

Directions:
1. Brush pork chops with oil and rub with ranch seasoning.
2. Place pork chops into the multi-level air fryer basket.
3. Place multi-level air fryer basket into the inner pot of the instant pot.
4. Secure pot with air fryer lid, select air fry mode then cook at 390 F for 5 minutes. Flip pork chops halfway through.
5. Serve and enjoy.

Nutritional Value (Amount per Serving):
- Calories 321
- Fat 26.9 g
- Carbohydrates 0 g
- Sugar 0 g
- Protein 18 g
- Cholesterol 69 mg

Herb Seasoned Pork Chops

Preparation Time: 10 minutes
Cooking Time: 16 minutes
Serve: 4
Ingredients:
- 4 pork chops
- 1 tsp smoked paprika
- 1 tsp rosemary
- 2 tsp oregano
- 2 tsp thyme
- 2 tsp sage
- 2 tbsp olive oil
- 1 tsp garlic powder
- 1/2 tsp pepper
- 1 tsp salt

Directions:
1. Brush pork chops with olive oil.
2. In a small bowl, mix garlic powder, paprika, rosemary, oregano, thyme, sage, pepper, and salt and rub all over pork chops.
3. Place pork chops into the multi-level air fryer basket.
4. Place multi-level air fryer basket into the inner pot of the instant pot.
5. Secure pot with air fryer lid, select air fry mode then cook at 360 F for 16 minutes. Flip pork chops halfway through.
6. Serve and enjoy.

Nutritional Value (Amount per Serving):
- Calories 326
- Fat 27.2 g
- Carbohydrates 2.2 g
- Sugar 0.3 g
- Protein 18.4 g
- Cholesterol 69 mg

Cheese Mustard Pork Chops

Preparation Time: 10 minutes
Cooking Time: 12 minutes
Serve: 4
Ingredients:
- 4 pork chops, bone-in
- 2 tbsp olive oil
- 1/2 tsp Italian dried herbs
- 1 tsp ground mustard
- 1 tsp onion powder
- 2 tsp garlic powder
- 1 tsp paprika
- 1/2 cup parmesan cheese, grated
- 1/2 tsp pepper
- 1 tsp kosher salt

Directions:
1. In a shallow dish, mix parmesan cheese, paprika, garlic powder, onion powder, ground mustard, dried herbs, pepper, and salt.
2. Brush pork chops with oil and coat with parmesan cheese.

3. Place pork chops into the multi-level air fryer basket.
4. Place multi-level air fryer basket into the inner pot of the instant pot.
5. Secure pot with air fryer lid, select air fry mode then cook at 400 F for 12 minutes. Flip pork chops halfway through.
6. Serve and enjoy.

Nutritional Value (Amount per Serving):
- Calories 269
- Fat 17 g
- Carbohydrates 2.7 g
- Sugar 0.7 g
- Protein 26.4 g
- Cholesterol 72 mg

Crispy Crusted Pork Chops

Preparation Time: 10 minutes
Cooking Time: 12 minutes
Serve: 4
Ingredients:
- 1 egg
- 4 pork chops, boneless
- 1/2 tsp chili powder
- 1/2 tsp onion powder
- 1/2 tsp garlic powder
- 1 1/2 tsp smoked paprika
- 1 tbsp parmesan cheese, grated
- 1 cup breadcrumbs
- 1/4 tsp pepper
- 1/4 tsp salt

Directions:
1. In a shallow dish, mix breadcrumbs, parmesan cheese, paprika, garlic powder, onion powder, chili powder, pepper, and salt.
2. Add egg in a small bowl and whisk well.
3. Dip pork chop in egg then coats with breadcrumb mixture.
4. Place coated pork chops into the multi-level air fryer basket.
5. Place multi-level air fryer basket into the inner pot of the instant pot.
6. Secure pot with air fryer lid, select air fry mode then cook at 400 F for 12 minutes. Flip pork chops halfway through.
7. Serve and enjoy.

Nutritional Value (Amount per Serving):
- Calories 394
- Fat 23.2 g
- Carbohydrates 20.8 g
- Sugar 2.1 g
- Protein 24.2 g
- Cholesterol 112 mg

Delicious & Moist Pork Chops

Preparation Time: 10 minutes
Cooking Time: 12 minutes
Serve: 2
Ingredients:
- 2 pork chops, boneless
- 1 tbsp olive oil
- 1/8 tsp red pepper flakes, crushed
- 1/4 tsp onion powder
- 1/4 tsp garlic powder
- 1/2 tsp lemon zest
- 1/2 tsp paprika
- 3/4 tsp rosemary
- 1/4 tsp pepper
- 1/4 tsp salt

Directions:
1. Brush pork chops with oil.
2. In a small bowl, mix red pepper flakes, onion powder, garlic powder, lemon zest, paprika, rosemary, pepper, and salt and rub over pork chops.
3. Place pork chops into the multi-level air fryer basket.
4. Place multi-level air fryer basket into the inner pot of the instant pot.
5. Secure pot with air fryer lid, select air fry mode then cook at 390 F for 12 minutes. Flip pork chops halfway through.
6. Serve and enjoy.

Nutritional Value (Amount per Serving):
- Calories 323
- Fat 27.1 g
- Carbohydrates 1.4 g
- Sugar 0.3 g
- Protein 18.2 g
- Cholesterol 69 mg

Asian Pork Ribs

Preparation Time: 10 minutes
Cooking Time: 20 minutes
Serve: 3
Ingredients:
- 1 1/2 lbs pork ribs, cut into bite-size pieces
- 1 tbsp garlic, minced
- 2 1/2 tbsp brown sugar
- 2 tbsp sesame oil
- 1/2 cup soy sauce

Directions:
1. Add pork pieces and remaining ingredients into the zip-lock bag, seal bag, and place in the refrigerator overnight.
2. Remove pork pieces from the marinade and place them into the multi-level air fryer basket.
3. Place multi-level air fryer basket into the inner pot of the instant pot.
4. Secure pot with air fryer lid, select air fry mode then cook at 400 F for 20 minutes.
5. Serve and enjoy.

Nutritional Value (Amount per Serving):
- Calories 755
- Fat 49.3 g
- Carbohydrates 11.5 g
- Sugar 8 g
- Protein 62.9 g
- Cholesterol 234 mg

Marinated Pork Chops

Preparation Time: 10 minutes
Cooking Time: 20 minutes
Serve: 4
Ingredients:
- 4 pork chops

For marinade:
- 1 tbsp honey
- 1/2 small onion, chopped
- 1 tbsp garlic, chopped
- 3 tbsp lemongrass, chopped
- 3 tbsp sugar
- 2 tbsp soy sauce
- 3 tbsp fish sauce
- Pepper

Directions:
1. Add pork chops and marinade ingredients into the zip-lock bag, seal bag, and place in the refrigerator overnight.
2. Remove pork chops from marinade and place it into the multi-level air fryer basket.
3. Place multi-level air fryer basket into the inner pot of the instant pot.
4. Secure pot with air fryer lid, select air fry mode then cook at 400 F for 20 minutes. Flip pork chops halfway through.
5. Serve and enjoy.

Nutritional Value (Amount per Serving):
- Calories 325
- Fat 19.9 g
- Carbohydrates 16.9 g
- Sugar 14.3 g
- Protein 19.5 g
- Cholesterol 69 mg

Greek Ribeye Steak

Preparation Time: 10 minutes
Cooking Time: 10 minutes
Serve: 4
Ingredients:
- 1 lb ribeye steaks
- 1 tsp dried oregano
- 1 tbsp garlic, minced
- 1/4 cup fresh lemon juice
- 1/2 cup olive oil
- Pepper
- Salt

Directions:
1. Add ribeye steaks and remaining ingredients into the zip-lock bag, seal bag, and place in the refrigerator overnight.
2. Remove steaks from marinade and place it into the multi-level air fryer basket.
3. Place multi-level air fryer basket into the inner pot of the instant pot.
4. Secure pot with air fryer lid, select air fry mode then cook at 400 F for 10 minutes.
5. Serve and enjoy.

Nutritional Value (Amount per Serving):
- Calories 224
- Fat 75.3 g
- Carbohydrates 5.8 g
- Sugar 0.4 g
- Protein 62.7 g
- Cholesterol 0 mg

Cripsy Pork Belly Bites

Preparation Time: 10 minutes
Cooking Time: 18 minutes
Serve: 4
Ingredients:
- 1 lb pork belly, rinsed, pat dry & cut into 3/4-inch pieces
- 1/2 tsp garlic powder
- 1 tsp soy sauce
- Pepper
- Salt

Directions:
1. Add pork belly pieces and remaining ingredients into the large bowl and toss well.
2. Add pork belly pieces into the multi-level air fryer basket.
3. Place multi-level air fryer basket into the inner pot of the instant pot.
4. Secure pot with air fryer lid, select air fry mode then cook at 400 F for 18 minutes. Stir halfway through.
5. Serve and enjoy.

Nutritional Value (Amount per Serving):
- Calories 525
- Fat 30.5 g
- Carbohydrates 0.4 g
- Sugar 0.1 g
- Protein 52.5 g
- Cholesterol 131 mg

Crunchy Pork Belly Crack

Preparation Time: 10 minutes
Cooking Time: 15 minutes
Serve: 4
Ingredients:
- 1 lb pork belly strips, sliced
- 1/2 tsp pepper
- 1 tsp sea salt

Directions:
1. Season pork belly slices with pepper and salt and place into the multi-level air fryer basket.
2. Place multi-level air fryer basket into the inner pot of the instant pot.
3. Secure pot with air fryer lid, select air fry mode then cook at 390 F for 15 minutes. Flip pork belly slices after every 5 minutes.
4. Serve and enjoy.

Nutritional Value (Amount per Serving):
- Calories 597
- Fat 61.7 g

- Carbohydrates 0.2 g
- Sugar 0 g
- Protein 8 g
- Cholesterol 60 mg

Baked Pork Chops

Preparation Time: 10 minutes
Cooking Time: 30 minutes
Serve: 4
Ingredients:
- 1 lb pork ribs, boneless
- 1/2 tbsp onion powder
- 3/4 tbsp garlic powder
- Pepper
- Salt

Directions:
1. Season pork ribs with onion powder, garlic powder, pepper, and salt.
2. Place pork ribs into the multi-level air fryer basket.
3. Place multi-level air fryer basket into the inner pot of the instant pot.
4. Secure pot with air fryer lid, select bake mode then cook at 350 F for 25-30 minutes. Flip pork ribs halfway through.
5. Serve and enjoy.

Nutritional Value (Amount per Serving):
- Calories 318
- Fat 20.1 g
- Carbohydrates 1.9 g
- Sugar 0.7 g
- Protein 30.4 g
- Cholesterol 117 mg

Perfect Baked Pork Chops

Preparation Time: 10 minutes
Cooking Time: 25 minutes
Serve: 2
Ingredients:
- 2 pork chops, bone-in
- 1 tsp paprika
- 2 tsp brown sugar
- 1/2 tsp pepper
- 1/2 tsp salt

Directions:
1. Mix together paprika, brown sugar, pepper, and salt and rub over pork chops.
2. Place pork chops into the multi-level air fryer basket.
3. Place multi-level air fryer basket into the inner pot of the instant pot.
4. Secure pot with air fryer lid, select bake mode then cook at 325 F for 25 minutes. Flip pork chops after 15 minutes.
5. Serve and enjoy.

Nutritional Value (Amount per Serving):
- Calories 272
- Fat 20 g

- Carbohydrates 3.9 g
- Sugar 3 g
- Protein 18.2 g
- Cholesterol 69 mg

Delicious Mini Meatloaf

Preparation Time: 10 minutes
Cooking Time: 12 minutes
Serve: 4
Ingredients:
- 1 lb ground beef
- 1/4 cup BBQ sauce
- 1/2 tsp yellow mustard
- 1 tbsp Worcestershire sauce
- 1/2 tsp garlic powder
- 1/2 tsp onion powder
- 1 egg, lightly beaten
- 1/4 cup breadcrumbs
- 3/4 cup cheddar cheese, shredded
- 2 bacon slices, cooked & chopped
- 3 oz chili sauce
- 1/2 tsp salt

Directions:
1. Add all ingredients except BBQ sauce into the large bowl and mix until well combined.
2. Divide mixture into the 4 equal portions and give them loaf shape.
3. Place mini loves into the multi-level air fryer basket then spread a tablespoon of BBQ sauce on each loaf.
4. Place multi-level air fryer basket into the inner pot of the instant pot.
5. Secure pot with air fryer lid, select air fry mode then cook at 400 F for 12 minutes.
6. Serve and enjoy.

Nutritional Value (Amount per Serving):
- Calories 422
- Fat 19.7 g
- Carbohydrates 12.7 g
- Sugar 5.9 g
- Protein 45.7 g
- Cholesterol 175 mg

Steak & Mushrooms

Preparation Time: 10 minutes
Cooking Time: 18 minutes
Serve: 4
Ingredients:
- 1 lb steaks, cut into 1-inch pieces
- 8 oz mushrooms, cut in half
- 1/2 tsp garlic powder
- 1 tsp soy sauce
- 2 tbsp olive oil
- 1/8 tsp red chili flakes, crushed
- Pepper
- Salt

Directions:

1. Add steak pieces, mushrooms, garlic powder, soy sauce, oil, red chili flakes, pepper, and salt into the mixing bowl and toss well.
2. Add steak and mushroom mixture into the multi-level air fryer basket.
3. Place multi-level air fryer basket into the inner pot of the instant pot.
4. Secure pot with air fryer lid, select air fry mode then cook at 400 F for 18 minutes. Stir halfway through.
5. Serve and enjoy.

Nutritional Value (Amount per Serving):
- Calories 300
- Fat 12.8 g
- Carbohydrates 2.2 g
- Sugar 1.1 g
- Protein 42.9 g
- Cholesterol 102 mg

Tasty & Juicy Steak

Preparation Time: 10 minutes
Cooking Time: 14 minutes
Serve: 2

Ingredients:
- 2 rib-eye steaks
- 1/4 tsp garlic powder
- 1/4 tsp onion powder
- 1 tbsp olive oil
- Pepper
- Salt

Directions:
1. Brush steaks with olive oil.
2. Mix together garlic powder, onion powder, pepper, and salt and rub all over the steaks.
3. Place steaks into the multi-level air fryer basket.
4. Place multi-level air fryer basket into the inner pot of the instant pot.
5. Secure pot with air fryer lid, select air fry mode then cook at 400 F for 14 minutes. Flip steaks halfway through.
6. Serve and enjoy.

Nutritional Value (Amount per Serving):
- Calories 372
- Fat 32 g
- Carbohydrates 0.5 g
- Sugar 0.2 g
- Protein 20.1 g
- Cholesterol 75 mg

Air Fry Steak Bites

Preparation Time: 10 minutes
Cooking Time: 7 minutes
Serve: 4

Ingredients:
- 1 lb steak, cut into 1-inch pieces
- 1 1/2 tbsp steak seasoning
- 3 tbsp butter, melted

Directions:

1. Add steak pieces, steak seasoning, and melted butter into the large bowl and toss well.
2. Transfer steak pieces into the multi-level air fryer basket.
3. Place multi-level air fryer basket into the inner pot of the instant pot.
4. Secure pot with air fryer lid, select air fry mode then cook at 350 F for 7 minutes.
5. Serve and enjoy.

Nutritional Value (Amount per Serving):
- Calories 302
- Fat 14.3 g
- Carbohydrates 0 g
- Sugar 0 g
- Protein 41.1 g
- Cholesterol 125 mg

Mexican Steak Fajitas

Preparation Time: 10 minutes
Cooking Time: 8 minutes
Serve: 4

Ingredients:
- 1 lb beef flank steak, sliced
- 1 tsp garlic powder
- 1 tsp paprika
- 1 1/2 tsp ground cumin
- 1/4 tsp pepper
- 1/2 tbsp chili powder
- 2 tbsp olive oil
- 1/2 onion, sliced
- 2 bell peppers, sliced
- 1/2 tsp dry sriracha
- 1 tsp salt

Directions:
1. Add sliced flank steak and remaining ingredients into the mixing bowl and mix well.
2. Add steak mixture into the multi-level air fryer basket.
3. Place multi-level air fryer basket into the inner pot of the instant pot.
4. Secure pot with air fryer lid, select air fry mode then cook at 390 F for 8 minutes. Stir steak mixture after 5 minutes.
5. Serve and enjoy.

Nutritional Value (Amount per Serving):
- Calories 306
- Fat 14.7 g
- Carbohydrates 7.7 g
- Sugar 3.9 g
- Protein 35.6 g
- Cholesterol 101 mg

Meatballs

Preparation Time: 10 minutes
Cooking Time: 14 minutes
Serve: 4

Ingredients:
- 1 egg

- 1 lb ground beef
- 1/4 cup breadcrumbs
- 1/2 onion, diced
- 1 tsp garlic powder
- Pepper
- Salt

Directions:
1. Add all ingredients into the bowl and mix until well combined.
2. Make small balls from mixture and place into the multi-level air fryer basket.
3. Place multi-level air fryer basket into the inner pot of the instant pot.
4. Secure pot with air fryer lid, select air fry mode then cook at 390 F for 14 minutes.
5. Serve and enjoy.

Nutritional Value (Amount per Serving):
- Calories 261
- Fat 8.5 g
- Carbohydrates 6.8 g
- Sugar 1.3 g
- Protein 37 g
- Cholesterol 142 mg

Steak Bites with Potatoes

Preparation Time: 10 minutes
Cooking Time: 20 minutes
Serve: 4
Ingredients:
- 1 lb steaks, cut into 1/2-inch pieces
- 1/2 lb potatoes, cut into 1/2-inch pieces
- 1/2 tsp garlic powder
- 1 tsp soy sauce
- 2 tbsp olive oil
- Pepper
- Salt

Directions:
1. Add potatoes into the boiling water and cook for 5 minutes. Drain well and set aside.
2. Add potatoes, steak, garlic powder, soy sauce, oil, pepper, and salt into the large bowl and toss well.
3. Add potatoes and steak mixture into the multi-level air fryer basket.
4. Place multi-level air fryer basket into the inner pot of the instant pot.
5. Secure pot with air fryer lid, select air fry mode then cook at 400 F for 20 minutes. Stir halfway through.
6. Serve and enjoy.

Nutritional Value (Amount per Serving):
- Calories 327
- Fat 12.7 g
- Carbohydrates 9.3 g
- Sugar 0.8 g
- Protein 42.1 g
- Cholesterol 102 mg

Beef with Veggies

Preparation Time: 10 minutes
Cooking Time: 8 minutes
Serve: 4
Ingredients:
- 1 lb sirloin steak, cut into strips
- 1/4 cup water
- 1/3 cup brown sugar
- 1 tsp sesame oil
- 1/4 cup vinegar
- 1/2 cup soy sauce
- 1/4 tsp red chili flakes
- 2 tbsp ginger, grated
- 1 tbsp garlic, minced
- 1 bell pepper, sliced
- 1/2 onion, sliced
- 2 tbsp cornstarch

Directions:
1. Add all ingredients into the zip-lock bag, seal bag shake well and place in the refrigerator overnight.
2. Remove steaks, bell pepper, and onion from marinade and place into the multi-level air fryer basket.
3. Place multi-level air fryer basket into the inner pot of the instant pot.
4. Secure pot with air fryer lid, select air fry mode then cook at 400 F for 8 minutes. Stir halfway through.
5. Serve and enjoy.

Nutritional Value (Amount per Serving):
- Calories 329
- Fat 8.5 g
- Carbohydrates 24.2 g
- Sugar 14.5 g
- Protein 37.3 g
- Cholesterol 101 mg

Marinated Steak Fajitas

Preparation Time: 10 minutes
Cooking Time: 17 minutes
Serve: 4
Ingredients:
- 1 1/2 lbs flank steak, sliced
- 1 onion, sliced
- 1 bell pepper, sliced
- 1/2 tsp paprika
- 1 tsp ground cumin
- 1/2 tsp chili powder
- 1 tbsp garlic, minced
- 1 tbsp soy sauce
- 1 tbsp olive oil
- 2 tbsp fresh lime juice
- 1/4 cup pineapple juice
- Pepper
- Salt

Directions:

1. Add all ingredients into the zip-lock bag, seal bag shake well and place in the refrigerator overnight.
2. Line multi-level air fryer basket with parchment paper.
3. Remove steaks, bell pepper, and onion from marinade and place into the multi-level air fryer basket.
4. Place multi-level air fryer basket into the inner pot of the instant pot.
5. Secure pot with air fryer lid, select air fry mode then cook at 400 F for 17 minutes. Stir after 10 minutes.
6. Serve and enjoy.

Nutritional Value (Amount per Serving):
- Calories 403
- Fat 18 g
- Carbohydrates 10.2 g
- Sugar 4.8 g
- Protein 48.6 g
- Cholesterol 94 mg

Meatballs

Preparation Time: 10 minutes
Cooking Time: 15 minutes
Serve: 4
Ingredients:
- 1 lb ground beef
- 1/2 tsp Italian seasoning
- 1 tsp garlic, minced
- 1/4 cup milk
- 1/2 cup parmesan cheese, grated
- 1/2 cup breadcrumbs
- Pepper
- Salt

Directions:
1. Add all ingredients into the bowl and mix until well combined.
2. Make 1 1/2-inch ball from the mixture and place it into the multi-level air fryer basket.
3. Place multi-level air fryer basket into the inner pot of the instant pot.
4. Secure pot with air fryer lid, select air fry mode then cook at 375 F for 15 minutes.
5. Serve and enjoy.

Nutritional Value (Amount per Serving):
- Calories 311
- Fat 10.5 g
- Carbohydrates 11.2 g
- Sugar 1.6 g
- Protein 40.4 g
- Cholesterol 111 mg

Beef Skewers

Preparation Time: 10 minutes
Cooking Time: 14 minutes
Serve: 4
Ingredients:
- 1 lb round steak, cut into pieces
- 2 tbsp olive oil
- 1/2 tsp garlic powder
- 1/4 cup water
- 1/4 cup pineapple juice
- 1/2 cup soy sauce
- 3/4 cup brown sugar

Directions:
1. Add all ingredients into the zip-lock bag, seal bag, and place in the refrigerator overnight.
2. Remove steak pieces from marinade and thread onto the skewers.
3. Place steak skewers into the multi-level air fryer basket.
4. Place multi-level air fryer basket into the inner pot of the instant pot.
5. Secure pot with air fryer lid, select air fry mode then cook at 400 F for 14 minutes. Flip skewers halfway through.
6. Serve and enjoy.

Nutritional Value (Amount per Serving):
- Calories 435
- Fat 17.9 g
- Carbohydrates 31.4 g
- Sugar 28.6 g
- Protein 36.4 g
- Cholesterol 96 mg

Easy Beef Patties

Preparation Time: 10 minutes
Cooking Time: 13 minutes
Serve: 4
Ingredients:
- 1 lb ground beef
- 1/4 tsp chili powder
- 1/2 tsp garlic powder
- 1/2 tsp onion powder
- 1 tbsp parsley, chopped
- Pepper
- Salt

Directions:
1. Add all ingredients into the bowl and mix until well combined.
2. Make 4 even shapes of patties from mixture and place into the multi-level air fryer basket.
3. Place multi-level air fryer basket into the inner pot of the instant pot.
4. Secure pot with air fryer lid, select air fry mode then cook at 400 F for 13 minutes. Turn patties after 10 minutes.
5. Serve and enjoy.

Nutritional Value (Amount per Serving):
- Calories 214
- Fat 7.1 g
- Carbohydrates 0.7 g
- Sugar 0.2 g
- Protein 34.5 g
- Cholesterol 101 mg

Meatballs

Preparation Time: 10 minutes
Cooking Time: 10 minutes
Serve: 4
Ingredients:
- 2 eggs
- 1/2 lb ground pork
- 1 lb ground beef
- 1/2 cup parmesan cheese, grated
- 1/2 tbsp Italian seasoning
- 1/2 tsp onion powder
- 1/2 tsp garlic powder
- 1/2 cup breadcrumbs
- Pepper
- Salt

Directions:
1. Add all ingredients into the bowl and mix until well combined.
2. Make small balls from mixture and place into the multi-level air fryer basket.
3. Place multi-level air fryer basket into the inner pot of the instant pot.
4. Secure pot with air fryer lid, select air fry mode then cook at 400 F for 10 minutes.
5. Serve and enjoy.

Nutritional Value (Amount per Serving):
- Calories 384
- Fat 14.9 g
- Carbohydrates 11 g
- Sugar 1.4 g
- Protein 57.5 g
- Cholesterol 234 mg

Tasty Pork Riblets

Preparation Time: 10 minutes
Cooking Time: 12 minutes
Serve: 4
Ingredients:
- 1 lb pork riblets, cut into single pieces
- 4 garlic cloves, cut in half
- 1 1/2 tbsp sugar
- 3 tbsp dry sherry
- 1 tsp dark soy sauce
- 1 tbsp oyster sauce
- 2 tbsp soy sauce

Directions:
1. Add all ingredients into the zip-lock bag, seal bag, and place in the refrigerator overnight.
2. Remove riblets from marinade and place into the multi-level air fryer basket.
3. Place multi-level air fryer basket into the inner pot of the instant pot.
4. Secure pot with air fryer lid, select air fry mode then cook at 360 F for 12 minutes. Stir halfway through.
5. Serve and enjoy.

Nutritional Value (Amount per Serving):
- Calories 128
- Fat 6.8 g
- Carbohydrates 10.1 g
- Sugar 7.2 g
- Protein 5.5 g
- Cholesterol 20 mg

Meatballs

Preparation Time: 10 minutes
Cooking Time: 20 minutes
Serve: 4
Ingredients:
- 1 egg
- 1 lb ground beef
- 2 tbsp parmesan cheese, grated
- 2 tsp Italian seasoning
- 1/4 cup rolled oats
- 1/2 cup frozen spinach, thawed
- 1 tsp garlic, minced
- 1/2 onion, minced
- 4 oz mushrooms, chopped
- 3/4 cup cooked quinoa

Directions:
1. Add all ingredients into the bowl and mix until well combined.
2. Make small balls from mixture and place into the multi-level air fryer basket.
3. Place multi-level air fryer basket into the inner pot of the instant pot.
4. Secure pot with air fryer lid, select bake mode then cook at 380 F for 15-20 minutes.
5. Serve and enjoy.

Nutritional Value (Amount per Serving):
- Calories 395
- Fat 12 g
- Carbohydrates 27 g
- Sugar 1.4 g
- Protein 43.3 g
- Cholesterol 146 mg

Healthy Pork Patties

Preparation Time: 10 minutes
Cooking Time: 35 minutes
Serve: 6
Ingredients:
- 1 egg
- 2 1/4 lbs ground pork
- 1/2 cup breadcrumbs
- 1 tsp garlic powder
- 1 tsp paprika
- 1 onion, minced
- 1 carrot, minced
- 1 tsp salt

Directions:
1. Add all ingredients into the bowl and mix until well combined.
2. Line multi-level air fryer basket with parchment paper.

3. Make the equal shape of patties from the mixture and place it into the multi-level air fryer basket.
4. Place multi-level air fryer basket into the inner pot of the instant pot.
5. Secure pot with air fryer lid, select bake mode then cook at 375 F for 25-35 minutes.
6. Serve and enjoy.

Nutritional Value (Amount per Serving):
- Calories 303
- Fat 7.3 g
- Carbohydrates 9.8 g
- Sugar 2.1 g
- Protein 47.1 g
- Cholesterol 151 mg

Juicy & Tender Lamb Chops

Preparation Time: 10 minutes
Cooking Time: 15 minutes
Serve: 4
Ingredients:
- 8 loin lamb chops
- 1 tbsp fresh lime juice
- 1 tsp dried mix herbs
- 1/2 tsp olive oil
- 2 tbsp Dijon mustard
- Pepper
- Salt

Directions:
1. In a small bowl, mix together lime juice, mix herbs, oil, Dijon mustard, pepper, and salt.
2. Brush lamb chops with the lime juice mixture and place it into the multi-level air fryer basket.
3. Place multi-level air fryer basket into the inner pot of the instant pot.
4. Secure pot with air fryer lid, select air fry mode then cook at 390 F for 15 minutes.
5. Serve and enjoy.

Nutritional Value (Amount per Serving):
- Calories 653
- Fat 52.9 g
- Carbohydrates 1.4 g
- Sugar 0.3 g
- Protein 38.4 g
- Cholesterol 160 mg

Flavors Rosemary Thyme Lamb Chops

Preparation Time: 10 minutes
Cooking Time: 10 minutes
Serve: 4
Ingredients:
- 1 lb lamb chops
- 2 tbsp fresh lime juice
- 2 tbsp olive oil
- 1 tsp ground coriander
- 1 tsp oregano
- 1 tsp dried thyme
- 1 tsp dried rosemary
- 1 tsp salt

Directions:
1. Add lamb chops and remaining ingredients into the zip-lock bag, seal bag, and place in the refrigerator overnight.
2. Place marinated lamb chops into the multi-level air fryer basket.
3. Place multi-level air fryer basket into the inner pot of the instant pot.
4. Secure pot with air fryer lid, select air fry mode then cook at 390 F for 10 minutes. Flip lamb chops halfway through.
5. Serve and enjoy.

Nutritional Value (Amount per Serving):
- Calories 279
- Fat 15.4 g
- Carbohydrates 2.4 g
- Sugar 0.4 g
- Protein 32 g
- Cholesterol 102 mg

Herb Pork Chops

Preparation Time: 10 minutes
Cooking Time: 16 minutes
Serve: 4
Ingredients:
- 4 pork chops
- 1 tsp garlic powder
- 1 tsp paprika
- 1 tsp rosemary
- 2 tsp oregano
- 2 tsp thyme
- 2 tsp sage
- 1/2 tsp pepper
- 1 tsp salt

Directions:
1. In a small bowl, mix garlic powder, paprika, rosemary, oregano, thyme, sage, pepper, and salt and rub over pork chops.
2. Place pork chops into the multi-level air fryer basket.
3. Place multi-level air fryer basket into the inner pot of the instant pot.
4. Secure pot with air fryer lid, select air fry mode then cook at 360 F for 16 minutes. Flip pork chops halfway through.
5. Serve and enjoy.

Nutritional Value (Amount per Serving):
- Calories 266
- Fat 20.2 g
- Carbohydrates 2.2 g
- Sugar 0.3 g
- Protein 18.4 g
- Cholesterol 69 mg

Classic Lamb Chops

Preparation Time: 10 minutes
Cooking Time: 10 minutes
Serve: 4
Ingredients:
- 2 lbs lamb chops
- 2 tsp garlic, minced
- 2 tsp dried oregano
- 1/4 cup fresh lime juice
- 1/4 cup olive oil
- 1/2 tsp pepper
- 1 tsp salt

Directions:
1. Add lamb chops, garlic, oregano, lime juice, oil, pepper, and salt into the zip-lock bag, seal bag, and place in the refrigerator overnight.
2. Place marinated lamb chops into the multi-level air fryer basket.
3. Place multi-level air fryer basket into the inner pot of the instant pot.
4. Secure pot with air fryer lid, select air fry mode then cook at 400 F for 10 minutes. Flip lamb chops halfway through.
5. Serve and enjoy.

Nutritional Value (Amount per Serving):
- Calories 536
- Fat 29.3 g
- Carbohydrates 1.3 g
- Sugar 0.1 g
- Protein 63.9 g
- Cholesterol 204 mg

Onion Pork Chops

Preparation Time: 10 minutes
Cooking Time: 35 minutes
Serve: 2
Ingredients:
- 2 pork chops
- 2 tbsp brown sugar
- 2 1/2 tbsp ketchup
- 2 onion, sliced
- Pepper
- Salt

Directions:
1. Line multi-level air fryer basket with parchment paper.
2. Season pork chops with pepper and salt.
3. Place pork chops in a multi-level air fryer basket.
4. Mix together ketchup and brown sugar and pour over pork chops.
5. Add sliced onion on top of pork chops.
6. Place multi-level air fryer basket into the inner pot of the instant pot.
7. Secure pot with air fryer lid, select air fry mode then cook at 375 F for 35 minutes.
8. Serve and enjoy.

Nutritional Value (Amount per Serving):
- Calories 353
- Fat 20.1 g
- Carbohydrates 23.9 g
- Sugar 17.7 g
- Protein 19.5 g
- Cholesterol 69 mg

Beef Zucchini Burgers

Preparation Time: 10 minutes
Cooking Time: 35 minutes
Serve: 6
Ingredients:
- 2 eggs, lightly beaten
- 1/2 onion, chopped
- 2 zucchini, grated & squeeze out all liquid
- 3/4 lb ground beef
- 1/2 tsp chili powder
- 1 tsp curry powder
- 1 cup breadcrumbs
- Pepper
- Salt

Directions:
1. Add all ingredients into the large bowl and mix until well combined.
2. Make 6 equal shapes of patties from the meat mixture and place it into the multi-level air fryer basket.
3. Place multi-level air fryer basket into the inner pot of the instant pot.
4. Secure pot with air fryer lid, select bake mode then cook at 380 F for 35 minutes. Flip patties after 20 minutes.
5. Serve and enjoy.

Nutritional Value (Amount per Serving):
- Calories 213
- Fat 6.2 g
- Carbohydrates 16.4 g
- Sugar 2.8 g
- Protein 22.4 g
- Cholesterol 105 mg

Meatballs

Preparation Time: 10 minutes
Cooking Time: 15 minutes
Serve: 4
Ingredients:
- 1 lb ground pork
- 1 tsp paprika
- 1 tsp garlic powder
- 1 tsp onion powder
- 1/2 tsp ground cumin
- 1/2 tsp coriander
- 1/2 tsp dried thyme
- Pepper
- Salt

Directions:
1. Add all ingredients into the large bowl and mix until well combined.
2. Make small balls from the meat mixture and place it into the multi-level air fryer basket.

3. Place multi-level air fryer basket into the inner pot of the instant pot.
4. Secure pot with air fryer lid, select bake mode then cook at 380 F for 15 minutes.
5. Serve and enjoy.

Nutritional Value (Amount per Serving):
- Calories 320
- Fat 9.2 g
- Carbohydrates 24.7 g
- Sugar 4.2 g
- Protein 33.6 g
- Cholesterol 158 mg

Cinnamon Lamb Chops

Preparation Time: 10 minutes
Cooking Time: 30 minutes
Serve: 4

Ingredients:
- 4 lamb chops
- 1 tsp ginger
- 1/4 cup brown sugar
- 1 tsp garlic powder
- 1 tsp ground cinnamon
- 1 1/2 tsp tarragon
- Pepper
- Salt

Directions:
1. Add lamb chops and remaining ingredients into the zip-lock bag, seal bag, and place in the refrigerator overnight.
2. Place marinated lamb chops into the multi-level air fryer basket.
3. Place multi-level air fryer basket into the inner pot.
4. Secure pot with air fryer lid, select bake mode then cook at 375 F for 30 minutes. Flip lamb chops after 20 minutes.
5. Serve and enjoy.

Nutritional Value (Amount per Serving):
- Calories 251
- Fat 8.4 g
- Carbohydrates 10.3 g
- Sugar 9 g
- Protein 32.1 g
- Cholesterol 102 mg

Crispy Pork Chops

Preparation Time: 10 minutes
Cooking Time: 15 minutes
Serve: 2

Ingredients:
- 2 pork chops, bone-in
- 1 tbsp olive oil
- 1 cup pork rinds, crushed
- 1/2 tsp garlic powder
- 1/2 tsp onion powder
- 1/2 tsp paprika
- 1/2 tsp parsley

Directions:
1. In a large bowl, mix together pork rinds, garlic powder, onion powder, parsley, and paprika.
2. Brush pork chops with oil and coat with crushed pork rind.
3. Place coated pork chops into the multi-level air fryer basket.
4. Place multi-level air fryer basket into the inner pot of the instant pot.
5. Secure pot with air fryer lid, select air fry mode then cook at 400 F for 15 minutes. Flip pork chops after 10 minutes.
6. Serve and enjoy.

Nutritional Value (Amount per Serving):
- Calories 362
- Fat 29.5 g
- Carbohydrates 1.3 g
- Sugar 0.4 g
- Protein 22.8 g
- Cholesterol 79 mg

Cheese Cracker Crust Pork Chops

Preparation Time: 10 minutes
Cooking Time: 30 minutes
Serve: 3

Ingredients:
- 1 egg, lightly beaten
- 3 pork chops, boneless
- 4 tbsp parmesan cheese, grated
- 2 tbsp milk
- 1/2 cup crackers, crushed
- Pepper
- Salt

Directions:
1. In a small bowl, whisk the egg with milk.
2. In a shallow dish, mix together cheese, crackers, pepper, and salt.
3. Dip pork chops in egg then coat with cheese mixture.
4. Place coated pork chops into the multi-level air fryer basket.
5. Place multi-level air fryer basket into the inner pot of the instant pot.
6. Secure pot with air fryer lid, select bake mode then cook at 350 F for 30 minutes. Flip pork chops halfway through.
7. Serve and enjoy.

Nutritional Value (Amount per Serving):
- Calories 358
- Fat 25.8 g
- Carbohydrates 7.2 g
- Sugar 0.8 g
- Protein 23.3 g
- Cholesterol 130 mg

Meatballs

Preparation Time: 10 minutes
Cooking Time: 15 minutes
Serve: 4

Ingredients:
- 1 lb ground lamb
- 1 tsp onion powder
- 1 tsp garlic, minced
- 1/2 tsp ground coriander
- 1 tsp ground cumin
- Pepper
- Salt

Directions:
1. Add all ingredients into the large bowl and mix until well combined.
2. Make small balls from the meat mixture and place it into the multi-level air fryer basket.
3. Place multi-level air fryer basket into the inner pot of the instant pot.
4. Secure pot with air fryer lid, select bake mode then cook at 380 F for 15 minutes.
5. Serve and enjoy.

Nutritional Value (Amount per Serving):
- Calories 218
- Fat 8.5 g
- Carbohydrates 1.4 g
- Sugar 0.2 g
- Protein 32.1 g
- Cholesterol 102 mg

Cheesy Beef Patties

Preparation Time: 10 minutes
Cooking Time: 15 minutes
Serve: 6

Ingredients:
- 2 lbs ground beef
- 1 cup cheddar cheese, grated
- 1 tsp onion powder
- 1 tsp garlic powder
- Pepper
- Salt

Directions:
1. Line multi-level air fryer basket with parchment paper.
2. Add all ingredients into the large bowl and mix until well combined.
3. Make 6 equal shapes of patties from the meat mixture and place it into the multi-level air fryer basket.
4. Place multi-level air fryer basket into the inner pot of the instant pot.
5. Secure pot with air fryer lid, select bake mode then cook at 380 F for 15 minutes.
6. Serve and enjoy.

Nutritional Value (Amount per Serving):
- Calories 360
- Fat 15.7 g
- Carbohydrates 0.9 g
- Sugar 0.4 g
- Protein 50.7 g
- Cholesterol 155 mg

Meatballs

Preparation Time: 10 minutes
Cooking Time: 20 minutes
Serve: 4

Ingredients:
- 1 lb ground beef
- 1/2 small onion, chopped
- 1 egg, lightly beaten
- 2 garlic cloves, minced
- 1 tbsp basil, chopped
- 1/4 cup parmesan cheese, grated
- 1 tbsp Italian parsley, chopped
- 1 tbsp rosemary, chopped
- 2 tbsp milk
- 1/2 cup breadcrumbs
- Pepper
- Salt

Directions:
1. Line multi-level air fryer basket with parchment paper.
2. Add all ingredients into the bowl and mix until well combined.
3. Make small balls from the meat mixture and place it into the multi-level air fryer basket.
4. Place multi-level air fryer basket into the inner pot of the instant pot.
5. Secure pot with air fryer lid, select bake mode then cook at 375 F for 20 minutes.
6. Serve and enjoy.

Nutritional Value (Amount per Serving):
- Calories 311
- Fat 10.4 g
- Carbohydrates 12.3 g
- Sugar 1.7 g
- Protein 39.9 g
- Cholesterol 147 mg

Meatballs

Preparation Time: 10 minutes
Cooking Time: 12 minutes
Serve: 6

Ingredients:
- 2 eggs, lightly beaten
- 2 lbs ground beef
- 3 oz parmesan cheese, shredded
- 2 oz pork rind, crushed
- Pepper
- Salt

Directions:
1. Add all ingredients into the bowl and mix until well combined.
2. Make small balls from mixture and place into the multi-level air fryer basket.
3. Place multi-level air fryer basket into the inner pot of the instant pot.
4. Secure pot with air fryer lid, select air fry mode then cook at 350 F for 12 minutes.
5. Serve and enjoy.

Nutritional Value (Amount per Serving):
- Calories 401
- Fat 17.3 g
- Carbohydrates 0.6 g
- Sugar 0.1 g
- Protein 58.4 g
- Cholesterol 213 mg

Delicious Beef Kebabs

Preparation Time: 10 minutes
Cooking Time: 10 minutes
Serve: 4
Ingredients:
- 1 lb beef ribs, cut into 1-inch pieces
- 1/2 onion, cut into pieces
- 1 green pepper, cut into pieces
- 1/3 cup sour cream

Directions:
1. Add beef cubes and sour cream into the bowl and mix well, cover and place in the refrigerator overnight.
2. Thread marinated meat, onion, and bell peppers onto the skewers.
3. Place skewers into the multi-level air fryer basket.
4. Place multi-level air fryer basket into the inner pot of the instant pot.
5. Secure pot with air fryer lid, select air fry mode then cook at 400 F for 10 minutes. Flip kebabs halfway through.
6. Serve and enjoy.

Nutritional Value (Amount per Serving):
- Calories 371
- Fat 30.2 g
- Carbohydrates 5 g
- Sugar 2.3 g
- Protein 20.6 g
- Cholesterol 84 mg

Meatballs

Preparation Time: 10 minutes
Cooking Time: 10 minutes
Serve: 4
Ingredients:
- 1 egg, lightly beaten
- 1 lb ground beef
- 1/4 cup onion, chopped
- 2 tbsp taco seasoning
- 1 tbsp garlic, minced
- 1/2 cup cheddar cheese, shredded
- 1/4 cup cilantro, chopped
- Pepper
- Salt

Directions:
1. Add ground beef and remaining ingredients into the large bowl and mix until well combined.
2. Make small meatballs from meat mixture and place it into a multi-level air fryer basket.
3. Place multi-level air fryer basket into the inner pot of the instant pot.
4. Secure pot with air fryer lid, select air fry mode then cook at 400 F for 10 minutes.
5. Serve and enjoy.

Nutritional Value (Amount per Serving):
- Calories 301
- Fat 13.5 g
- Carbohydrates 2.5 g
- Sugar 0.5 g
- Protein 40.1 g
- Cholesterol 159 mg

Honey Garlic Pork Chops

Preparation Time: 10 minutes
Cooking Time: 12 minutes
Serve: 4
Ingredients:
- 4 pork chops
- 2 tbsp lemon juice
- 1/4 cup honey
- 1 tsp garlic, minced
- 1 tbsp olive oil
- 1 tbsp sweet chili sauce
- Pepper
- Salt

Directions:
1. Season pork chops with pepper and salt.
2. Place pork chops into the multi-level air fryer basket.
3. Place multi-level air fryer basket into the inner pot of the instant pot.
4. Secure pot with air fryer lid, select air fry mode then cook at 400 F for 12 minutes. Flip pork chops halfway through.
5. Meanwhile, heat oil in a pan over medium heat. Add garlic and saute for 1 minute.
6. Add lemon juice, honey, and sweet chili sauce and stir well and cook for 3 minutes.
7. Pour sauce over pork chops and serve.

Nutritional Value (Amount per Serving):
- Calories 361
- Fat 23.4 g
- Carbohydrates 19.4 g
- Sugar 19.1 g
- Protein 18.1 g
- Cholesterol 69 mg

Pork Tenderloin

Preparation Time: 10 minutes
Cooking Time: 20 minutes
Serve: 4
Ingredients:
- 1 1/4 lb pork tenderloin
- 1 tsp ground mustard
- 1 tbsp paprika
- 2 tbsp brown sugar
- 1/2 tbsp olive oil

- 1/4 tsp garlic powder
- 1/2 tsp onion powder
- Pepper
- Salt

Directions:
1. In a small bowl, mix together garlic powder, onion powder, ground mustard, paprika, brown sugar, pepper, and salt.
2. Coat pork tenderloin with oil and rub with spice mixture.
3. Place pork tenderloin into the multi-level air fryer basket.
4. Place multi-level air fryer basket into the inner pot of the instant pot.
5. Secure pot with air fryer lid, select air fry mode then cook at 400 F for 20 minutes.
6. Slice and serve.

Nutritional Value (Amount per Serving):
- Calories 245
- Fat 7.2 g
- Carbohydrates 6.1 g
- Sugar 4.8 g
- Protein 37.6 g
- Cholesterol 103 mg

Basil Pork Loin

Preparation Time: 10 minutes
Cooking Time: 18 minutes
Serve: 8

Ingredients:
- 2 lbs pork chops
- 1 tsp basil
- 1 tsp garlic powder
- 3 tbsp brown sugar
- 1 tsp salt

Directions:
1. Mix together brown sugar, basil, garlic powder, and salt and rub over pork chops.
2. Place pork chops into the multi-level air fryer basket.
3. Place multi-level air fryer basket into the inner pot of the instant pot.
4. Secure pot with air fryer lid, select air fry mode then cook at 400 F for 18 minutes. Flip pork chops after 8 minutes.
5. Serve and enjoy.

Nutritional Value (Amount per Serving):
- Calories 377
- Fat 28.2 g
- Carbohydrates 3.6 g
- Sugar 3.4 g
- Protein 25.5 g
- Cholesterol 98 mg

Pork Belly Strips

Preparation Time: 10 minutes
Cooking Time: 15 minutes
Serve: 4
Ingredients:
- 1 lb pork belly strips
- 1/4 tsp garlic powder
- Pepper
- Salt

Directions:
1. Season pork belly strips with garlic powder, pepper, and salt and place into the multi-level air fryer basket.
2. Place multi-level air fryer basket into the inner pot of the instant pot.
3. Secure pot with air fryer lid, select air fry mode then cook at 380 F for 15 minutes.
4. Serve and enjoy.

Nutritional Value (Amount per Serving):
- Calories 598
- Fat 61.7 g
- Carbohydrates 0.2 g
- Sugar 0 g
- Protein 8 g
- Cholesterol 60 mg

Cajun Pork Chops

Preparation Time: 10 minutes
Cooking Time: 9 minutes
Serve: 2

Ingredients:
- 2 pork chops, boneless
- 1 tsp Cajun seasoning
- 3 tbsp parmesan cheese, grated
- 1/3 cup almond flour
- 1 tsp dried mixed herbs
- 1 tsp paprika
- 1 tbsp olive oil

Directions:
1. In a bowl, mix together parmesan cheese, almond flour, paprika, mixed herbs, and Cajun seasoning.
2. Brush pork chops with oil and coat with parmesan cheese.
3. Place coated pork chops into the multi-level air fryer basket.
4. Place multi-level air fryer basket into the inner pot of the instant pot.
5. Secure pot with air fryer lid, select air fry mode then cook at 350 F for 9 minutes. Flip pork chops halfway through.
6. Serve and enjoy.

Nutritional Value (Amount per Serving):
- Calories 383
- Fat 31.8 g
- Carbohydrates 2.2 g
- Sugar 0.3 g
- Protein 22.8 g
- Cholesterol 77 mg

Honey Ginger Pork Shoulder

Preparation Time: 10 minutes
Cooking Time: 15 minutes

Serve: 4
Ingredients:
- 1 lb pork shoulder, boneless
- 2 tsp garlic, minced
- 1 tbsp wine
- 1 tbsp sugar
- 2 tbsp soy sauce
- 4 tbsp honey
- 1 tsp Chinese five-spice
- 2 tsp ginger, minced

Directions:
1. Add all ingredients except pork into the zip-lock bag and mix well and place it in the refrigerator overnight.
2. Remove pork from marinade and place it into the multi-level air fryer basket.
3. Place multi-level air fryer basket into the inner pot of the instant pot.
4. Secure pot with air fryer lid, select air fry mode then cook at 380 F for 15 minutes. Flip pork shoulder halfway through.
5. Serve and enjoy.

Nutritional Value (Amount per Serving):
- Calories 419
- Fat 24.3 g
- Carbohydrates 22.1 g
- Sugar 20.5 g
- Protein 27.1 g
- Cholesterol 102 mg

Flavors Beef Strips

Preparation Time: 10 minutes
Cooking Time: 25 minutes
Serve: 4
Ingredients:
- 1 lb beef stew meat, cut into strips
- 1 garlic clove, minced
- 1/2 lime juice
- 1 tbsp olive oil
- 1/2 tbsp chives, chopped
- 1/2 tbsp ground cumin
- 1 tbsp garlic powder
- Pepper
- Salt

Directions:
1. Add the meat into the large bowl.
2. Add remaining ingredients over meat and toss well.
3. Add beef strips into the multi-level air fryer basket.
4. Place multi-level air fryer basket into the inner pot of the instant pot.
5. Secure pot with air fryer lid, select air fry mode then cook at 380 F for 25 minutes. Flip beef strips halfway through.
6. Serve and enjoy.

Nutritional Value (Amount per Serving):
- Calories 253
- Fat 10.8 g
- Carbohydrates 2.6 g
- Sugar 0.6 g
- Protein 35 g
- Cholesterol 101 mg

Easy Mustard Pork Chops

Preparation Time: 10 minutes
Cooking Time: 30 minutes
Serve: 4
Ingredients:
- 1 lb pork chops
- 2 tbsp brown mustard
- 1 cup flour
- 1 tsp garlic salt

Directions:
1. Mix together flour and salt.
2. Coat one side of pork chops with flour and place it into the multi-level air fryer basket.
3. Spread mustard on top of pork chops.
4. Place multi-level air fryer basket into the inner pot of the instant pot.
5. Secure pot with air fryer lid, select bake mode then cook at 350 F for 30 minutes.
6. Serve and enjoy.

Nutritional Value (Amount per Serving):
- Calories 479
- Fat 28.5 g
- Carbohydrates 98 g
- Sugar 0.3 g
- Protein 28.8 g
- Cholesterol 98 mg

Chapter 5: Fish & Seafood

Parmesan Shrimp

Preparation Time: 10 minutes
Cooking Time: 12 minutes
Serve: 4
Ingredients:
- 1 lb shrimp, peeled & deveined
- 2 tbsp parsley, minced
- 2 tbsp parmesan cheese, grated
- 1/8 tsp garlic powder
- 2 tbsp olive oil
- 1/2 tsp pepper
- 1/2 tsp salt

Directions:
1. Add shrimp and remaining ingredients into the mixing bowl and toss well.
2. Add shrimp into the multi-level air fryer basket.
3. Place multi-level air fryer basket into the inner pot of the instant pot.
4. Secure pot with air fryer lid, select air fry mode then cook at 400 F for 12 minutes. Stir shrimp halfway through.
5. Serve and enjoy.

Nutritional Value (Amount per Serving):
- Calories 205
- Fat 9.5 g
- Carbohydrates 2.2 g
- Sugar 0 g
- Protein 26.8 g
- Cholesterol 241 mg

Quick & Healthy Salmon

Preparation Time: 10 minutes
Cooking Time: 15 minutes
Serve: 2
Ingredients:
- 2 salmon fillets
- 1 tbsp olive oil
- 1 garlic clove, minced
- Pepper
- Salt

Directions:
1. In a small bowl, mix oil, garlic, pepper, and salt.
2. Brush salmon fillets with olive oil mixture and place it into the multi-level air fryer basket.
3. Place multi-level air fryer basket into the inner pot of the instant pot.
4. Secure pot with air fryer lid, select air fry mode then cook at 400 F for 15 minutes.
5. Serve and enjoy.

Nutritional Value (Amount per Serving):
- Calories 298
- Fat 18 g
- Carbohydrates 0.5 g
- Sugar 0 g
- Protein 34.6 g
- Cholesterol 78 mg

Easy Tuna Cakes

Preparation Time: 10 minutes
Cooking Time: 12 minutes
Serve: 4
Ingredients:
- 2 eggs
- 12 oz can tuna chunk in water, drain
- 1/2 onion, diced
- 2 tbsp fresh lime juice
- 1/4 cup mayonnaise
- 1/2 cup breadcrumbs
- 1/4 tsp pepper
- 1/2 tsp salt

Directions:
1. Line multi-level air fryer basket with parchment paper.
2. Add all ingredients into the mixing bowl and mix until well combined.
3. Make patties from mixture and place into the multi-level air fryer basket.
4. Place multi-level air fryer basket into the inner pot of the instant pot.
5. Secure pot with air fryer lid, select air fry mode then cook at 375 F for 12 minutes. Flip patties halfway through.
6. Serve and enjoy.

Nutritional Value (Amount per Serving):
- Calories 229
- Fat 7.8 g
- Carbohydrates 16.6 g
- Sugar 2.9 g
- Protein 21.7 g
- Cholesterol 131 mg

Crispy White Fish Fillets

Preparation Time: 10 minutes
Cooking Time: 17 minutes
Serve: 4
Ingredients:
- 4 white fish fillets, cut in half
- 3/4 cup cornmeal
- 1/2 tsp pepper
- 1/2 tsp garlic powder
- 1 tsp paprika
- 2 tsp old bay seasoning
- 1/4 cup flour
- 1 1/2 tsp salt

Directions:
1. Add cornmeal, pepper, garlic powder, paprika, old bay seasoning, flour, and salt into the zip-lock bag, seal bag, and shake well.
2. Add fish fillets into the bag, seal bag, and shake until fish is well coated.

3. Remove coated fish fillets from the bag and place it into the multi-level air fryer basket.
4. Place multi-level air fryer basket into the inner pot of the instant pot.
5. Secure pot with air fryer lid, select air fry mode then cook at 400 F for 17 minutes. Flip fish fillets after 10 minutes.
6. Serve and enjoy.

Nutritional Value (Amount per Serving):
- Calories 379
- Fat 12.6 g
- Carbohydrates 24.3 g
- Sugar 0.3 g
- Protein 40.5 g
- Cholesterol 119 mg

Quick Taco Shrimp

Preparation Time: 10 minutes
Cooking Time: 6 minutes
Serve: 4

Ingredients:
- 1 lb shrimp, peeled & deveined
- 1/2 tsp garlic powder
- 1/4 tsp onion powder
- 1/4 tsp cumin
- 1/2 tsp chili powder
- 2 tbsp olive oil
- Pepper
- Salt

Directions:
1. Toss shrimp with onion powder, cumin, garlic powder, chili powder, oil, pepper, and salt.
2. Add shrimp into the multi-level air fryer basket.
3. Place multi-level air fryer basket into the inner pot of the instant pot.
4. Secure pot with air fryer lid, select air fry mode then cook at 400 F for 6 minutes.
5. Serve and enjoy.

Nutritional Value (Amount per Serving):
- Calories 198
- Fat 9 g
- Carbohydrates 2.4 g
- Sugar 0.2 g
- Protein 26 g
- Cholesterol 239 mg

Delicious Crab Cakes

Preparation Time: 10 minutes
Cooking Time: 10 minutes
Serve: 4

Ingredients:
- 8 oz lump crab
- 1 tsp old bay seasoning
- 1 tbsp Dijon mustard
- 2 tbsp breadcrumbs
- 2 tbsp mayonnaise
- 2 green onion, chopped
- 1/4 cup bell pepper, chopped

Directions:
1. Add all ingredients into the mixing bowl and mix until well combined.
2. Line multi-level air fryer basket with parchment paper.
3. Make 4 equal shapes of patties from the mixture and place it into the multi-level air fryer basket.
4. Place multi-level air fryer basket into the inner pot of the instant pot.
5. Secure pot with air fryer lid, select air fry mode then cook at 370 F for 10 minutes.
6. Serve and enjoy.

Nutritional Value (Amount per Serving):
- Calories 85
- Fat 3.3 g
- Carbohydrates 6.5 g
- Sugar 2.3 g
- Protein 8 g
- Cholesterol 53 mg

Perfect Air Fryer Salmon

Preparation Time: 10 minutes
Cooking Time: 12 minutes
Serve: 2

Ingredients:
- 2 salmon fillets
- 3 tbsp coconut aminos
- 1 garlic, minced
- 1 tsp ginger, grated
- 1/2 tsp hot sauce

Directions:
1. In a shallow dish, mix coconut aminos, garlic, ginger, and hot sauce.
2. Add salmon fillets into the marinade, coat well, and let it sit for 30 minutes.
3. Remove salmon fillets from marinade and place it into the multi-level air fryer basket.
4. Place multi-level air fryer basket into the inner pot of the instant pot.
5. Secure pot with air fryer lid, select air fry mode then cook at 400 F for 6 minutes.
6. Brush salmon fillets with marinade and air fry for 6 minutes more.
7. Serve and enjoy.

Nutritional Value (Amount per Serving):
- Calories 268
- Fat 11.1 g
- Carbohydrates 6.7 g
- Sugar 0.1 g
- Protein 34.9 g
- Cholesterol 78 mg

Healthy Coconut Shrimp

Preparation Time: 10 minutes
Cooking Time: 12 minutes
Serve: 4

Ingredients:

- 1 lb shrimp, peeled & deveined
- 1/4 cup breadcrumbs
- 3/4 cup shredded coconut
- 2 eggs, lightly beaten
- 1/4 cup flour
- 1/4 tsp pepper
- 1/2 tsp salt

Directions:
1. Line multi-level air fryer basket with parchment paper.
2. In a small bowl, add egg and whisk well.
3. In a shallow dish, mix flour, pepper, and salt.
4. In a separate shallow dish, mix breadcrumbs and shredded coconut.
5. Coat shrimp with flour, then dip in egg, and finally coat with breadcrumbs.
6. Place coated shrimp into the multi-level air fryer basket.
7. Place multi-level air fryer basket into the inner pot of the instant pot.
8. Secure pot with air fryer lid, select air fry mode then cook at 360 F for 12 minutes. Flip shrimp halfway through.
9. Serve and enjoy.

Nutritional Value (Amount per Serving):
- Calories 275
- Fat 9.6 g
- Carbohydrates 15.1 g
- Sugar 1.5 g
- Protein 30.8 g
- Cholesterol 321 mg

Simple Garlic Butter Salmon

Preparation Time: 10 minutes
Cooking Time: 10 minutes
Serve: 2

Ingredients:
- 2 salmon fillets, boneless
- 1 tsp parsley, chopped
- 1 tsp garlic, minced
- 2 tbsp butter, melted
- Pepper
- Salt

Directions:
1. In a small bowl, mix butter, garlic, and parsley.
2. Season salmon with pepper and salt and brush with melted butter mixture.
3. Place salmon fillets into the multi-level air fryer basket.
4. Place multi-level air fryer basket into the inner pot of the instant pot.
5. Secure pot with air fryer lid, select air fry mode then cook at 360 F for 10 minutes.
6. Serve and enjoy.

Nutritional Value (Amount per Serving):
- Calories 340
- Fat 22.5 g
- Carbohydrates 0.5 g
- Sugar 0 g
- Protein 34.8 g
- Cholesterol 109 mg

Herbed Salmon

Preparation Time: 10 minutes
Cooking Time: 6 minutes
Serve: 2

Ingredients:
- 8 oz salmon fillets
- 1 tbsp butter
- 2 tbsp olive oil
- 1/4 tsp paprika
- 1 tsp herb de Provence
- 1/4 tsp pepper
- 1/4 tsp salt

Directions:
1. Brush salmon fillets with oil and rub with paprika, herb de Provence, pepper, and salt.
2. Place salmon fillets into the multi-level air fryer basket.
3. Place multi-level air fryer basket into the inner pot of the instant pot.
4. Secure pot with air fryer lid, select air fry mode then cook at 390 F for 5-8 minutes.
5. Melt butter and pour over salmon fillets and serve.

Nutritional Value (Amount per Serving):
- Calories 322
- Fat 26.8 g
- Carbohydrates 0.3 g
- Sugar 0 g
- Protein 22.1 g
- Cholesterol 65 mg

Air Fryer Cod

Preparation Time: 10 minutes
Cooking Time: 10 minutes
Serve: 1

Ingredients:
- 3 oz cod fillet
- 1 lemon, sliced
- Pepper
- Salt

Directions:
1. Season cod with pepper and salt and place into the multi-level air fryer basket. Top with sliced lemon.
2. Place multi-level air fryer basket into the inner pot of the instant pot.
3. Secure pot with air fryer lid, select air fry mode then cook at 375 F for 10 minutes.
4. Serve and enjoy.

Nutritional Value (Amount per Serving):
- Calories 85
- Fat 0.9 g
- Carbohydrates 5.5 g
- Sugar 1.5 g

- Protein 15.8 g
- Cholesterol 42 mg

Healthy Salmon Patties

Preparation Time: 10 minutes
Cooking Time: 8 minutes
Serve: 6
Ingredients:
- 14 oz can salmon, drain & mince
- 1 egg, lightly beaten
- 1 tsp paprika
- 3 green onions, minced
- 3 tbsp parsley, chopped
- Pepper
- Salt

Directions:
1. Line multi-level air fryer basket with parchment paper.
2. Add all ingredients into the mixing bowl and mix until well combined.
3. Make 6 equal shapes of patties from the mixture and place it into the multi-level air fryer basket.
4. Place multi-level air fryer basket into the inner pot of the instant pot.
5. Secure pot with air fryer lid, select air fry mode then cook at 360 F for 8 minutes. Flip patties halfway through.
6. Serve and enjoy.

Nutritional Value (Amount per Serving):
- Calories 102
- Fat 4.9 g
- Carbohydrates 0.9 g
- Sugar 0.3 g
- Protein 14 g
- Cholesterol 56 mg

Honey Glazed Fish Fillets

Preparation Time: 10 minutes
Cooking Time: 8 minutes
Serve: 4
Ingredients:
- 4 salmon fillets, skin-on
- 1 tsp sesame seeds
- 1 tbsp honey
- 2 tsp soy sauce
- Pepper
- Salt

Directions:
1. Season salmon fillets with pepper and salt and brush with soy sauce.
2. Place salmon fillets into the multi-level air fryer basket.
3. Place multi-level air fryer basket into the inner pot of the instant pot.
4. Secure pot with air fryer lid, select air fry mode then cook at 375 F for 8 minutes.
5. Brush salmon fillets with honey and sprinkle with sesame seeds.
6. Serve and enjoy.

Nutritional Value (Amount per Serving):
- Calories 257
- Fat 11.4 g
- Carbohydrates 4.7 g
- Sugar 4.4 g
- Protein 34.9 g
- Cholesterol 78 mg

Dijon Crab Cakes

Preparation Time: 10 minutes
Cooking Time: 14 minutes
Serve: 4
Ingredients:
- 1 egg
- 1 lb crabmeat
- 1/2 cup crackers, crushed
- 2 tsp soy sauce
- 1 tsp Dijon mustard
- 1 tsp dry mustard
- 1/3 cup mayonnaise

Directions:
1. Line multi-level air fryer basket with parchment paper.
2. Add all ingredients into the bowl and mix until well combined. Place mixture in the refrigerator for 1 hour.
3. Make 4 equal shapes of patties from the mixture and place it into the multi-level air fryer basket.
4. Place multi-level air fryer basket into the inner pot of the instant pot.
5. Secure pot with air fryer lid, select air fry mode then cook at 350 F for 14 minutes. Flip patties halfway through.
6. Serve and enjoy.

Nutritional Value (Amount per Serving):
- Calories 245
- Fat 10.4 g
- Carbohydrates 27.1 g
- Sugar 8.7 g
- Protein 11.2 g
- Cholesterol 69 mg

Breaded Cod

Preparation Time: 10 minutes
Cooking Time: 12 minutes
Serve: 3
Ingredients:
- 3 cod fillets
- 1/4 cup parmesan cheese, grated
- 1 tsp garlic herb seasoning
- 1 egg, lightly beaten
- 1/2 cup breadcrumbs
- Pepper
- Salt

Directions:
1. In a small bowl, add egg and whisk well.

2. In a shallow dish, mix parmesan cheese, garlic herb seasoning, breadcrumbs, pepper, and salt.
3. Dip cod fillet in egg and coat with parmesan cheese mixture.
4. Place coated cod fillets into the multi-level air fryer basket.
5. Place multi-level air fryer basket into the inner pot of the instant pot.
6. Secure pot with air fryer lid, select air fry mode then cook at 380 F for 12 minutes. Flip fish fillets halfway through.
7. Serve and enjoy.

Nutritional Value (Amount per Serving):
- Calories 206
- Fat 5 g
- Carbohydrates 13.4 g
- Sugar 1.2 g
- Protein 26.7 g
- Cholesterol 115 mg

Shrimp Fajitas

Preparation Time: 10 minutes
Cooking Time: 22 minutes
Serve: 12

Ingredients:
- 1 lb shrimp, peeled and deveined
- 2 tbsp taco seasoning
- 1/2 cup onion, diced
- 2 bell pepper, diced
- 1 tbsp olive oil

Directions:
1. Add shrimp and remaining ingredients into the mixing bowl and toss well.
2. Add shrimp mixture into the multi-level air fryer basket.
3. Place multi-level air fryer basket into the inner pot of the instant pot.
4. Secure pot with air fryer lid, select air fry mode then cook at 390 F for 22 minutes. Stir shrimp mixture after 12 minutes.
5. Serve and enjoy.

Nutritional Value (Amount per Serving):
- Calories 66
- Fat 2 g
- Carbohydrates 2.8 g
- Sugar 1.2 g
- Protein 9 g
- Cholesterol 80 mg

Delicious Lemon Pepper Shrimp

Preparation Time: 10 minutes
Cooking Time: 8 minutes
Serve: 2

Ingredients:
- 12 oz shrimp, peeled & deveined
- 1/4 tsp garlic powder
- 1/4 tsp paprika
- 1 tsp lemon pepper
- 1 lemon juice
- 1/2 tbsp olive oil

Directions:
1. Add shrimp and remaining ingredients into the bowl and toss well.
2. Add shrimp into the multi-level air fryer basket.
3. Place multi-level air fryer basket into the inner pot of the instant pot.
4. Secure pot with air fryer lid, select air fry mode then cook at 400 F for 8 minutes.
5. Serve and enjoy.

Nutritional Value (Amount per Serving):
- Calories 242
- Fat 6.6 g
- Carbohydrates 4.1 g
- Sugar 0.6 g
- Protein 39.1 g
- Cholesterol 358 mg

Shrimp with Pepper & Zucchini

Preparation Time: 10 minutes
Cooking Time: 15 minutes
Serve: 4

Ingredients:
- 1 lb shrimp, peeled & deveined
- 1 bell pepper, sliced
- 1 zucchini, sliced
- 1/4 cup parmesan cheese, grated
- 1 tbsp Italian seasoning
- 1 tbsp garlic, minced
- 1 tbsp olive oil
- Pepper
- Salt

Directions:
1. Add shrimp and remaining ingredients into the mixing bowl and toss well.
2. Add shrimp mixture into the multi-level air fryer basket.
3. Place multi-level air fryer basket into the inner pot of the instant pot.
4. Secure pot with air fryer lid, select air fry mode then cook at 390 F for 15 minutes. Stir shrimp mixture halfway through.
5. Serve and enjoy.

Nutritional Value (Amount per Serving):
- Calories 212
- Fat 7.8 g
- Carbohydrates 245 g
- Sugar 2.2 g
- Protein 28.6 g
- Cholesterol 245 mg

Old Bay Shrimp

Preparation Time: 10 minutes
Cooking Time: 10 minutes
Serve: 4

Ingredients:
- 1 lb shrimp, peeled & deveined

- 1 tbsp old bay seasoning
- 1/2 tbsp garlic, minced
- 1/2 tbsp lemon juice
- 1/2 tbsp olive oil

Directions:
1. Add shrimp and remaining ingredients into the mixing bowl and toss well.
2. Add shrimp into the multi-level air fryer basket.
3. Place multi-level air fryer basket into the inner pot of the instant pot.
4. Secure pot with air fryer lid, select air fry mode then cook at 390 F for 10 minutes.
5. Serve and enjoy.

Nutritional Value (Amount per Serving):
- Calories 152
- Fat 3.7 g
- Carbohydrates 2.1 g
- Sugar 0.1 g
- Protein 25.9 g
- Cholesterol 239 mg

Shrimp with Sausage & Peppers

Preparation Time: 10 minutes
Cooking Time: 12 minutes
Serve: 4

Ingredients:
- 1/2 lb shrimp
- 1/2 bell pepper, sliced
- 1/2 onion, sliced
- 1/2 zucchini, sliced
- 1/2 squash, sliced
- 1/2 sausage, sliced
- 1 tsp old bay seasoning
- 1 tbsp olive oil

Directions:
1. Add shrimp and remaining ingredients into the mixing bowl and toss well.
2. Add shrimp mixture into the multi-level air fryer basket.
3. Place multi-level air fryer basket into the inner pot of the instant pot.
4. Secure pot with air fryer lid, select air fry mode then cook at 400 F for 12 minutes.
5. Serve and enjoy.

Nutritional Value (Amount per Serving):
- Calories 127
- Fat 5.6 g
- Carbohydrates 4.9 g
- Sugar 2.2 g
- Protein 14.5 g
- Cholesterol 122 mg

Rosemary Garlic Shrimp

Preparation Time: 10 minutes
Cooking Time: 10 minutes
Serve: 4

Ingredients:
- 1 lb shrimp, peeled and deveined
- 1/2 tbsp fresh rosemary, chopped
- 1 tsp garlic, minced
- 1 tbsp olive oil
- Pepper
- Salt

Directions:
1. Add shrimp and remaining ingredients in a large bowl and toss well.
2. Add shrimp into the multi-level air fryer basket.
3. Place multi-level air fryer basket into the inner pot of the instant pot.
4. Secure pot with air fryer lid, select bake mode then cook at 380 F for 10 minutes.
5. Serve and enjoy.

Nutritional Value (Amount per Serving):
- Calories 167
- Fat 5.5 g
- Carbohydrates 2.2 g
- Sugar 0 g
- Protein 25.9 g
- Cholesterol 239 mg

Garlic Tomato Shrimp

Preparation Time: 10 minutes
Cooking Time: 25 minutes
Serve: 4

Ingredients:
- 1 lb shrimp, peeled
- 1 tbsp garlic, sliced
- 2 cups cherry tomatoes
- 1 tbsp olive oil
- Pepper
- Salt

Directions:
1. Add shrimp, oil, garlic, tomatoes, pepper, and salt into the bowl and toss well.
2. Line multi-level air fryer basket with parchment paper.
3. Transfer shrimp mixture into the multi-level air fryer basket.
4. Place multi-level air fryer basket into the inner pot of the instant pot.
5. Secure pot with air fryer lid, select bake mode then cook at 380 F for 25 minutes.
6. Serve and enjoy.

Nutritional Value (Amount per Serving):
- Calories 184
- Fat 5.6 g
- Carbohydrates 5.9 g
- Sugar 2.4 g
- Protein 26.8 g
- Cholesterol 239 mg

Cajun Shrimp

Preparation Time: 10 minutes
Cooking Time: 10 minutes

Serve: 4
Ingredients:
- 1 lb shrimp, deveined & peeled
- 3/4 tbsp Cajun seasoning
- 2 tbsp olive oil
- Salt

Directions:
1. Toss shrimp, Cajun seasoning, and oil into the bowl.
2. Add shrimp into the multi-level air fryer basket.
3. Place multi-level air fryer basket into the inner pot of the instant pot.
4. Secure pot with air fryer lid, select bake mode then cook at 350 F for 10 minutes.
5. Serve and enjoy.

Nutritional Value (Amount per Serving):
- Calories 195
- Fat 8.9 g
- Carbohydrates 1.7 g
- Sugar 0 g
- Protein 25.9 g
- Cholesterol 239 mg

Spicy Lemon Pepper Shrimp

Preparation Time: 10 minutes
Cooking Time: 6 minutes
Serve: 4

Ingredients:
- 1 lb shrimp
- 1 tsp steak seasoning
- 1/4 tsp red pepper flakes
- 1 tsp garlic, minced
- 2 tsp olive oil
- 1 tbsp parsley, chopped
- 2 tsp fresh lemon juice
- 1 tsp lemon zest, grated
- Pepper
- Salt

Directions:
1. Add shrimp and remaining ingredients into the bowl and toss well.
2. Add shrimp into the multi-level air fryer basket.
3. Place multi-level air fryer basket into the inner pot of the instant pot.
4. Secure pot with air fryer lid, select air fry mode then cook at 400 F for 6 minutes.
5. Serve and enjoy.

Nutritional Value (Amount per Serving):
- Calories 157
- Fat 4.3 g
- Carbohydrates 2.2 g
- Sugar 0.1 g
- Protein 25.9 g
- Cholesterol 239 mg

Lemon Pepper Tilapia

Preparation Time: 10 minutes
Cooking Time: 10 minutes
Serve: 2

Ingredients:
- 2 tilapia fillets
- 1/2 tsp lemon pepper seasoning

Directions:
1. Season tilapia fillets with lemon pepper seasoning and place into the multi-level air fryer basket.
2. Place multi-level air fryer basket into the inner pot of the instant pot.
3. Secure pot with air fryer lid, select air fry mode then cook at 360 F for 10 minutes.
4. Serve and enjoy.

Nutritional Value (Amount per Serving):
- Calories 94
- Fat 1 g
- Carbohydrates 0.3 g
- Sugar 0 g
- Protein 21.1 g
- Cholesterol 55 mg

Delicious Tuna Patties

Preparation Time: 10 minutes
Cooking Time: 10 minutes
Serve: 10

Ingredients:
- 15 oz can tuna, drained and flaked
- 3 tbsp parmesan cheese, grated
- 1/2 cup breadcrumbs
- 1 tbsp lemon juice
- 2 eggs, lightly beaten
- 1/2 tsp dried herbs
- 1/2 tsp garlic powder
- 2 tbsp onion, minced
- 1 celery stalk, chopped
- Pepper
- Salt

Directions:
1. Line multi-level air fryer basket with parchment paper.
2. Add all ingredients into the mixing bowl and mix until well combined.
3. Make small patties from tuna mixture and place it into the multi-level air fryer basket.
4. Place multi-level air fryer basket into the inner pot of the instant pot.
5. Secure pot with air fryer lid, select air fry mode then cook at 360 F for 10 minutes. Flip patties halfway through.
6. Serve and enjoy.

Nutritional Value (Amount per Serving):
- Calories 112
- Fat 3.3 g
- Carbohydrates 4.7 g
- Sugar 0.6 g
- Protein 15.5 g
- Cholesterol 52 mg

Chili Honey Salmon

Preparation Time: 10 minutes
Cooking Time: 12 minutes
Serve: 3
Ingredients:
- 3 salmon fillets
- 1/2 tsp chili powder
- 1/2 tsp turmeric
- 1 tsp ground coriander
- 1/4 cup honey
- 1 tbsp red pepper flakes
- Pepper
- Salt

Directions:
1. Add honey in an oven-safe bowl and microwave until just warm. Add red pepper flakes, chili powder, turmeric, coriander, pepper, and salt and stir well.
2. Brush salmon with honey mixture and place it into the multi-level air fryer basket.
3. Place multi-level air fryer basket into the inner pot of the instant pot.
4. Secure pot with air fryer lid, select air fry mode then cook at 400 F for 12 minutes.
5. Serve and enjoy.

Nutritional Value (Amount per Serving):
- Calories 330
- Fat 11.4 g
- Carbohydrates 24.8 g
- Sugar 23.4 g
- Protein 34.9 g
- Cholesterol 78 mg

Flavorful Marinated Fish Fillets

Preparation Time: 10 minutes
Cooking Time: 10 minutes
Serve: 2
Ingredients:
- 2 salmon fillets, skinless and boneless
- For marinade:
- 1 tsp garlic, minced
- 2 tbsp mirin
- 2 tbsp soy sauce
- 1 tbsp olive oil
- 2 tbsp green onion, minced
- 1 tbsp ginger, grated

Directions:
1. Add salmon and marinade ingredients into the zip-lock bag, seal bag, and place in the refrigerator for 30 minutes.
2. Remove salmon from marinade and place it into the multi-level air fryer basket.
3. Place multi-level air fryer basket into the inner pot of the instant pot.
4. Secure pot with air fryer lid, select air fry mode then cook at 360 F for 10 minutes.
5. Serve and enjoy.

Nutritional Value (Amount per Serving):
- Calories 342
- Fat 18.2 g
- Carbohydrates 11 g
- Sugar 4.5 g
- Protein 36 g
- Cholesterol 78 mg

Rosemary Basil Salmon

Preparation Time: 10 minutes
Cooking Time: 15 minutes
Serve: 4
Ingredients:
- 1 lbs salmon, cut into 4 pieces
- 1 tbsp olive oil
- 1/2 tbsp dried rosemary
- 1/4 tsp dried basil
- 1 tbsp dried chives
- Pepper
- Salt

Directions:
1. In a small bowl, mix olive oil, rosemary, basil, chives, pepper, and salt.
2. Brush salmon with oil mixture and place it into the multi-level air fryer basket.
3. Place multi-level air fryer basket into the inner pot of the instant pot.
4. Secure pot with air fryer lid, select air fry mode then cook at 400 F for 15 minutes.
5. Serve and enjoy.

Nutritional Value (Amount per Serving):
- Calories 229
- Fat 7.8 g
- Carbohydrates 16.6 g
- Sugar 2.9 g
- Protein 21.7 g
- Cholesterol 131 mg

Baked Fish Fillet with Pepper

Preparation Time: 10 minutes
Cooking Time: 30 minutes
Serve: 1
Ingredients:
- 8 oz frozen white fish fillet
- 1/2 tsp Italian seasoning
- 1 1/2 tbsp butter, melted
- 1 tbsp lemon juice
- 1 tbsp fresh parsley, chopped
- 1 tbsp roasted red bell pepper, diced

Directions:
1. Line multi-level air fryer basket with parchment paper.
2. In a small bowl, mix melted butter, lemon juice, parsley, and Italian seasoning.
3. Brush fish fillet with melted butter mixture and place it into the multi-level air fryer basket. Top with roasted bell pepper.
4. Place multi-level air fryer basket into the inner pot of the instant pot.

5. Secure pot with air fryer lid, select bake mode then cook at 380 F for 30 minutes.
6. Serve and enjoy.

Nutritional Value (Amount per Serving):
- Calories 182
- Fat 10.6 g
- Carbohydrates 0.3 g
- Sugar 0 g
- Protein 22 g
- Cholesterol 50 mg

Greek Fish Fillets

Preparation Time: 10 minutes
Cooking Time: 10 minutes
Serve: 4

Ingredients:
- 1 1/2 lbs salmon, cut into 4 pieces
- 1 tsp lemon zest
- 2 tbsp lemon juice
- 2 tbsp olive oil
- 1 tsp oregano
- 1 garlic clove, grated
- 1 tbsp yogurt
- 1/4 tsp pepper
- 1/4 tsp salt

Directions:
1. Add all ingredients into the zip-lock bag, seal bag, and place in the refrigerator for 30 minutes.
2. Line multi-level air fryer basket with parchment paper.
3. Place marinated fish fillets into the multi-level air fryer basket.
4. Place multi-level air fryer basket into the inner pot of the instant pot.
5. Secure pot with air fryer lid, select bake mode then cook at 380 F for 10 minutes.
6. Serve and enjoy.

Nutritional Value (Amount per Serving):
- Calories 292
- Fat 17.7 g
- Carbohydrates 1.1 g
- Sugar 0.5 g
- Protein 33.4 g
- Cholesterol 75 mg

Cheese Herb Cod

Preparation Time: 10 minutes
Cooking Time: 20 minutes
Serve: 4

Ingredients:
- 1 lb cod, cut into 4 pieces
- 1 tsp dried oregano
- 1 tbsp fresh lemon juice
- 1 tsp garlic, minced
- 1/2 cup parmesan cheese, grated
- 4 tbsp butter, melted
- 1 tbsp dried parsley

Directions:
1. In a small bowl, mix butter, garlic, and lemon juice.
2. In a shallow dish, mix parmesan cheese, oregano, and parsley.
3. Brush fish fillets with butter mixture and coat with parmesan cheese mixture and place into the multi-level air fryer basket.
4. Place multi-level air fryer basket into the inner pot of the instant pot.
5. Secure pot with air fryer lid, select bake mode then cook at 380 F for 20 minutes.
6. Serve and enjoy.

Nutritional Value (Amount per Serving):
- Calories 260
- Fat 15 g
- Carbohydrates 1 g
- Sugar 0.1 g
- Protein 29.8 g
- Cholesterol 101 mg

Delicious Air Fry Prawns

Preparation Time: 10 minutes
Cooking Time: 6 minutes
Serve: 4

Ingredients:
- 12 prawns
- 3 tbsp mayonnaise
- 1 tsp chili powder
- 1 tsp red chili flakes
- 1 tbsp vinegar
- 1 tbsp ketchup
- 1/2 tsp sea salt

Directions:
1. In a bowl, toss prawns with chili flakes, chili powder, and salt.
2. Add shrimp into the multi-level air fryer basket.
3. Place multi-level air fryer basket into the inner pot of the instant pot.
4. Secure pot with air fryer lid, select air fry mode then cook at 350 F for 6 minutes. Stir halfway through.
5. In a small bowl, mix mayonnaise, vinegar, and ketchup and serve with prawns.

Nutritional Value (Amount per Serving):
- Calories 128
- Fat 4.9 g
- Carbohydrates 5 g
- Sugar 1.6 g
- Protein 15.3 g
- Cholesterol 142 mg

Cheese Garlic Shrimp

Preparation Time: 10 minutes
Cooking Time: 10 minutes
Serve: 3

Ingredients:
- 1 lb shrimp, peeled and deveined
- 1/4 cup parmesan cheese, grated

- 3 garlic cloves, minced
- 1 tbsp olive oil
- 1/4 tsp oregano
- 1/2 tsp pepper
- 1/2 tsp onion powder
- 1/2 tsp basil

Directions:
1. Line multi-level air fryer basket with parchment paper.
2. Add all ingredients into the bowl and toss well.
3. Add shrimp into the multi-level air fryer basket.
4. Place multi-level air fryer basket into the inner pot of the instant pot.
5. Secure pot with air fryer lid, select air fry mode then cook at 350 F for 10 minutes.
6. Serve and enjoy.

Nutritional Value (Amount per Serving):
- Calories 251
- Fat 8.9 g
- Carbohydrates 4.2 g
- Sugar 0.2 g
- Protein 37.1 g
- Cholesterol 324 mg

Tasty Tuna Patties

Preparation Time: 10 minutes
Cooking Time: 6 minutes
Serve: 4

Ingredients:
- 8 oz can tuna, drained
- 1/4 cup breadcrumbs
- 1 tbsp mustard
- 1 egg, lightly beaten
- Pepper
- Salt

Directions:
1. Line multi-level air fryer basket with parchment paper.
2. Add all ingredients into the large bowl and mix until well combined.
3. Make 4 equal shapes of patties from the mixture and place it into the multi-level air fryer basket.
4. Place multi-level air fryer basket into the inner pot of the instant pot.
5. Secure pot with air fryer lid, select air fry mode then cook at 400 F for 6 minutes. Flip patties halfway through.
6. Serve and enjoy.

Nutritional Value (Amount per Serving):
- Calories 121
- Fat 2.7 g
- Carbohydrates 5.9 g
- Sugar 0.7 g
- Protein 17.4 g
- Cholesterol 58 mg

Delicious Blackened Shrimp

Preparation Time: 10 minutes
Cooking Time: 6 minutes
Serve: 4

Ingredients:
- 1 lb shrimp, peeled and deveined
- 1 tsp garlic powder
- 1 tsp onion powder
- 2 tbsp olive oil
- 2 tsp paprika
- 1/4 tsp cayenne
- 1 tsp dried oregano
- Pepper
- Salt

Directions:
1. In a bowl, toss shrimp with remaining ingredients.
2. Add shrimp into the multi-level air fryer basket.
3. Place multi-level air fryer basket into the inner pot of the instant pot.
4. Secure pot with air fryer lid, select air fry mode then cook at 400 F for 6 minutes.
5. Serve and enjoy.

Nutritional Value (Amount per Serving):
- Calories 204
- Fat 9.1 g
- Carbohydrates 3.6 g
- Sugar 0.5 g
- Protein 26.2 g
- Cholesterol 239 mg

Cajun Fish Fillets

Preparation Time: 10 minutes
Cooking Time: 15 minutes
Serve: 2

Ingredients:
- 2 catfish fillets
- 6 tbsp cornmeal
- 1 1/2 tsp Cajun seasoning
- 1 tbsp olive oil

Directions:
1. In a shallow dish, mix cornmeal and cajun seasoning.
2. Brush fish fillets with oil and coat with cornmeal mixture.
3. Place coated fish fillets into the multi-level air fryer basket.
4. Place multi-level air fryer basket into the inner pot of the instant pot.
5. Secure pot with air fryer lid, select air fry mode then cook at 380 F for 15 minutes. Flip fish fillets halfway through.
6. Serve and enjoy.

Nutritional Value (Amount per Serving):
- Calories 359
- Fat 20 g
- Carbohydrates 17.6 g

- Sugar 0.2 g
- Protein 26.8 g
- Cholesterol 75 mg

Air Fry Scallops

Preparation Time: 10 minutes
Cooking Time: 4 minutes
Serve: 4
Ingredients:
- 1 lb sea scallops
- 1/2 tsp garlic powder
- 1/2 cup crackers, crushed
- 2 tbsp butter, melted
- 1/2 tsp old bay seasoning

Directions:
1. In a shallow dish, mix crushed crackers, garlic powder, and old bay seasoning.
2. Toss scallops with melted butter and coat with cracker mixture.
3. Place coated scallops into the multi-level air fryer basket.
4. Place multi-level air fryer basket into the inner pot of the instant pot.
5. Secure pot with air fryer lid, select air fry mode then cook at 380 F for 4 minutes.
6. Serve and enjoy.

Nutritional Value (Amount per Serving):
- Calories 191
- Fat 8.6 g
- Carbohydrates 7.7 g
- Sugar 0.2 g
- Protein 19.7 g
- Cholesterol 53 mg

White Fish Fillets

Preparation Time: 10 minutes
Cooking Time: 12 minutes
Serve: 2
Ingredients:
- 12 oz white fish fillets
- 1/2 tsp lemon pepper seasoning
- 1/2 tsp onion powder
- 1/2 tsp garlic powder
- 1 tbsp olive oil
- Pepper
- Salt

Directions:
1. Brush fish fillets with olive oil and season with garlic powder, onion powder, lemon pepper seasoning, pepper, and salt.
2. Place fish fillets into the multi-level air fryer basket.
3. Place multi-level air fryer basket into the inner pot of the instant pot.
4. Secure pot with air fryer lid, select air fry mode then cook at 360 F for 12 minutes.
5. Serve and enjoy.

Nutritional Value (Amount per Serving):
- Calories 358

- Fat 19.8 g
- Carbohydrates 1.4 g
- Sugar 0.4 g
- Protein 41.9 g
- Cholesterol 131 mg

Spicy Scallops

Preparation Time: 10 minutes
Cooking Time: 6 minutes
Serve: 1
Ingredients:
- 4 scallops, rinsed and pat dry
- 1/8 tsp Pepper
- 1 tsp olive oil
- 1/2 tsp Cajun seasoning
- Salt

Directions:
1. Toss scallops with pepper, oil, cajun seasoning, and salt.
2. Add scallops into the multi-level air fryer basket.
3. Place multi-level air fryer basket into the inner pot of the instant pot.
4. Secure pot with air fryer lid, select air fry mode then cook at 400 F for 6 minutes.
5. Serve and enjoy.

Nutritional Value (Amount per Serving):
- Calories 146
- Fat 5.6 g
- Carbohydrates 3 g
- Sugar 0 g
- Protein 20.2 g
- Cholesterol 40 mg

Shrimp with Vegetables

Preparation Time: 10 minutes
Cooking Time: 20 minutes
Serve: 2
Ingredients:
- 25 shrimp, peeled and deveined
- 1 1/2 cups frozen mix vegetables
- 1/2 tbsp Cajun seasoning

Directions:
1. Toss shrimp, vegetables, and cajun seasoning into the bowl.
2. Add shrimp and vegetable mixture into the multi-level air fryer basket.
3. Place multi-level air fryer basket into the inner pot of the instant pot.
4. Secure pot with air fryer lid, select air fry mode then cook at 350 F for 20 minutes. Stir halfway through.
5. Serve and enjoy.

Nutritional Value (Amount per Serving):
- Calories 416
- Fat 4.9 g
- Carbohydrates 22 g
- Sugar 4.3 g

- Protein 66.6 g
- Cholesterol 579 mg

Miso White Fish Fillets

Preparation Time: 10 minutes
Cooking Time: 10 minutes
Serve: 2
Ingredients:
- 2 white fish fillets
- 2 tbsp brown sugar
- 2 tbsp miso
- 1 tbsp garlic, chopped

Directions:
1. Add all ingredients to the zip-lock bag and place the refrigerator for overnight.
2. Place marinated fish fillets into the multi-level air fryer basket.
3. Place multi-level air fryer basket into the inner pot of the instant pot.
4. Secure pot with air fryer lid, select air fry mode then cook at 380 F for 10 minutes.
5. Serve and enjoy.

Nutritional Value (Amount per Serving):
- Calories 340
- Fat 12.6 g
- Carbohydrates 14.8 g
- Sugar 9.8 g
- Protein 40 g
- Cholesterol 119 mg

Air Fry Tilapia

Preparation Time: 10 minutes
Cooking Time: 7 minutes
Serve: 2
Ingredients:
- 2 tilapia fillets
- 1/4 tsp lemon pepper
- 1/2 tsp old bay seasoning
- 1/2 tbsp butter, melted
- Pepper
- Salt

Directions:
1. Brush tilapia with butter and season with lemon pepper, old bay seasoning, pepper, and salt.
2. Place tilapia fillets into the multi-level air fryer basket.
3. Place multi-level air fryer basket into the inner pot of the instant pot.
4. Secure pot with air fryer lid, select air fry mode then cook at 400 F for 7 minutes.
5. Serve and enjoy.

Nutritional Value (Amount per Serving):
- Calories 102
- Fat 2 g
- Carbohydrates 0.2 g
- Sugar 0 g
- Protein 21.1 g
- Cholesterol 58 mg

Tasty Crab Patties

Preparation Time: 10 minutes
Cooking Time: 12 minutes
Serve: 2
Ingredients:
- 3/4 cup crabmeat, drained
- 1 large egg whites
- 2 green onions, chopped
- 1/2 celery stalk, chopped
- 1/2 medium sweet red pepper, chopped
- 1/4 cup breadcrumbs
- 18 tsp wasabi
- 1 1/2 tbsp mayonnaise
- 1/8 tsp salt

Directions:
1. Line multi-level air fryer basket with parchment paper.
2. Add all ingredients into the mixing bowl and mix until well combined.
3. Make patties from mixture and place into the multi-level air fryer basket.
4. Place multi-level air fryer basket into the inner pot of the instant pot.
5. Secure pot with air fryer lid, select air fry mode then cook at 375 F for 12 minutes. Flip halfway through.
6. Serve and enjoy.

Nutritional Value (Amount per Serving):
- Calories 177
- Fat 4.9 g
- Carbohydrates 26.5 g
- Sugar 5.6 g
- Protein 7.9 g
- Cholesterol 9 mg

Smoked Paprika Salmon

Preparation Time: 10 minutes
Cooking Time: 7 minutes
Serve: 2
Ingredients:
- 2 salmon fillets
- 2 tsp olive oil
- 2 tsp smoked paprika
- Pepper
- Salt

Directions:
1. Brush salmon fillets with oil and season with paprika, pepper, and salt.
2. Place salmon fillets into the multi-level air fryer basket.
3. Place multi-level air fryer basket into the inner pot of the instant pot.
4. Secure pot with air fryer lid, select air fry mode then cook at 380 F for 7 minutes.
5. Serve and enjoy.

Nutritional Value (Amount per Serving):
- Calories 282
- Fat 15.9 g

- Carbohydrates 1.2 g
- Sugar 0.2 g
- Protein 34.9 g
- Cholesterol 78 mg

Pesto Fish Fillets

Preparation Time: 10 minutes
Cooking Time: 20 minutes
Serve: 2
Ingredients:
- 2 salmon fillets
- 1/4 cup parmesan cheese, grated

For pesto:
- 1/4 cup pine nuts
- 1/4 cup olive oil
- 1 1/2 cups fresh basil leaves
- 2 garlic cloves, peeled and chopped
- 1/4 cup parmesan cheese, grated
- 1/2 tsp pepper
- 1/2 tsp salt

Directions:
1. Line multi-level air fryer basket with parchment paper.
2. Add pesto ingredients into the blender and blend until smooth.
3. Place salmon fillet into the multi-level air fryer basket. Spread pesto and parmesan cheese on top of fish fillets.
4. Place multi-level air fryer basket into the inner pot of the instant pot.
5. Secure pot with air fryer lid, select bake mode then cook at 380 F for 20 minutes.
6. Serve and enjoy.

Nutritional Value (Amount per Serving):
- Calories 648
- Fat 52.8 g
- Carbohydrates 4.8 g
- Sugar 0.7 g
- Protein 44.9 g
- Cholesterol 95 mg

Easy Shrimp Scampi

Preparation Time: 10 minutes
Cooking Time: 13 minutes
Serve: 4
Ingredients:
- 1 lb shrimp, peeled and deveined
- 1/4 cup parmesan cheese, grated
- 8 garlic cloves, peeled
- 2 tbsp olive oil
- 1 fresh lemon, cut into wedges

Directions:
1. Line multi-level air fryer basket with parchment paper.
2. Add all ingredients except parmesan cheese into the bowl and toss well.
3. Transfer shrimp mixture into the multi-level air fryer basket.
4. Place multi-level air fryer basket into the inner pot of the instant pot.
5. Secure pot with air fryer lid, select bake mode then cook at 380 F for 13 minutes.
6. Top with cheese and serve.

Nutritional Value (Amount per Serving):
- Calories 226
- Fat 10.2 g
- Carbohydrates 5.3 g
- Sugar 0.4 g
- Protein 28.2 g
- Cholesterol 243 mg

Mediterranean Fish Fillet

Preparation Time: 10 minutes
Cooking Time: 20 minutes
Serve: 1
Ingredients:
- 4 oz salmon fillet
- 1 tbsp olive oil
- 1 garlic clove, sliced
- 1/4 onion, diced
- 1/2 lemon juice
- 4 grape tomatoes
- 1 tbsp fresh parsley, chopped
- Pepper
- Salt

Directions:
1. Line multi-level air fryer basket with parchment paper.
2. Add salmon and remaining ingredients into the mixing bowl and mix well. Let it sit for 1 hour.
3. Place salmon mixture into the multi-level air fryer basket.
4. Place multi-level air fryer basket into the inner pot of the instant pot.
5. Secure pot with air fryer lid, select bake mode then cook at 350 F for 20 minutes.
6. Serve and enjoy.

Nutritional Value (Amount per Serving):
- Calories 381
- Fat 22.3 g
- Carbohydrates 23.5 g
- Sugar 14.5 g
- Protein 27.1 g
- Cholesterol 50 mg

Citrusy Salmon

Preparation Time: 10 minutes
Cooking Time: 22 minutes
Serve: 4
Ingredients:
- 2 lbs salmon fillet, skinless and boneless
- 2 fresh lemon juice
- 1 chili, sliced
- 1 orange juice
- 1 tbsp olive oil
- Pepper

- Salt

Directions:
1. Line multi-level air fryer basket with parchment paper.
2. In a small bowl, mix lemon juice, chili, orange juice, oil, pepper, and salt.
3. Place salmon fillets into the multi-level air fryer basket. Brush salmon fillets with lemon juice mixture.
4. Place multi-level air fryer basket into the inner pot of the instant pot.
5. Secure pot with air fryer lid, select bake mode then cook at 350 F for 22 minutes.
6. Serve and enjoy.

Nutritional Value (Amount per Serving):
- Calories 351
- Fat 18 g
- Carbohydrates 3.3 g
- Sugar 2.4 g
- Protein 44.6 g
- Cholesterol 101 mg

Easy Lemon Garlic Shrimp

Preparation Time: 10 minutes
Cooking Time: 15 minutes
Serve: 4

Ingredients:
- 1 lb shrimp, peeled and deveined
- 1/4 tsp garlic powder
- 1/2 fresh lemon
- 1 tbsp olive oil
- Pepper
- Salt

Directions:
1. In a bowl, toss shrimp with garlic powder, olive oil, pepper, and salt.
2. Add shrimp into the multi-level air fryer basket.
3. Place multi-level air fryer basket into the inner pot of the instant pot.
4. Secure pot with air fryer lid, select air fry mode then cook at 400 F for 15 minutes. Stir halfway through.
5. Pour lemon juice over shrimp and serve.

Nutritional Value (Amount per Serving):
- Calories 168
- Fat 5.4 g
- Carbohydrates 2.6 g
- Sugar 0.2 g
- Protein 25.9 g
- Cholesterol 239 mg

Delicious Fish Sticks

Preparation Time: 10 minutes
Cooking Time: 15 minutes
Serve: 5

Ingredients:
- 12 oz tilapia fish fillet, cut into fish sticks
- 1 tsp paprika
- 1 tsp garlic powder
- 1/4 cup mayonnaise
- 1/2 cup parmesan cheese, grated
- 3.5 oz pork rind, crushed

Directions:
1. In a shallow bowl, mix parmesan cheese, crushed pork rind, paprika, and garlic powder.
2. In a bowl, mix fish pieces and mayonnaise.
3. Coat fish pieces with parmesan cheese mixture and place them into the multi-level air fryer basket.
4. Place multi-level air fryer basket into the inner pot of the instant pot.
5. Secure pot with air fryer lid, select air fry mode then cook at 380 F for 15 minutes.
6. Serve and enjoy.

Nutritional Value (Amount per Serving):
- Calories 342
- Fat 20.2 g
- Carbohydrates 17.6 g
- Sugar 1.5 g
- Protein 23.1 g
- Cholesterol 53 mg

Cheesy Baked Tilapia

Preparation Time: 10 minutes
Cooking Time: 15 minutes
Serve: 6

Ingredients:
- 6 tilapia fillets
- 1/4 tsp onion powder
- 1 tsp garlic, minced
- 1/2 cup mayonnaise
- 1/2 cup Asiago cheese, grated
- 1/4 tsp basil
- 1/4 tsp thyme
- 1/8 tsp pepper
- 1/4 tsp salt

Directions:
1. Line multi-level air fryer basket with parchment paper.
2. In a small bowl, mix together the cheese, basil, thyme, onion powder, garlic, mayonnaise, pepper, and salt.
3. Place fish fillets into the multi-level air fryer basket. Spread cheese mixture on top of fish fillets.
4. Place multi-level air fryer basket into the inner pot of the instant pot.
5. Secure pot with air fryer lid, select bake mode then cook at 350 F for 15 minutes.
6. Serve and enjoy.

Nutritional Value (Amount per Serving):
- Calories 179
- Fat 8.2 g
- Carbohydrates 5 g
- Sugar 1.3 g
- Protein 21.8 g
- Cholesterol 62 mg

Pecan Crust Halibut Fillets

Preparation Time: 10 minutes
Cooking Time: 12 minutes
Serve: 2
Ingredients:
- 2 halibut fillets
- 1/4 cup parmesan cheese, grated
- 1/4 cup pecans
- 2 tbsp butter
- 1/2 lemon juice
- 1 tsp garlic, minced
- Pepper
- Salt

Directions:
1. Add pecans, lemon juice, garlic, parmesan cheese, and butter into the food processor and process until well blended.
2. Place fish fillets into the multi-level air fryer basket. Spread pecan mixture on top of fish fillets.
3. Place multi-level air fryer basket into the inner pot of the instant pot.
4. Secure pot with air fryer lid, select bake mode then cook at 380 F for 12 minutes.
5. Serve and enjoy.

Nutritional Value (Amount per Serving):
- Calories 545
- Fat 29.7 g
- Carbohydrates 2.9 g
- Sugar 0.7 g
- Protein 65.8 g
- Cholesterol 132 mg

Bagel Seasoned Fish Fillets

Preparation Time: 10 minutes
Cooking Time: 10 minutes
Serve: 4
Ingredients:
- 4 white fish fillets
- 1 tsp lemon pepper seasoning
- 2 tbsp almond flour
- 1/4 cup bagel seasoning
- 1 tbsp mayonnaise

Directions:
1. Line multi-level air fryer basket with parchment paper.
2. In a small bowl, mix together bagel seasoning, almond flour, and lemon pepper seasoning.
3. Brush mayonnaise over fish fillets.
4. Sprinkle bagel seasoning mixture over fish fillets.
5. Place fish fillets into the multi-level air fryer basket.
6. Place multi-level air fryer basket into the inner pot of the instant pot.
7. Secure pot with air fryer lid, select bake mode then cook at 380 F for 10 minutes.
8. Serve and enjoy.

Nutritional Value (Amount per Serving):
- Calories 375
- Fat 19.9 g
- Carbohydrates 7.2 g
- Sugar 1 g
- Protein 41.3 g
- Cholesterol 120 mg

Tasty Pesto Scallops

Preparation Time: 10 minutes
Cooking Time: 7 minutes
Serve: 4
Ingredients:
- 1 lb sea scallops
- 1/4 cup basil pesto
- 1 tbsp olive oil
- 2 tsp garlic, minced
- 3 tbsp heavy cream
- 1/2 tsp pepper
- 1 tsp salt

Directions:
1. Line multi-level air fryer basket with parchment paper.
2. In a small pan, mix together oil, cream, garlic, pesto, pepper, and salt, and simmer for 2 minutes.
3. Add scallops into the multi-level air fryer basket.
4. Place multi-level air fryer basket into the inner pot of the instant pot.
5. Secure pot with air fryer lid, select air fry mode then cook at 320 F for 7 minutes. Flip scallops after 5 minutes.
6. Pour pesto mixture over scallops and serve.

Nutritional Value (Amount per Serving):
- Calories 172
- Fat 8.6 g
- Carbohydrates 3.7 g
- Sugar 0 g
- Protein 19.4 g
- Cholesterol 53 mg

Cheese Crust Salmon

Preparation Time: 10 minutes
Cooking Time: 14 minutes
Serve: 4
Ingredients:
- 4 salmon fillets
- 2 tbsp parmesan cheese, grated
- 2 tbsp crushed pork rind
- 4 tbsp mayonnaise
- 2 tsp Italian seasoning

Directions:
1. Line multi-level air fryer basket with parchment paper.
2. Spread mayonnaise on top of fish fillets.
3. Sprinkle with cheese, Italian seasoning, and crushed pork rind.

4. Place fish fillets into the multi-level air fryer basket.
5. Place multi-level air fryer basket into the inner pot of the instant pot.
6. Secure pot with air fryer lid, select bake mode then cook at 375 F for 14 minutes.
7. Serve and enjoy.

Nutritional Value (Amount per Serving):
- Calories 338
- Fat 19 g
- Carbohydrates 3.9 g
- Sugar 1.1 g
- Protein 38.5 g
- Cholesterol 93 mg

Baked Halibut Fillets

Preparation Time: 10 minutes
Cooking Time: 12 minutes
Serve: 4

Ingredients:
- 1 lb halibut fillets
- 1/4 tsp pepper
- 1/4 cup olive oil
- 1/4 tsp garlic powder
- 1/4 tsp smoked paprika
- 1 lemon juice
- 1/2 tsp salt

Directions:
1. In a small bowl, mix together olive oil, lemon juice, pepper, paprika, garlic powder, and salt and rub over fish fillets.
2. Place fish fillets into the multi-level air fryer basket.
3. Place multi-level air fryer basket into the inner pot of the instant pot.
4. Secure pot with air fryer lid, select bake mode then cook at 380 F for 12 minutes.
5. Serve and enjoy.

Nutritional Value (Amount per Serving):
- Calories 238
- Fat 15.4 g
- Carbohydrates 0.5 g
- Sugar 0.3 g
- Protein 24 g
- Cholesterol 36 mg

Basil Mahi Mahi

Preparation Time: 10 minutes
Cooking Time: 30 minutes
Serve: 4

Ingredients:
- 4 Mahi Mahi fillets
- 1 tbsp dried basil
- 1 tsp onion powder
- 1 tsp garlic powder
- 1 tsp turmeric
- 1 tsp pepper
- 1 tsp salt

Directions:
1. In a small bowl, mix together onion powder, garlic powder, turmeric, basil, pepper, and salt and rub over fish fillets.
2. Place fish fillets into the multi-level air fryer basket.
3. Place multi-level air fryer basket into the inner pot of the instant pot.
4. Secure pot with air fryer lid, select bake mode then cook at 350 F for 30 minutes.
5. Serve and enjoy.

Nutritional Value (Amount per Serving):
- Calories 97
- Fat 1 g
- Carbohydrates 1.7 g
- Sugar 0.4 g
- Protein 19.2 g
- Cholesterol 86 mg

Cheese Paprika Cod

Preparation Time: 10 minutes
Cooking Time: 15 minutes
Serve: 4

Ingredients:
- 4 cod fillets
- 2 tsp smoked paprika
- 3/4 cup parmesan cheese, grated
- 1 tbsp olive oil
- 1 tbsp parsley, chopped
- 1/4 tsp sea salt

Directions:
1. In a dish, mix together parmesan cheese, paprika, parsley, and salt.
2. Brush fish fillets with oil and coat with cheese mixture.
3. Place fillets into the multi-level air fryer basket.
4. Place multi-level air fryer basket into the inner pot of the instant pot.
5. Secure pot with air fryer lid, select bake mode then cook at 380 F for 15 minutes.
6. Serve and enjoy.

Nutritional Value (Amount per Serving):
- Calories 178
- Fat 8.3 g
- Carbohydrates 1.3 g
- Sugar 0.1 g
- Protein 25.6 g
- Cholesterol 67 mg

Blackened Fish Fillets

Preparation Time: 10 minutes
Cooking Time: 14 minutes
Serve: 3

Ingredients:
- 3 tilapia fillets
- 1 tsp garlic powder
- 1 tsp onion powder
- 2 1/2 tbsp paprika

- 1 tbsp dried parsley flakes
- 1/4 tsp cayenne pepper
- 1 tbsp olive oil
- 1/2 tsp pepper
- 1 tsp salt

Directions:
1. In a small bowl, mix together paprika, pepper, onion powder, garlic powder, cayenne, parsley, pepper, and salt.
2. Brush fish fillets with oil and rub with spice mixture.
3. Place fish fillets into the multi-level air fryer basket.
4. Place multi-level air fryer basket into the inner pot of the instant pot.
5. Secure pot with air fryer lid, select bake mode then cook at 380 F for 14 minutes.
6. Serve and enjoy.

Nutritional Value (Amount per Serving):
- Calories 157
- Fat 6.5 g
- Carbohydrates 4.9 g
- Sugar 1.1 g
- Protein 22.2 g
- Cholesterol 55 mg

Chapter 6: Vegetables & Side Dishes

Herb Mushrooms

Preparation Time: 10 minutes
Cooking Time: 25 minutes
Serve: 2
Ingredients:
- 1 lbs mushrooms, wash, dry, and cut into quarter
- 1 tsp herb de Provence
- 1/4 tsp garlic powder
- 1/4 tsp onion powder
- 1/2 tbsp olive oil
- 1 tbsp vinegar

Directions
1. Line multi-level air fryer basket with parchment paper.
2. Add all ingredients to the bowl and toss well.
3. Add mushrooms into the multi-level air fryer basket.
4. Place multi-level air fryer basket into the inner pot of the instant pot.
5. Secure pot with air fryer lid, select air fry mode then cook at 350 F for 25 minutes. Stir mushrooms halfway through.
6. Serve and enjoy.

Nutritional Value (Amount per Serving):
- Calories 86
- Fat 4.4 g
- Carbohydrates 8 g
- Sugar 4.1 g
- Protein 7.7 g
- Cholesterol 0 mg

Lemon Garlic Brussels Sprouts

Preparation Time: 10 minutes
Cooking Time: 12 minutes
Serve: 2
Ingredients:
- 1/2 lb Brussels sprouts, remove stems & cut in half
- 1/4 tsp black pepper
- 1 tbsp olive oil
- 1/2 tsp garlic powder
- 1 tbsp lemon juice
- 1/2 tsp salt

Directions:
1. Line multi-level air fryer basket with parchment paper.
2. Add brussels sprouts and remaining ingredients into the bowl and toss well.
3. Add brussels sprouts into the multi-level air fryer basket.
4. Place multi-level air fryer basket into the inner pot of the instant pot.
5. Secure pot with air fryer lid, select air fry mode then cook at 360 F for 12 minutes. Stir halfway through.
6. Serve and enjoy.

Nutritional Value (Amount per Serving):
- Calories 114
- Fat 7.5 g
- Carbohydrates 11.2 g
- Sugar 2.8 g
- Protein 4.1 g
- Cholesterol 0 mg

Cheesy Veggie Fritters

Preparation Time: 10 minutes
Cooking Time: 15 minutes
Serve: 2
Ingredients:
- 1 egg, lightly beaten
- 1/4 tsp garlic powder
- 1/4 cup cheddar cheese, shredded
- 1/2 tbsp breadcrumbs
- 1 1/2 cups frozen vegetable, steam & mashed
- Pepper
- Salt

Directions:
1. Line multi-level air fryer basket with parchment paper.
2. Add all ingredients into the mixing bowl and mix until well combined.
3. Make small patties from mixture and place into the multi-level air fryer basket.
4. Place multi-level air fryer basket into the inner pot of the instant pot.
5. Secure pot with air fryer lid, select air fry mode then cook at 390 F for 15 minutes. Flip patties halfway through.
6. Serve and enjoy.

Nutritional Value (Amount per Serving):
- Calories 185
- Fat 7.2 g
- Carbohydrates 19.7 g
- Sugar 4.7 g
- Protein 10.5 g
- Cholesterol 97 mg

Potato Patties

Preparation Time: 10 minutes
Cooking Time: 12 minutes
Serve: 2
Ingredients:
- 1 cup potatoes, boiled, peeled, and mashed
- 2 cups kale, chopped
- 1 garlic clove, minced
- 1 tsp olive oil
- 1 tbsp milk
- Pepper

- Salt

Directions:
1. Line multi-level air fryer basket with parchment paper.
2. Heat oil in a pan over medium-high heat. Add garlic and kale and saute for 2 minutes.
3. Transfer sauteed kale and garlic into the large bowl.
4. Add remaining ingredients into the bowl and mix until well combined.
5. Make small patties from mixture and place into the multi-level air fryer basket.
6. Place multi-level air fryer basket into the inner pot of the instant pot.
7. Secure pot with air fryer lid, select air fry mode then cook at 400 F for 12 minutes. Flip patties halfway through.
8. Serve and enjoy.

Nutritional Value (Amount per Serving):
- Calories 111
- Fat 2.6 g
- Carbohydrates 19.7 g
- Sugar 1.2 g
- Protein 3.6 g
- Cholesterol 1 mg

Air Fry Corn

Preparation Time: 10 minutes
Cooking Time: 10 minutes
Serve: 2

Ingredients:
- 2 ears of corn, remove husks, wash, and pat dry
- 1 tbsp fresh lemon juice
- Salt

Directions:
1. Line multi-level air fryer basket with parchment paper.
2. Cut the corn to fit in a multi-level air fryer basket.
3. Spray corn with cooking spray and place it into the multi-level air fryer basket.
4. Place multi-level air fryer basket into the inner pot of the instant pot.
5. Secure pot with air fryer lid, select air fry mode then cook at 400 F for 10 minutes.
6. Drizzle lemon juice over corn.
7. Season corn with salt and serve.

Nutritional Value (Amount per Serving):
- Calories 134
- Fat 1.9 g
- Carbohydrates 29.2 g
- Sugar 5.2 g
- Protein 5.1 g
- Cholesterol 0 mg

Simple Crisp Tofu

Preparation Time: 10 minutes
Cooking Time: 15 minutes
Serve: 4

Ingredients:
- 15 oz tofu, cut into bite-sized pieces
- 2 tbsp soy sauce
- 1 tbsp olive oil

Directions:
1. Line multi-level air fryer basket with parchment paper.
2. Add tofu, oil, and soy sauce in a bowl and toss well. Set aside for 15 minutes.
3. Add tofu into the multi-level air fryer basket.
4. Place multi-level air fryer basket into the inner pot of the instant pot.
5. Secure pot with air fryer lid, select air fry mode then cook at 370 F for 15 minutes. Stir halfway through.
6. Serve and enjoy.

Nutritional Value (Amount per Serving):
- Calories 87
- Fat 6.4 g
- Carbohydrates 1.9 g
- Sugar 0.6 g
- Protein 7.4 g
- Cholesterol 0 mg

Spicy Sweet Potato Fries

Preparation Time: 10 minutes
Cooking Time: 16 minutes
Serve: 2

Ingredients:
- 2 sweet potatoes, peeled and cut into fries shape
- 1/4 tsp garlic powder
- 1/4 tsp onion powder
- 1 tbsp olive oil
- 1/2 tsp chili powder
- Salt

Directions:
1. Line multi-level air fryer basket with parchment paper.
2. Add sweet potatoes and remaining ingredients into the mixing bowl and toss until well coated.
3. Add sweet potato fries into the multi-level air fryer basket.
4. Place multi-level air fryer basket into the inner pot of the instant pot.
5. Secure pot with air fryer lid, select bake mode then cook at 380 F for 16 minutes. Stir halfway through.
6. Serve and enjoy.

Nutritional Value (Amount per Serving):
- Calories 241
- Fat 7.4 g
- Carbohydrates 42.7 g
- Sugar 1 g
- Protein 2.5 g
- Cholesterol 0 mg

Zucchini Cheese Burger

Preparation Time: 10 minutes
Cooking Time: 25 minutes
Serve: 6
Ingredients:
- 1 cup zucchini, shredded and squeeze out all liquid
- 1 egg, lightly beaten
- 1/4 cup parmesan cheese, grated
- 1/2 tbsp Dijon mustard
- 1/2 tbsp mayonnaise
- 1/2 cup breadcrumbs
- 2 tbsp onion, minced
- Pepper
- Salt

Directions:
1. Line multi-level air fryer basket with parchment paper.
2. Add all ingredients into the bowl and mix until well combined.
3. Make small patties from mixture and place into the multi-level air fryer basket.
4. Place multi-level air fryer basket into the inner pot of the instant pot.
5. Secure pot with air fryer lid, select bake mode then cook at 380 F for 25 minutes. Flip patties after 15 minutes.
6. Serve and enjoy.

Nutritional Value (Amount per Serving):
- Calories 68
- Fat 2.5 g
- Carbohydrates 8 g
- Sugar 1.2 g
- Protein 3.7 g
- Cholesterol 30 mg

Roasted Cauliflower

Preparation Time: 10 minutes
Cooking Time: 12 minutes
Serve: 2
Ingredients:
- 3 cups cauliflower florets
- 1/2 tsp dried oregano
- 1 1/2 tsp olive oil
- 1/4 tsp chili powder
- 1/4 tsp garlic powder
- Pepper
- Salt

Directions:
1. Line multi-level air fryer basket with parchment paper.
2. Add cauliflower and remaining ingredients into the bowl and toss well.
3. Add cauliflower florets into the multi-level air fryer basket.
4. Place multi-level air fryer basket into the inner pot of the instant pot.
5. Secure pot with air fryer lid, select roast mode then cook at 380 F for 12 minutes. Stir halfway through.
6. Serve and enjoy.

Nutritional Value (Amount per Serving):
- Calories 71
- Fat 3.8 g
- Carbohydrates 8.7 g
- Sugar 3.7 g
- Protein 3.1 g
- Cholesterol 0 mg

Roasted Potatoes

Preparation Time: 10 minutes
Cooking Time: 15 minutes
Serve: 4
Ingredients:
- 4 cups baby potatoes, cut each potato into four pieces
- 1 tbsp garlic, minced
- 2 tsp dried rosemary, minced
- 1/2 tsp chili powder
- 1/4 tsp paprika
- 3 tbsp olive oil
- Pepper
- Salt

Directions:
1. Line multi-level air fryer basket with parchment paper.
2. Add baby potatoes and remaining ingredients into the bowl and toss well.
3. Add baby potatoes into the multi-level air fryer basket.
4. Place multi-level air fryer basket into the inner pot of the instant pot.
5. Secure pot with air fryer lid, select roast mode then cook at 380 F for 15 minutes.
6. Serve and enjoy.

Nutritional Value (Amount per Serving):
- Calories 119
- Fat 10.7 g
- Carbohydrates 6.1 g
- Sugar 0.1 g
- Protein 1.2 g
- Cholesterol 0 mg

Roasted Asparagus

Preparation Time: 10 minutes
Cooking Time: 15 minutes
Serve: 4
Ingredients:
- 25 asparagus spears, cut the ends
- 1 tbsp olive oil
- Pepper
- Salt

Directions:
1. Line multi-level air fryer basket with parchment paper.

2. Brush asparagus spears with oil and season with pepper and salt.
3. Place asparagus spears into the multi-level air fryer basket.
4. Place multi-level air fryer basket into the inner pot of the instant pot.
5. Secure pot with air fryer lid, select roast mode then cook at 400 F for 15 minutes
6. Serve and enjoy.

Nutritional Value (Amount per Serving):
- Calories 60
- Fat 3.7 g
- Carbohydrates 5.8 g
- Sugar 2.8 g
- Protein 3.3 g
- Cholesterol 0 mg

Roasted Carrots & Potatoes

Preparation Time: 10 minutes
Cooking Time: 40 minutes
Serve: 2

Ingredients:
- 1/2 lb carrots, peeled & cut into chunks
- 1/2 onion, diced
- 1 tbsp olive oil
- 1/2 lb potatoes, cut into 1-inch cubes
- 1/2 tsp Italian seasoning
- 1/4 tsp garlic powder
- Pepper
- Salt

Directions:
1. Line multi-level air fryer basket with parchment paper.
2. In a large bowl, toss potatoes, garlic powder, carrots, Italian seasoning, oil, onion, pepper, and salt.
3. Transfer potato carrot mixture into the multi-level air fryer basket.
4. Place multi-level air fryer basket into the inner pot of the instant pot.
5. Secure pot with air fryer lid, select roast mode then cook at 400 F for 40 minutes. Stir halfway through.
6. Serve and enjoy.

Nutritional Value (Amount per Serving):
- Calories 201
- Fat 7.5 g
- Carbohydrates 32 g
- Sugar 8.2 g
- Protein 3.2 g
- Cholesterol 1 mg

Spicy Brussels Sprouts

Preparation Time: 10 minutes
Cooking Time: 14 minutes
Serve: 2

Ingredients:
- 1/2 lb Brussels sprouts, trimmed and halved
- 1/4 tsp cayenne
- 1/2 tsp chili powder
- 1/2 tbsp olive oil
- Pepper
- Salt

Directions:
1. Line multi-level air fryer basket with parchment paper.
2. Add brussels sprouts and remaining ingredients into the large bowl and toss well.
3. Add Brussels sprouts into the multi-level air fryer basket.
4. Place multi-level air fryer basket into the inner pot of the instant pot.
5. Secure pot with air fryer lid, select air fry mode then cook at 370 F for 14 minutes. Stir halfway through.
6. Serve and enjoy.

Nutritional Value (Amount per Serving):
- Calories 82
- Fat 4 g
- Carbohydrates 10.8 g
- Sugar 2.5 g
- Protein 4 g
- Cholesterol 0 mg

Flavorful Ranch Potatoes

Preparation Time: 10 minutes
Cooking Time: 20 minutes
Serve: 2

Ingredients:
- 1/2 lb baby potatoes, wash and cut in half
- 1/4 tsp garlic powder
- 1/2 tbsp olive oil
- 1/4 tsp parsley
- 1/4 tsp smoked paprika
- 1/4 tsp onion powder
- Salt

Directions:
1. Line multi-level air fryer basket with parchment paper.
2. Add all ingredients into the mixing bowl and toss well.
3. Spread potatoes into the multi-level air fryer basket.
4. Place multi-level air fryer basket into the inner pot of the instant pot.
5. Secure pot with air fryer lid, select air fry mode then cook at 400 F for 20 minutes. Stir halfway through.
6. Serve and enjoy.

Nutritional Value (Amount per Serving):
- Calories 99
- Fat 3.6 g
- Carbohydrates 14.8 g
- Sugar 0.2 g
- Protein 3 g
- Cholesterol 0 mg

Broccoli Fritters

Preparation Time: 10 minutes
Cooking Time: 30 minutes
Serve: 4
Ingredients:
- 3 cups broccoli florets, steam & chopped
- 2 cups cheddar cheese, shredded
- 1/4 cup breadcrumbs
- 2 eggs, lightly beaten
- 2 garlic cloves, minced
- Pepper
- Salt

Directions:
1. Line multi-level air fryer basket with parchment paper.
2. Add all ingredients into the bowl and mix until well combined.
3. Make patties from mixture and place into the multi-level air fryer basket.
4. Place multi-level air fryer basket into the inner pot of the instant pot.
5. Secure pot with air fryer lid, select bake mode then cook at 375 F for 30 minutes. Flip patties halfway through.
6. Serve and enjoy.

Nutritional Value (Amount per Serving):
- Calories 311
- Fat 21.5 g
- Carbohydrates 10.8 g
- Sugar 2.1 g
- Protein 19.8 g
- Cholesterol 141 mg

Roasted Mushrooms & Cauliflower

Preparation Time: 10 minutes
Cooking Time: 25 minutes
Serve: 6
Ingredients:
- 2 cups cauliflower florets
- 2 cups cherry tomatoes
- 1 lb mushrooms, cleaned
- 1 tbsp Italian seasoning
- 2 tbsp olive oil
- 8 garlic cloves, peeled
- Pepper
- Salt

Directions:
1. Line multi-level air fryer basket with parchment paper.
2. In a large bowl, toss cauliflower, cherry tomatoes, mushrooms, Italian seasoning, oil, garlic, pepper, and salt.
3. Add cauliflower mixture into the multi-level air fryer basket.
4. Place multi-level air fryer basket into the inner pot of the instant pot.
5. Secure pot with air fryer lid, select roast mode then cook at 380 F for 25 minutes. Stir halfway through.
6. Serve and enjoy.

Nutritional Value (Amount per Serving):
- Calories 88
- Fat 5.8 g
- Carbohydrates 8.2 g
- Sugar 3.9 g
- Protein 3.8 g
- Cholesterol 2 mg

Cauliflower Tomato Roast

Preparation Time: 10 minutes
Cooking Time: 20 minutes
Serve: 4
Ingredients:
- 4 cups cauliflower florets
- 1 tbsp capers, drained
- 3 tbsp olive oil
- 1/2 cup grape tomatoes, halved
- 1 tbsp garlic, sliced
- 1/4 tsp onion powder
- Pepper
- Salt

Directions:
1. Line multi-level air fryer basket with parchment paper.
2. Toss cauliflower florets with remaining ingredients into the mixing bowl.
3. Add cauliflower floret mixture into the multi-level air fryer basket.
4. Place multi-level air fryer basket into the inner pot of the instant pot.
5. Secure pot with air fryer lid, select roast mode then cook at 380 F for 20 minutes. Stir halfway through.
6. Serve and enjoy.

Nutritional Value (Amount per Serving):
- Calories 123
- Fat 10.7 g
- Carbohydrates 7.1 g
- Sugar 3.1 g
- Protein 2.4 g
- Cholesterol 0 mg

Healthy Roasted Asparagus

Preparation Time: 10 minutes
Cooking Time: 12 minutes
Serve: 4
Ingredients:
- 1 lb asparagus, wash, trimmed, and cut the ends
- 1 tbsp dried parsley
- 1 tsp garlic, minced
- 2 tbsp olive oil
- 3 oz Asiago cheese, shaved
- 1 tsp dried oregano

- Pepper
- Salt

Directions:
1. Line multi-level air fryer basket with parchment paper.
2. Brush asparagus with oil and season with pepper and salt.
3. Place asparagus into the multi-level air fryer basket.
4. Spread cheese, oregano, parsley, and garlic over asparagus.
5. Place multi-level air fryer basket into the inner pot of the instant pot.
6. Secure pot with air fryer lid, select bake mode then cook at 380 F for 12 minutes.
7. Serve and enjoy.

Nutritional Value (Amount per Serving):
- Calories 161
- Fat 13.3 g
- Carbohydrates 5 g
- Sugar 2.2 g
- Protein 7.9 g
- Cholesterol 19 mg

Roasted Cauliflower & Pepper

Preparation Time: 10 minutes
Cooking Time: 30 minutes
Serve: 4

Ingredients:
- 1 cauliflower head, cut into florets
- 1/2 onion, sliced
- 1 bell pepper, cut into 1-inch pieces
- 2 tsp olive oil
- 2 tbsp vinegar
- 3 tbsp balsamic vinegar
- Pepper
- Salt

Directions:
1. Line multi-level air fryer basket with parchment paper.
2. Add all ingredients into the zip-lock bag.
3. Seal the bag and shake well and place it in the refrigerator for 1 hour.
4. Add cauliflower mixture into the multi-level air fryer basket.
5. Place multi-level air fryer basket into the inner pot of the instant pot.
6. Secure pot with air fryer lid, select bake mode then cook at 380 F for 30 minutes. Stir halfway through.
7. Serve and enjoy.

Nutritional Value (Amount per Serving):
- Calories 56
- Fat 2.5 g
- Carbohydrates 7.2 g
- Sugar 3.8 g
- Protein 1.8 g
- Cholesterol 0 mg

Easy Roasted Broccoli

Preparation Time: 10 minutes
Cooking Time: 20 minutes
Serve: 6

Ingredients:
- 4 cups broccoli florets
- 1/2 tsp garlic powder
- 3 tbsp olive oil
- 1/4 tsp onion powder
- 1 tsp Italian seasoning
- 1/4 tsp pepper
- 1 tsp salt

Directions:
1. Line multi-level air fryer basket with parchment paper.
2. Add broccoli and remaining ingredients into the mixing bowl and toss well.
3. Add broccoli florets into the multi-level air fryer basket.
4. Place multi-level air fryer basket into the inner pot of the instant pot.
5. Secure pot with air fryer lid, select bake mode then cook at 380 F for 20 minutes. Stir halfway through.
6. Serve and enjoy.

Nutritional Value (Amount per Serving):
- Calories 84
- Fat 7.4 g
- Carbohydrates 4.4 g
- Sugar 1.2 g
- Protein 1.8 g
- Cholesterol 1 mg

Air Fry Bell Peppers

Preparation Time: 10 minutes
Cooking Time: 8 minutes
Serve: 3

Ingredients:
- 3 cups red bell peppers, cut into chunks
- 1 tsp olive oil
- 1/4 tsp chili powder
- 1/4 tsp garlic powder
- Pepper
- Salt

Directions:
1. Line multi-level air fryer basket with parchment paper.
2. Add all ingredients into the large bowl and toss well.
3. Add bell peppers into the multi-level air fryer basket.
4. Place multi-level air fryer basket into the inner pot of the instant pot.
5. Secure pot with air fryer lid, select air fry mode then cook at 360 F for 8 minutes. Stir halfway through.
6. Serve and enjoy.

Nutritional Value (Amount per Serving):

- Calories 53
- Fat 1.9 g
- Carbohydrates 9.3 g
- Sugar 6.1 g
- Protein 1.3 g
- Cholesterol 0 mg

Tasty Eggplant Cubes

Preparation Time: 10 minutes
Cooking Time: 12 minutes
Serve: 2
Ingredients:
- 1 eggplant, cut into cubes
- 1/4 tsp paprika
- 1/2 tsp garlic powder
- 1/4 tsp onion powder
- 1 tbsp olive oil

Directions:
1. Line multi-level air fryer basket with parchment paper.
2. Add all ingredients into the large bowl and toss well.
3. Add eggplant into the multi-level air fryer basket.
4. Place multi-level air fryer basket into the inner pot of the instant pot.
5. Secure pot with air fryer lid, select air fry mode then cook at 390 F for 12 minutes. Stir halfway through.
6. Serve and enjoy.

Nutritional Value (Amount per Serving):
- Calories 121
- Fat 7.5 g
- Carbohydrates 14.4 g
- Sugar 7.2 g
- Protein 2.4 g
- Cholesterol 0 mg

Air Fry Green Beans

Preparation Time: 10 minutes
Cooking Time: 10 minutes
Serve: 2
Ingredients:
- 8 oz green beans, trimmed and cut in half
- 1 tsp sesame oil

Directions:
1. Line multi-level air fryer basket with parchment paper.
2. Brush green beans with sesame oil.
3. Add green beans into the multi-level air fryer basket.
4. Place multi-level air fryer basket into the inner pot of the instant pot.
5. Secure pot with air fryer lid, select air fry mode then cook at 400 F for 10 minutes. Flip green beans halfway through.
6. Serve and enjoy.

Nutritional Value (Amount per Serving):
- Calories 55
- Fat 2.4 g
- Carbohydrates 8.1 g
- Sugar 1.6 g
- Protein 2.1 g
- Cholesterol 0 mg

Air Fried Okra

Preparation Time: 10 minutes
Cooking Time: 10 minutes
Serve: 2
Ingredients:
- 3 cups okra, wash, dry & sliced
- 1 tsp fresh lemon juice
- 1/2 tsp chili powder
- 1 tsp ground cumin
- 1 tbsp olive oil
- Salt

Directions:
1. Line multi-level air fryer basket with parchment paper.
2. Add okra, chili powder, cumin, oil, and salt into the bowl and toss well.
3. Add okra into the multi-level air fryer basket.
4. Place multi-level air fryer basket into the inner pot of the instant pot.
5. Secure pot with air fryer lid, select air fry mode then cook at 390 F for 10 minutes.
6. Drizzle lemon juice over okra and serve.

Nutritional Value (Amount per Serving):
- Calories 127
- Fat 7.7 g
- Carbohydrates 12.1 g
- Sugar 2.3 g
- Protein 3.2 g
- Cholesterol 0 mg

Garlicky Baby Potatoes

Preparation Time: 10 minutes
Cooking Time: 20 minutes
Serve: 4
Ingredients:
- 1 lb baby potatoes, cut into quarters
- 3/4 tsp granulated garlic
- 1/2 tsp dried parsley
- 1 tbsp olive oil
- 1/4 tsp salt

Directions:
1. Line multi-level air fryer basket with parchment paper.
2. In a bowl, toss baby potatoes with oil, garlic, parsley, and salt.
3. Add baby potatoes into the multi-level air fryer basket.
4. Place multi-level air fryer basket into the inner pot of the instant pot.
5. Secure pot with air fryer lid, select air fry mode then cook at 350 F for 20 minutes. Stir halfway through.

6. Serve and enjoy.
Nutritional Value (Amount per Serving):
- Calories 98
- Fat 3.6 g
- Carbohydrates 14.5 g
- Sugar 0.1 g
- Protein 3 g
- Cholesterol 0 mg

Spicy Cauliflower Florets

Preparation Time: 10 minutes
Cooking Time: 15 minutes
Serve: 4
Ingredients:
- 1 medium cauliflower head, cut into florets
- 1 tsp olive oil
- 1/4 cup hot sauce
- 1 tbsp flour
- 1 tsp garlic powder
- 1/2 tsp sea salt

Directions:
1. Line multi-level air fryer basket with parchment paper.
2. In a bowl, add cauliflower florets, garlic powder, oil, hot sauce, flour, and salt and toss until well coated.
3. Add cauliflower florets into the multi-level air fryer basket.
4. Place multi-level air fryer basket into the inner pot of the instant pot.
5. Secure pot with air fryer lid, select air fry mode then cook at 400 F for 15 minutes.
6. Serve and enjoy.

Nutritional Value (Amount per Serving):
- Calories 57
- Fat 1.4 g
- Carbohydrates 9.9 g
- Sugar 3.8 g
- Protein 3.2 g
- Cholesterol 0 mg

Sweet Potatoes & Brussels Sprouts

Preparation Time: 10 minutes
Cooking Time: 15 minutes
Serve: 6
Ingredients:
- 1 lb sweet potatoes, peeled and diced into 1/2-inch cubes
- 1 lb Brussels sprouts, remove stem & cut into quarter
- 1/4 tsp garlic powder
- 1 tsp chili powder
- 2 tbsp olive oil
- Pepper
- Salt

Directions:
1. Line multi-level air fryer basket with parchment paper.
2. Add sweet potatoes, brussels sprouts, and remaining ingredients into the bowl and toss well.
3. Add sweet potatoes and brussels sprouts into the multi-level air fryer basket.
4. Place multi-level air fryer basket into the inner pot of the instant pot.
5. Secure pot with air fryer lid, select air fry mode then cook at 380 F for 15 minutes. Stir halfway through.
6. Serve and enjoy.

Nutritional Value (Amount per Serving):
- Calories 164
- Fat 5.1 g
- Carbohydrates 28.3 g
- Sugar 2.1 g
- Protein 3.8 g
- Cholesterol 0 mg

Spicy Brussels Sprouts

Preparation Time: 10 minutes
Cooking Time: 15 minutes
Serve: 4
Ingredients:
- 1 lb Brussels sprouts, cut in half
- 1 tbsp olive oil
- 2 tbsp honey
- 1 tbsp gochujang
- 1/2 tsp salt

Directions:
1. Line multi-level air fryer basket with parchment paper.
2. In a large bowl, mix oil, honey, gochujang, and salt.
3. Add Brussels sprouts into the bowl and toss well.
4. Add Brussels sprouts into the multi-level air fryer basket.
5. Place multi-level air fryer basket into the inner pot of the instant pot.
6. Secure pot with air fryer lid, select air fry mode then cook at 360 F for 15 minutes.
7. Serve and enjoy.

Nutritional Value (Amount per Serving):
- Calories 115
- Fat 3.9 g
- Carbohydrates 19.9 g
- Sugar 11.7 g
- Protein 4 g
- Cholesterol 0 mg

Crispy Green Beans

Preparation Time: 10 minutes
Cooking Time: 5 minutes
Serve: 6
Ingredients:
- 1 lb green beans, rinsed
- 1/2 cup flour
- 2 eggs, lightly beaten
- 1 tbsp garlic powder

- 1/2 cup parmesan cheese, grated
- 1 cup breadcrumbs

Directions:
1. Line multi-level air fryer basket with parchment paper.
2. In a shallow bowl, whisk eggs.
3. In a dish, mix breadcrumbs, garlic powder, and cheese.
4. In a separate dish, add flour.
5. Coat green beans with flour then dip in egg and finally coat with breadcrumbs.
6. Place coated green beans into the multi-level air fryer basket.
7. Place multi-level air fryer basket into the inner pot of the instant pot.
8. Secure pot with air fryer lid, select air fry mode then cook at 390 F for 5 minutes.
9. Serve and enjoy.

Nutritional Value (Amount per Serving):
- Calories 182
- Fat 4.2 g
- Carbohydrates 27.7 g
- Sugar 2.7 g
- Protein 9.4 g
- Cholesterol 60 mg

Chili Lime Sweet Potatoes

Preparation Time: 10 minutes
Cooking Time: 15 minutes
Serve: 4

Ingredients:
- 2 sweet potatoes, peeled & cut into 1-inch pieces
- 1 tbsp chili powder
- 2 tbsp olive oil
- 2 tsp fresh lime juice
- 1 tsp cumin

Directions:
1. Line multi-level air fryer basket with parchment paper.
2. In a bowl, add sweet potatoes, lime juice, cumin, chili powder, and olive oil and toss well.
3. Add sweet potatoes into the multi-level air fryer basket.
4. Place multi-level air fryer basket into the inner pot of the instant pot.
5. Secure pot with air fryer lid, select air fry mode then cook at 380 F for 15 minutes. Stir halfway through.
6. Serve and enjoy.

Nutritional Value (Amount per Serving):
- Calories 162
- Fat 7.6 g
- Carbohydrates 24 g
- Sugar 0.9 g
- Protein 1.6 g
- Cholesterol 0 mg

Healthy Air Fry Mushrooms

Preparation Time: 10 minutes
Cooking Time: 12 minutes
Serve: 2

Ingredients:
- 8 oz mushrooms, clean and cut into quarters
- 1 tsp soy sauce
- 1/4 tsp onion powder
- 1/2 tsp garlic powder
- 1 tbsp olive oil
- 1/4 tsp paprika
- Pepper
- Salt

Directions:
1. Line multi-level air fryer basket with parchment paper.
2. Add mushrooms and remaining ingredients into the bowl and toss well.
3. Transfer mushrooms into the multi-level air fryer basket.
4. Place multi-level air fryer basket into the inner pot of the instant pot.
5. Secure pot with air fryer lid, select air fry mode then cook at 380 F for 12 minutes. Stir halfway through.
6. Serve and enjoy.

Nutritional Value (Amount per Serving):
- Calories 90
- Fat 7.4 g
- Carbohydrates 4.9 g
- Sugar 2.3 g
- Protein 3.9 g
- Cholesterol 0 mg

Tasty Butternut Squash

Preparation Time: 10 minutes
Cooking Time: 15 minutes
Serve: 4

Ingredients:
- 4 cups butternut squash, cut into 1-inch pieces
- 1 tbsp brown sugar
- 2 tbsp olive oil
- 1 tsp Chinese 5 spice powder

Directions:
1. Line multi-level air fryer basket with parchment paper.
2. Add squash and remaining ingredients into the bowl and toss well.
3. Add squash into the multi-level air fryer basket.
4. Place multi-level air fryer basket into the inner pot of the instant pot.
5. Secure pot with air fryer lid, select air fry mode then cook at 400 F for 15 minutes. Stir halfway through.
6. Serve and enjoy.

Nutritional Value (Amount per Serving):
- Calories 132

- Fat 7.1 g
- Carbohydrates 18.6 g
- Sugar 5.3 g
- Protein 1.4 g
- Cholesterol 0 mg

Zucchini Cheese Patties

Preparation Time: 10 minutes
Cooking Time: 10 minutes
Serve: 4
Ingredients:
- 1 1/4 cups zucchini, grated and squeezed out all liquid
- 1 egg, lightly beaten
- 1.5 oz feta cheese, crumbled
- 2 cups ground oats
- 1 tsp oregano
- 5 basil leaves, chopped
- 1 tsp lemon rind
- Pepper
- Salt

Directions:
1. Line multi-level air fryer basket with parchment paper.
2. Add all ingredients into the bowl and mix until well combined.
3. Make small patties from mixture and place into the multi-level air fryer basket.
4. Place multi-level air fryer basket into the inner pot of the instant pot.
5. Secure pot with air fryer lid, select air fry mode then cook at 400 F for 10 minutes.
6. Serve and enjoy.

Nutritional Value (Amount per Serving):
- Calories 611
- Fat 43.5 g
- Carbohydrates 34.1 g
- Sugar 1.2 g
- Protein 19.4 g
- Cholesterol 50 mg

Rosemary Potatoes

Preparation Time: 10 minutes
Cooking Time: 15 minutes
Serve: 4
Ingredients:
- 4 cups baby potatoes, cut into pieces
- 2 tsp dried rosemary, minced
- 3 tbsp olive oil
- Pepper
- Salt

Directions:
1. Line multi-level air fryer basket with parchment paper.
2. Add potatoes, rosemary, oil, pepper, and salt into the bowl and toss well.
3. Add potatoes into the multi-level air fryer basket.
4. Place multi-level air fryer basket into the inner pot of the instant pot.
5. Secure pot with air fryer lid, select air fry mode then cook at 400 F for 15 minutes.
6. Serve and enjoy.

Nutritional Value (Amount per Serving):
- Calories 114
- Fat 10.6 g
- Carbohydrates 5.1 g
- Sugar 0 g
- Protein 1 g
- Cholesterol 0 mg

Tofu Bites

Preparation Time: 10 minutes
Cooking Time: 15 minutes
Serve: 4
Ingredients:
- 15 oz tofu block, pressed and cut into bite-sized pieces
- 2 tbsp soy sauce
- 1/4 tsp garlic powder
- 1/4 tsp paprika
- 1 garlic clove, minced
- 1 tbsp olive oil

Directions:
1. Line multi-level air fryer basket with parchment paper.
2. Add tofu and remaining ingredients into the bowl and mix well. Set aside for 15 minutes.
3. Add tofu pieces into the multi-level air fryer basket.
4. Place multi-level air fryer basket into the inner pot of the instant pot.
5. Secure pot with air fryer lid, select air fry mode then cook at 375 F for 15 minutes. Stir halfway through.
6. Serve and enjoy.

Nutritional Value (Amount per Serving):
- Calories 190
- Fat 12.8 g
- Carbohydrates 5.6 g
- Sugar 0.2 g
- Protein 17.4 g
- Cholesterol 0 mg

Chickpea Zucchini Patties

Preparation Time: 10 minutes
Cooking Time: 12 minutes
Serve: 4
Ingredients:
- 1 large zucchini, grated & squeeze out all liquid
- 2 tbsp spring onion, sliced
- 7.5 oz can chickpeas, drained & mashed
- 1 tsp cumin
- 1 tsp mixed spice
- 1 tsp chili powder

- 3 tbsp coriander
- Pepper
- Salt

Directions:
1. Line multi-level air fryer basket with parchment paper.
2. Add all ingredients into the mixing bowl and mix until well combined.
3. Make 4 equal shapes of patties from the mixture into the multi-level air fryer basket.
4. Place multi-level air fryer basket into the inner pot of the instant pot.
5. Secure pot with air fryer lid, select air fry mode then cook at 400 F for 12 minutes. Flip patties halfway through.
6. Serve and enjoy.

Nutritional Value (Amount per Serving):
- Calories 81
- Fat 1 g
- Carbohydrates 15.6 g
- Sugar 1.5 g
- Protein 3.9 g
- Cholesterol 0 mg

Roasted Brussels Sprouts

Preparation Time: 10 minutes
Cooking Time: 35 minutes
Serve: 6

Ingredients:
- 2 cups Brussels sprouts, halved
- 1/4 cup olive oil
- 1/4 tsp cayenne pepper
- 1/4 tsp salt

Directions:
1. Line multi-level air fryer basket with parchment paper.
2. Add all ingredients into the bowl and toss well.
3. Add brussels sprouts into the multi-level air fryer basket.
4. Place multi-level air fryer basket into the inner pot of the instant pot.
5. Secure pot with air fryer lid, select roast mode then cook at 380 F for 30-35 minutes. Stir halfway through.
6. Serve and enjoy.

Nutritional Value (Amount per Serving):
- Calories 85
- Fat 8.5 g
- Carbohydrates 2.7 g
- Sugar 0.6 g
- Protein 1 g
- Cholesterol 0 mg

Old Bay Seasoned Cauliflower Florets

Preparation Time: 10 minutes
Cooking Time: 15 minutes
Serve: 4

Ingredients:
- 1 medium cauliflower head, cut into florets
- 1/4 tsp paprika
- 3 tbsp olive oil
- 1/2 tsp old bay seasoning
- Pepper
- Salt

Directions:
1. Line multi-level air fryer basket with parchment paper.
2. In a bowl, toss cauliflower with remaining ingredients.
3. Add cauliflower florets into the multi-level air fryer basket.
4. Place multi-level air fryer basket into the inner pot of the instant pot.
5. Secure pot with air fryer lid, select air fry mode then cook at 400 F for 15 minutes. Stir halfway through.
6. Serve and enjoy.

Nutritional Value (Amount per Serving):
- Calories 126
- Fat 10.7 g
- Carbohydrates 7.7 g
- Sugar 3.5 g
- Protein 2.9 g
- Cholesterol 0 mg

Tasty Herb Mushrooms

Preparation Time: 10 minutes
Cooking Time: 14 minutes
Serve: 4

Ingredients:
- 1 lb mushroom
- 1/2 tbsp vinegar
- 1 tsp rosemary, chopped
- 1 tbsp basil, minced
- 1 garlic clove, minced
- 1/4 tsp oregano
- Pepper
- Salt

Directions:
1. Line multi-level air fryer basket with parchment paper.
2. Add all ingredients into the bowl and toss well.
3. Add mushroom mixture into the multi-level air fryer basket.
4. Place multi-level air fryer basket into the inner pot of the instant pot.
5. Secure pot with air fryer lid, select air fry mode then cook at 350 F for 14 minutes. Stir halfway through.
6. Serve and enjoy.

Nutritional Value (Amount per Serving):
- Calories 27
- Fat 0.4 g
- Carbohydrates 4.3 g
- Sugar 2 g
- Protein 3.7 g

- Cholesterol 0 mg

Green Beans & Potatoes

Preparation Time: 10 minutes
Cooking Time: 30 minutes
Serve: 4
Ingredients:
- 1/2 lb green beans, trimmed and cut in half
- 3/4 lbs potatoes, peel & cut into cubes
- 1/2 tsp dried Italian herbs
- 1/2 tsp paprika
- 1 tbsp garlic, minced
- 2 tbsp olive oil
- 1/4 tsp pepper
- 1/2 tsp salt

Directions:
1. Line multi-level air fryer basket with parchment paper.
2. Add all ingredients into the mixing bowl and toss well.
3. Add green beans and potatoes into the multi-level air fryer basket.
4. Place multi-level air fryer basket into the inner pot of the instant pot.
5. Secure pot with air fryer lid, select bake mode then cook at 380 F for 30 minutes. Stir halfway through.
6. Serve and enjoy.

Nutritional Value (Amount per Serving):
- Calories 140
- Fat 7.2 g
- Carbohydrates 18.3 g
- Sugar 1.8 g
- Protein 2.6 g
- Cholesterol 0 mg

Simple Air Fry Cabbage

Preparation Time: 10 minutes
Cooking Time: 10 minutes
Serve: 2
Ingredients:
- 1/2 cabbage head, sliced into 2-inch slices
- 1 tbsp olive oil
- Pepper
- Salt

Directions:
1. Line multi-level air fryer basket with parchment paper.
2. Brush cabbage with oil and season with pepper and salt and place it into the multi-level air fryer basket.
3. Place multi-level air fryer basket into the inner pot of the instant pot.
4. Secure pot with air fryer lid, select air fry mode then cook at 375 F for 10 minutes. Flip cabbage halfway through.
5. Serve and enjoy.

Nutritional Value (Amount per Serving):
- Calories 105
- Fat 7.2 g
- Carbohydrates 10.4 g
- Sugar 5.7 g
- Protein 2.3 g
- Cholesterol 0 mg

Zucchini & Squash

Preparation Time: 10 minutes
Cooking Time: 25 minutes
Serve: 4
Ingredients:
- 1 lb zucchini, cut into 1/2-inch half-moons
- 1 lb yellow squash, cut into 1/2-inch half-moons
- 1 tbsp olive oil
- Pepper
- Salt

Directions:
1. Line multi-level air fryer basket with parchment paper.
2. In a bowl, add zucchini, squash, oil, pepper, and salt and toss well.
3. Add zucchini and squash into the multi-level air fryer basket.
4. Place multi-level air fryer basket into the inner pot of the instant pot.
5. Secure pot with air fryer lid, select bake mode then cook at 380 F for 25 minutes.
6. Serve and enjoy.

Nutritional Value (Amount per Serving):
- Calories 66
- Fat 3.9 g
- Carbohydrates 7.6 g
- Sugar 3.9 g
- Protein 2.7 g
- Cholesterol 0 mg

Bagel Seasoned Brussels Sprouts

Preparation Time: 10 minutes
Cooking Time: 15 minutes
Serve: 4
Ingredients:
- 2 cups Brussels sprouts, cut in half
- 2 tbsp olive oil
- 2 tbsp bagel seasoning
- 1/4 cup almonds, crushed
- 1/4 cup parmesan cheese, grated
- Salt

Directions:
1. Line multi-level air fryer basket with parchment paper.
2. Add brussels sprouts and remaining ingredients into the mixing bowl and toss well.
3. Add brussels sprouts into the multi-level air fryer basket.
4. Place multi-level air fryer basket into the inner pot of the instant pot.

5. Secure pot with air fryer lid, select air fry mode then cook at 375 F for 15 minutes. Stir halfway through.
6. Serve and enjoy.

Nutritional Value (Amount per Serving):
- Calories 139
- Fat 11.4 g
- Carbohydrates 7.1 g
- Sugar 1.3 g
- Protein 4.8 g
- Cholesterol 4 mg

Air Fry Mix Vegetables

Preparation Time: 10 minutes
Cooking Time: 10 minutes
Serve: 6

Ingredients:
- 2 cups mushrooms, cut in half
- 2 zucchini, sliced
- 3/4 tsp Italian seasoning
- 1/2 onion, sliced
- 2 squash, sliced
- 1/2 cup olive oil
- 1/2 tsp garlic salt

Directions:
1. Line multi-level air fryer basket with parchment paper.
2. Add vegetables and remaining ingredients into the bowl and toss well.
3. Add vegetables into the multi-level air fryer basket.
4. Place multi-level air fryer basket into the inner pot of the instant pot.
5. Secure pot with air fryer lid, select air fry mode then cook at 400 F for 10 minutes. Stir halfway through.
6. Serve and enjoy.

Nutritional Value (Amount per Serving):
- Calories 172
- Fat 17.2 g
- Carbohydrates 5.4 g
- Sugar 2.8 g
- Protein 2.2 g
- Cholesterol 0 mg

Simple & Healthy Asparagus

Preparation Time: 10 minutes
Cooking Time: 10 minutes
Serve: 4

Ingredients:
- 1 lb asparagus, ends trimmed and cut in half
- 2 tbsp olive oil
- 1 tbsp vinegar
- Pepper
- Salt

Directions:
1. Line multi-level air fryer basket with parchment paper.
2. Brush asparagus with oil and vinegar and season with pepper and salt.
3. Add asparagus into the multi-level air fryer basket.
4. Place multi-level air fryer basket into the inner pot of the instant pot.
5. Secure pot with air fryer lid, select air fry mode then cook at 400 F for 10 minutes. Stir halfway through.
6. Serve and enjoy.

Nutritional Value (Amount per Serving):
- Calories 84
- Fat 7.1 g
- Carbohydrates 4.5 g
- Sugar 2.2 g
- Protein 2.5 g
- Cholesterol 0 mg

Easy Green Beans

Preparation Time: 5 minutes
Cooking Time: 10 minutes
Serve: 2

Ingredients:
- 1 lb green beans, washed and ends trimmed
- 1 fresh lemon juice
- 1/4 tsp chili powder
- 1/4 tsp garlic powder
- 1/4 tsp olive oil
- Pepper
- Salt

Directions:
1. Line multi-level air fryer basket with parchment paper.
2. Add green beans and remaining ingredients into the large bowl and toss well.
3. Add green beans into the multi-level air fryer basket.
4. Place multi-level air fryer basket into the inner pot of the instant pot.
5. Secure pot with air fryer lid, select bake mode then cook at 380 F for 10 minutes. Stir green beans halfway through.
6. Serve and enjoy.

Nutritional Value (Amount per Serving):
- Calories 83
- Fat 1.1 g
- Carbohydrates 17.1 g
- Sugar 3.8 g
- Protein 4.4 g
- Cholesterol 0 mg

Flavorful Okra

Preparation Time: 10 minutes
Cooking Time: 10 minutes
Serve: 2

Ingredients:
- 1/2 lb okra, trimmed and sliced

- 1/2 tsp chili powder
- 1/2 tsp garlic powder
- 1/4 tsp paprika
- 1/4 tsp onion powder
- 1 tsp olive oil
- 1/8 tsp pepper
- 1/4 tsp salt

Directions:
1. Line multi-level air fryer basket with parchment paper.
2. Add all ingredients into the bowl and toss well.
3. Add okra into the multi-level air fryer basket.
4. Place multi-level air fryer basket into the inner pot of the instant pot.
5. Secure pot with air fryer lid, select air fry mode then cook at 350 F for 10 minutes. Stir halfway through.
6. Serve and enjoy.

Nutritional Value (Amount per Serving):
- Calories 72
- Fat 2.7 g
- Carbohydrates 9.8 g
- Sugar 2 g
- Protein 2.5 g
- Cholesterol 0 mg

Broccoli & Brussels Sprouts

Preparation Time: 10 minutes
Cooking Time: 30 minutes
Serve: 6

Ingredients:
- 1 lb Brussels sprouts, cut ends
- 1 lb broccoli, cut into florets
- 1/2 tsp pepper
- 3 tbsp olive oil
- 1 tsp paprika
- 1/2 onion, chopped
- 1 tsp garlic powder
- 3/4 tsp salt

Directions:
1. Line multi-level air fryer basket with parchment paper.
2. Add all ingredients into the bowl and toss well.
3. Add broccoli and brussels sprouts into the multi-level air fryer basket.
4. Place multi-level air fryer basket into the inner pot of the instant pot.
5. Secure pot with air fryer lid, select bake mode then cook at 380 F for 30 minutes. Stir halfway through.
6. Serve and enjoy.

Nutritional Value (Amount per Serving):
- Calories 125
- Fat 7.6 g
- Carbohydrates 13.4 g
- Sugar 3.5 g
- Protein 5 g
- Cholesterol 0 mg

Stuffed Peppers

Preparation Time: 10 minutes
Cooking Time: 45 minutes
Serve: 4

Ingredients:
- 4 eggs
- 2 bell peppers, sliced in half and remove seeds
- 1/2 cup ricotta cheese
- 1/4 cup baby spinach, chopped
- 1 tsp garlic powder
- 1/2 cup parmesan cheese, grated
- 1/2 cup mozzarella cheese, shredded

Directions:
1. Line multi-level air fryer basket with parchment paper.
2. Add cheeses, garlic powder, and eggs in a blender and blend until just combined.
3. Pour egg mixture into each pepper half and top with spinach.
4. Place stuffed peppers into the multi-level air fryer basket.
5. Place multi-level air fryer basket into the inner pot of the instant pot.
6. Secure pot with air fryer lid, select bake mode then cook at 375 F for 45 minutes.
7. Serve and enjoy.

Nutritional Value (Amount per Serving):
- Calories 174
- Fat 10 g
- Carbohydrates 7.5 g
- Sugar 3.6 g
- Protein 14.5 g
- Cholesterol 183 mg

Roasted Carrots

Preparation Time: 10 minutes
Cooking Time: 35 minutes
Serve: 6

Ingredients:
- 15 baby carrots
- 4 tbsp olive oil
- 1 tbsp dried basil
- 5 garlic cloves, minced
- 1 1/2 tsp salt

Directions:
1. Line multi-level air fryer basket with parchment paper.
2. In a bowl, oil, carrots, basil, garlic, and salt and toss well.
3. Add carrots into the multi-level air fryer basket.
4. Place multi-level air fryer basket into the inner pot of the instant pot.

5. Secure pot with air fryer lid, select bake mode then cook at 375 F for 35 minutes. Stir halfway through.
6. Serve and enjoy.

Nutritional Value (Amount per Serving):
- Calories 93
- Fat 9.4 g
- Carbohydrates 2.9 g
- Sugar 1.2 g
- Protein 0.3 g
- Cholesterol 0 mg

Potato Beans & Mushrooms

Preparation Time: 10 minutes
Cooking Time: 25 minutes
Serve: 4
Ingredients:
- 2 cups mushrooms, sliced
- 2 tsp garlic, minced
- 2 cups green beans, clean and cut into pieces
- 1 cup baby potatoes, cut in half
- 1/4 cup olive oil
- 1 tsp pepper
- 1 tsp sea salt

Directions:
1. Line multi-level air fryer basket with parchment paper.
2. Add all ingredients into the bowl and toss well.
3. Add potato bean mushroom mixture into the multi-level air fryer basket.
4. Place multi-level air fryer basket into the inner pot of the instant pot.
5. Secure pot with air fryer lid, select bake mode then cook at 380 F for 25 minutes. Stir halfway through.
6. Serve and enjoy.

Nutritional Value (Amount per Serving):
- Calories 142
- Fat 12.8 g
- Carbohydrates 7.1 g
- Sugar 1.4 g
- Protein 2.5 g
- Cholesterol 0 mg

Cheesy Zucchini Eggplant

Preparation Time: 10 minutes
Cooking Time: 35 minutes
Serve: 6
Ingredients:
- 1 eggplant, sliced
- 1 cup cherry tomatoes, halved
- 1 tbsp garlic, minced
- 4 tbsp parsley, chopped
- 4 tbsp basil, chopped
- 3 zucchini, sliced
- 3 oz Parmesan cheese, grated
- 1 tbsp olive oil
- 1/4 tsp pepper
- 1/4 tsp salt

Directions:
1. Line multi-level air fryer basket with parchment paper.
2. Add all ingredients into the large bowl and toss well.
3. Add vegetable mixture into the multi-level air fryer basket.
4. Place multi-level air fryer basket into the inner pot of the instant pot.
5. Secure pot with air fryer lid, select bake mode then cook at 350 F for 35 minutes. Stir halfway through.
6. Serve and enjoy.

Nutritional Value (Amount per Serving):
- Calories 109
- Fat 5.8 g
- Carbohydrates 10.2 g
- Sugar 4.8 g
- Protein 7 g
- Cholesterol 10 mg

Roasted Squash

Preparation Time: 10 minutes
Cooking Time: 30 minutes
Serve: 4
Ingredients:
- 1 lb summer squash, cut into 1-inch pieces
- 1/8 tsp paprika
- 1/8 tsp pepper
- 1/8 tsp garlic powder
- 3 tbsp olive oil
- 1 large lemon
- Pepper
- Salt

Directions:
1. Line multi-level air fryer basket with parchment paper.
2. Add squash and remaining ingredients into the bowl and toss well.
3. Add squash into the multi-level air fryer basket.
4. Place multi-level air fryer basket into the inner pot of the instant pot.
5. Secure pot with air fryer lid, select bake mode then cook at 380 F for 30 minutes. Stir halfway through.
6. Serve and enjoy.

Nutritional Value (Amount per Serving):
- Calories 116
- Fat 10.9 g
- Carbohydrates 5.9 g
- Sugar 4.4 g
- Protein 1.3 g
- Cholesterol 0 mg

Healthy Ratatouille

Preparation Time: 10 minutes
Cooking Time: 15 minutes
Serve: 6
Ingredients:
- 1 eggplant, diced
- 2 bell peppers, diced
- 1 1/2 tbsp olive oil
- 2 tbsp herb de Provence
- 1 tbsp garlic, chopped
- 1 tbsp vinegar
- 1 onion, diced
- 3 tomatoes, diced
- Pepper
- Salt

Directions:
1. Line multi-level air fryer basket with parchment paper.
2. Add all ingredients into the bowl and toss well.
3. Add vegetable mixture into the multi-level air fryer basket.
4. Place multi-level air fryer basket into the inner pot of the instant pot.
5. Secure pot with air fryer lid, select air fry mode then cook at 400 F for 15 minutes. Stir halfway through.
6. Serve and enjoy.

Nutritional Value (Amount per Serving):
- Calories 83
- Fat 3.9 g
- Carbohydrates 12.1 g
- Sugar 6.7 g
- Protein 2 g
- Cholesterol 0 mg

Healthy Artichoke Hearts

Preparation Time: 10 minutes
Cooking Time: 25 minutes
Serve: 6
Ingredients:
- 15 oz frozen artichoke hearts, defrosted
- 1 tbsp olive oil
- Pepper
- Salt

Directions:
1. Line multi-level air fryer basket with parchment paper.
2. Brush artichoke hearts with oil and season with pepper and salt.
3. Place artichoke hearts into the multi-level air fryer basket.
4. Place multi-level air fryer basket into the inner pot of the instant pot.
5. Secure pot with air fryer lid, select bake mode then cook at 380 F for 25 minutes.
6. Serve and enjoy.

Nutritional Value (Amount per Serving):
- Calories 53
- Fat 2.4 g
- Carbohydrates 7.5 g
- Sugar 0.7 g
- Protein 2.3 g
- Cholesterol 0 mg

Tasty Green Beans

Preparation Time: 10 minutes
Cooking Time: 10 minutes
Serve: 2
Ingredients:
- 8 oz green beans, trimmed and cut in half
- 1 tbsp tamari
- 1 tsp olive oil

Directions:
1. Line multi-level air fryer basket with parchment paper.
2. Add all ingredients into the large bowl and toss well.
3. Add green beans into the multi-level air fryer basket.
4. Place multi-level air fryer basket into the inner pot of the instant pot.
5. Secure pot with air fryer lid, select air fry mode then cook at 350 F for 10 minutes. Stir halfway through.
6. Serve and enjoy.

Nutritional Value (Amount per Serving):
- Calories 61
- Fat 2.5 g
- Carbohydrates 8.6 g
- Sugar 1.7 g
- Protein 3 g
- Cholesterol 0 mg

Cinnamon Butternut Squash

Preparation Time: 10 minutes
Cooking Time: 40 minutes
Serve: 4
Ingredients:
- 1 1/2 lbs butternut squash, cut into 1-inch pieces
- 1 tbsp maple syrup
- 1 tbsp olive oil
- 1/4 tsp cinnamon
- Pepper
- Salt

Directions:
1. Line multi-level air fryer basket with parchment paper.
2. In a bowl, toss squash cubes with remaining ingredients.
3. Add squash into the multi-level air fryer basket.
4. Place multi-level air fryer basket into the inner pot of the instant pot.

5. Secure pot with air fryer lid, select roast mode then cook at 380 F for 40 minutes. Stir halfway through.
6. Serve and enjoy.

Nutritional Value (Amount per Serving):
- Calories 120
- Fat 3.7 g
- Carbohydrates 23.4 g
- Sugar 6.7 g
- Protein 1.7 g
- Cholesterol 0 mg

Balsamic Vegetables

Preparation Time: 10 minutes
Cooking Time: 35 minutes
Serve: 4

Ingredients:
- 3 cups Brussels sprouts, cut in half
- 2 zucchini, cut into 1/2-inch thick half circles
- 2 bell peppers, cut into 2-inch chunks
- 8 oz mushrooms, cut in half
- 1 onion, cut into wedges
- 2 tbsp balsamic vinegar
- 1/4 cup olive oil
- 1/2 tsp salt

Directions:
1. Line multi-level air fryer basket with parchment paper.
2. Add all ingredients into the zip-lock bag, seal bag, and place in the refrigerator for 1 hour.
3. Add marinated vegetables into the multi-level air fryer basket.
4. Place multi-level air fryer basket into the inner pot of the instant pot.
5. Secure pot with air fryer lid, select bake mode then cook at 375 F for 35 minutes. Stir halfway through.
6. Serve and enjoy.

Nutritional Value (Amount per Serving):
- Calories 196
- Fat 13.4 g
- Carbohydrates 18.3 g
- Sugar 8.3 g
- Protein 6.1 g
- Cholesterol 0 mg

Healthy Root Vegetables

Preparation Time: 10 minutes
Cooking Time: 30 minutes
Serve: 4

Ingredients:
- 1 parsnip, cut into 1-inch chunks
- 3 carrots, cut into 1-inch pieces
- 1 1/2 tsp Italian seasoning
- 1 onion, cut into wedges
- 1 rutabaga, peeled and cut into 1-inch pieces
- 1 tbsp olive oil
- 2 tbsp vinegar
- Pepper
- Salt

Directions:
1. Line multi-level air fryer basket with parchment paper.
2. In a bowl, toss vegetables with remaining ingredients.
3. Add vegetables into the multi-level air fryer basket.
4. Place multi-level air fryer basket into the inner pot of the instant pot.
5. Secure pot with air fryer lid, select bake mode then cook at 380 F for 30 minutes. Stir halfway through.
6. Serve and enjoy.

Nutritional Value (Amount per Serving):
- Calories 126
- Fat 4.3 g
- Carbohydrates 21.2 g
- Sugar 10.6 g
- Protein 2.3 g
- Cholesterol 1 mg

Roasted Vegetables

Preparation Time: 10 minutes
Cooking Time: 30 minutes
Serve: 3

Ingredients:
- 10 oz mix frozen vegetables
- 1/2 tsp pepper
- 1/2 tsp onion powder
- 1/2 tsp garlic powder
- 2 tbsp olive oil
- 1/2 tsp salt

Directions:
1. Line multi-level air fryer basket with parchment paper.
2. Add all ingredients into the mixing bowl and toss well.
3. Add vegetables into the multi-level air fryer basket.
4. Place multi-level air fryer basket into the inner pot of the instant pot.
5. Secure pot with air fryer lid, select roast mode then cook at 380 F for 30 minutes. Stir halfway through.
6. Serve and enjoy.

Nutritional Value (Amount per Serving):
- Calories 145
- Fat 9.5 g
- Carbohydrates 13.3 g
- Sugar 3.2 g
- Protein 2.9 g
- Cholesterol 0 mg

Chapter 7: Snacks & Appetizers

Spicy Cashew Nuts

Preparation Time: 10 minutes
Cooking Time: 5 minutes
Serve: 3
Ingredients:
- 1 1/2 cup cashews
- 1 tbsp olive oil
- 1/2 tsp ground cumin
- 1/2 tsp smoked paprika
- 1/2 tsp salt

Directions:
1. Line multi-level air fryer basket with parchment paper.
2. Add cashews and remaining ingredients into the bowl and toss well.
3. Add cashews into the multi-level air fryer basket.
4. Place multi-level air fryer basket into the inner pot of the instant pot.
5. Secure pot with air fryer lid, select air fry mode then cook at 330 F for 5 minutes.
6. Serve and enjoy.

Nutritional Value (Amount per Serving):
- Calories 436
- Fat 36.6 g
- Carbohydrates 22.7 g
- Sugar 3.5 g
- Protein 10.6 g
- Cholesterol 0 mg

Tasty Hassel Back Potatoes

Preparation Time: 10 minutes
Cooking Time: 30 minutes
Serve: 4
Ingredients:
- 4 potatoes, peel & make 6-8 cuts on top of potatoes
- 1/4 cup Asiago cheese, shredded
- 1 tbsp olive oil
- Pepper
- Salt

Directions:
1. Line multi-level air fryer basket with parchment paper.
2. Brush potatoes with olive oil. Season with pepper and salt.
3. Place potatoes into the multi-level air fryer basket.
4. Place multi-level air fryer basket into the inner pot of the instant pot.
5. Secure pot with air fryer lid, select air fry mode then cook at 350 F for 30 minutes.
6. Sprinkle cheese on top of potatoes and serve.

Nutritional Value (Amount per Serving):
- Calories 183
- Fat 4.2 g
- Carbohydrates 33.5 g
- Sugar 2.5 g
- Protein 4 g
- Cholesterol 2 mg

Crunchy Chickpeas

Preparation Time: 10 minutes
Cooking Time: 10 minutes
Serve: 4
Ingredients:
- 14 oz can chickpeas, drained
- 1/2 tsp onion powder
- 1 tbsp olive oil
- 1/4 tsp paprika
- 1/2 tsp garlic powder
- Pepper
- Salt

Directions:
1. Line multi-level air fryer basket with parchment paper.
2. Toss chickpeas with remaining ingredients and add into the multi-level air fryer basket.
3. Place multi-level air fryer basket into the inner pot of the instant pot.
4. Secure pot with air fryer lid, select air fry mode then cook at 390 F for 10 minutes. Stir halfway through.
5. Serve and enjoy.

Nutritional Value (Amount per Serving):
- Calories 151
- Fat 4.7 g
- Carbohydrates 23 g
- Sugar 0.2 g
- Protein 5 g
- Cholesterol 0 mg

Cauliflower Hummus

Preparation Time: 10 minutes
Cooking Time: 30 minutes
Serve: 8
Ingredients:
- 1 cauliflower head, cut into florets
- 3 tbsp olive oil
- 2 tbsp fresh lime juice
- 1/3 cup tahini
- 1 tsp garlic, chopped
- Pepper
- Salt

Directions:
1. Line multi-level air fryer basket with parchment paper.
2. Add cauliflower florets into the multi-level air fryer basket.
3. Place multi-level air fryer basket into the inner pot of the instant pot.

4. Secure pot with air fryer lid, select roast mode then cook at 380 F for 30 minutes. Stir halfway through.
5. Add cauliflower and remaining ingredients into the food processor process until smooth.
6. Serve and enjoy.

Nutritional Value (Amount per Serving):
- Calories 116
- Fat 10.7 g
- Carbohydrates 4.9 g
- Sugar 1 g
- Protein 2.4 g
- Cholesterol 0 mg

Crispy Tofu

Preparation Time: 10 minutes
Cooking Time: 15 minutes
Serve: 2
Ingredients:
- 7.5 oz extra-firm tofu, pressed and cut into cubes
- 1/2 tsp sesame oil
- 1 tbsp rice vinegar
- Pepper
- Salt

Directions:
1. Line multi-level air fryer basket with parchment paper.
2. In a bowl, toss tofu with remaining ingredients. Let it sit for 15 minutes.
3. Add tofu into the multi-level air fryer basket.
4. Place multi-level air fryer basket into the inner pot of the instant pot.
5. Secure pot with air fryer lid, select air fry mode then cook at 400 F for 15 minutes. Stir halfway through.
6. Serve and enjoy.

Nutritional Value (Amount per Serving):
- Calories 112
- Fat 7.3 g
- Carbohydrates 2.2 g
- Sugar 0.5 g
- Protein 10.5 g
- Cholesterol 0 mg

Honey Cinnamon Potato Bites

Preparation Time: 10 minutes
Cooking Time: 15 minutes
Serve: 2
Ingredients:
- 2 sweet potato, diced into 1-inch cubes
- 1 1/2 tsp cinnamon
- 2 tbsp olive oil
- 2 tbsp honey
- 1 tsp red chili flakes

Directions:
1. Line multi-level air fryer basket with parchment paper.
2. Add all ingredients into the bowl and toss well.
3. Add sweet potato into the multi-level air fryer basket.
4. Place multi-level air fryer basket into the inner pot of the instant pot.
5. Secure pot with air fryer lid, select air fry mode then cook at 350 F for 15 minutes. Stir halfway through.
6. Serve and enjoy.

Nutritional Value (Amount per Serving):
- Calories 291
- Fat 14.2 g
- Carbohydrates 42.3 g
- Sugar 24.7 g
- Protein 2.4 g
- Cholesterol 0 mg

Air Fry Nuts

Preparation Time: 10 minutes
Cooking Time: 4 minutes
Serve: 2
Ingredients:
- 2 cup mixed nuts
- 1/2 tsp chili powder
- 1 tbsp olive oil
- 1 tsp pepper
- 1 tsp salt

Directions:
1. Line multi-level air fryer basket with parchment paper.
2. In a bowl, add all ingredients and toss well.
3. Add nuts into the multi-level air fryer basket.
4. Place multi-level air fryer basket into the inner pot of the instant pot.
5. Secure pot with air fryer lid, select air fry mode then cook at 350 F for 4 minutes. Stir halfway through.
6. Serve and enjoy.

Nutritional Value (Amount per Serving):
- Calories 950
- Fat 88 g
- Carbohydrates 33.1 g
- Sugar 6.4 g
- Protein 22.5 g
- Cholesterol 0 mg

Spicy Walnuts

Preparation Time: 10 minutes
Cooking Time: 5 minutes
Serve: 6
Ingredients:
- 2 cups walnuts
- 1 tsp olive oil
- 1/8 tsp paprika
- 1/4 tsp chili powder
- Pepper

- Salt

Directions:
1. Line multi-level air fryer basket with parchment paper.
2. Add walnuts, paprika, chili powder, oil, pepper, and salt into the bowl and toss well.
3. Add walnuts into the multi-level air fryer basket.
4. Place multi-level air fryer basket into the inner pot of the instant pot.
5. Secure pot with air fryer lid, select air fry mode then cook at 320 F for 5 minutes.
6. Serve and enjoy.

Nutritional Value (Amount per Serving):
- Calories 295
- Fat 4.1 g
- Carbohydrates 55.2 g
- Sugar 0.6 g
- Protein 9.5 g
- Cholesterol 1 mg

Tasty Roasted Olives

Preparation Time: 10 minutes
Cooking Time: 5 minutes
Serve: 4

Ingredients:
- 2 cups olives
- 2 tbsp olive oil
- 1/2 tsp red chili flakes
- 2 tsp garlic, minced
- Pepper
- Salt

Directions:
1. Line multi-level air fryer basket with parchment paper.
2. Add olives and remaining ingredients into the bowl and toss well.
3. Add olives into the multi-level air fryer basket.
4. Place multi-level air fryer basket into the inner pot of the instant pot.
5. Secure pot with air fryer lid, select air fry mode then cook at 300 F for 5 minutes.
6. Serve and enjoy.

Nutritional Value (Amount per Serving):
- Calories 139
- Fat 14.2 g
- Carbohydrates 4.7 g
- Sugar 0 g
- Protein 0.7 g
- Cholesterol 0 mg

Sweet Potato Quinoa Patties

Preparation Time: 10 minutes
Cooking Time: 60 minutes
Serve: 6

Ingredients:
- 2 cups cooked quinoa
- 2 cups sweet potatoes, mashed
- 1/4 cup celery, diced
- 1/4 cup scallions, chopped
- 1/4 cup parsley, chopped
- 1/4 cup flour
- 2 tsp Italian seasoning
- 1 garlic clove, minced
- Pepper
- Salt

Directions:
1. Line multi-level air fryer basket with parchment paper.
2. Add all ingredients into the mixing bowl and mix until well combined.
3. Make 6 equal shapes of patties from the mixture and place it into the multi-level air fryer basket.
4. Place multi-level air fryer basket into the inner pot of the instant pot.
5. Secure pot with air fryer lid, select bake mode then cook at 375 F for 60 minutes. Flip patties halfway through.
6. Serve and enjoy.

Nutritional Value (Amount per Serving):
- Calories 295
- Fat 4.1 g
- Carbohydrates 55.2 g
- Sugar 0.6 g
- Protein 9.5 g
- Cholesterol 1 mg

Tasty Carrot Fries

Preparation Time: 10 minutes
Cooking Time: 25 minutes
Serve: 4

Ingredients:
- 2 large carrots, peel and cut into fries shape
- 1/2 tbsp paprika
- 1 tbsp olive oil
- 1/2 tsp salt

Directions:
1. Line multi-level air fryer basket with parchment paper.
2. Add carrots, paprika, oil, and salt into the mixing bowl and toss well.
3. Add carrots into the multi-level air fryer basket.
4. Place multi-level air fryer basket into the inner pot of the instant pot.
5. Secure pot with air fryer lid, select bake mode then cook at 380 F for 25 minutes. Stir halfway through.
6. Serve and enjoy.

Nutritional Value (Amount per Serving):
- Calories 47
- Fat 3.6 g
- Carbohydrates 4 g
- Sugar 1.9 g
- Protein 0.4 g
- Cholesterol 0 mg

Delicious Jalapeno Poppers

Preparation Time: 10 minutes
Cooking Time: 7 minutes
Serve: 2
Ingredients:
- 5 jalapeno peppers, cut in half & remove seeds
- 1/4 tsp paprika
- 1/2 tsp chili powder
- 1 tsp garlic powder
- 1/2 cup cheddar cheese, shredded
- 4 oz cream cheese
- 1 tsp salt

Directions:
1. Line multi-level air fryer basket with parchment paper.
2. In a small bowl, mix cream cheese, cheddar cheese, garlic powder, chili powder, paprika, and salt.
3. Stuff cream cheese mixture into each jalapeno half.
4. Place stuffed jalapeno peppers into the multi-level air fryer basket.
5. Place multi-level air fryer basket into the inner pot of the instant pot.
6. Secure pot with air fryer lid, select air fry mode then cook at 350 F for 7 minutes.
7. Serve and enjoy.

Nutritional Value (Amount per Serving):
- Calories 334
- Fat 29.8 g
- Carbohydrates 6 g
- Sugar 1.9 g
- Protein 12.2 g
- Cholesterol 92 mg

Maple Chickpeas

Preparation Time: 10 minutes
Cooking Time: 12 minutes
Serve: 4
Ingredients:
- 14 oz can chickpeas, rinsed, drained and pat dry
- 1 tbsp maple syrup
- 1 tbsp olive oil
- Pepper
- Salt

Directions:
1. Line multi-level air fryer basket with parchment paper.
2. Add chickpeas into the multi-level air fryer basket.
3. Place multi-level air fryer basket into the inner pot of the instant pot.
4. Secure pot with air fryer lid, select air fry mode then cook at 375 F for 12 minutes. Stir halfway through.
5. In a bowl, add chickpeas, maple syrup, oil, pepper, and salt and toss well.
6. Serve and enjoy.

Nutritional Value (Amount per Serving):
- Calories 161
- Fat 4.6 g
- Carbohydrates 25.8 g
- Sugar 3 g
- Protein 4.9 g
- Cholesterol 0 mg

Spicy Potato Fries

Preparation Time: 10 minutes
Cooking Time: 16 minutes
Serve: 2
Ingredients:
- 2 sweet potatoes, peeled and cut into fries shape
- 1 tbsp olive oil
- 1/4 tsp chili powder
- 1/4 tsp paprika
- 1/8 tsp cayenne
- Pepper
- Salt

Directions:
1. Line multi-level air fryer basket with parchment paper.
2. Add sweet potato fries and remaining ingredients into the mixing bowl and toss well.
3. Add sweet potato fries into the multi-level air fryer basket.
4. Place multi-level air fryer basket into the inner pot of the instant pot.
5. Secure pot with air fryer lid, select air fry mode then cook at 375 F for 16 minutes.
6. Serve and enjoy.

Nutritional Value (Amount per Serving):
- Calories 239
- Fat 7.4 g
- Carbohydrates 42.2 g
- Sugar 0.8 g
- Protein 2.4 g
- Cholesterol 0 mg

Tasty Potato Wedges

Preparation Time: 10 minutes
Cooking Time: 15 minutes
Serve: 4
Ingredients:
- 2 potatoes, cut into wedges
- 1/2 tsp paprika
- 1 1/2 tbsp olive oil
- 1/4 tsp pepper
- 1 tsp sea salt

Directions:
1. Line multi-level air fryer basket with parchment paper.
2. Soak potato wedges into the water for half-hour. Drain well and pat dry.

3. In a bowl, toss potato wedges with remaining ingredients.
4. Add potato wedges into the multi-level air fryer basket.
5. Place multi-level air fryer basket into the inner pot of the instant pot.
6. Secure pot with air fryer lid, select air fry mode then cook at 400 F for 15 minutes. Stir halfway through.
7. Serve and enjoy.

Nutritional Value (Amount per Serving):
- Calories 120
- Fat 5.4 g
- Carbohydrates 17 g
- Sugar 1.3 g
- Protein 1.8 g
- Cholesterol 0 mg

Vegetable Skewers

Preparation Time: 10 minutes
Cooking Time: 10 minutes
Serve: 4

Ingredients:
- 1 red bell peppers, cut into pieces
- 1 yellow bell peppers, cut into pieces
- 1 eggplant, cut into pieces
- 1/2 onion, cut into pieces
- 1 zucchini, cut into pieces
- 1 tbsp olive oil
- Pepper
- Salt

Directions:
1. Line multi-level air fryer basket with parchment paper.
2. Thread vegetables onto the skewers and brush with oil. Season with pepper and salt.
3. Place vegetable skewers into the multi-level air fryer basket.
4. Place multi-level air fryer basket into the inner pot of the instant pot.
5. Secure pot with air fryer lid, select air fry mode then cook at 390 F for 10 minutes. Flip Skewers halfway through.
6. Serve and enjoy.

Nutritional Value (Amount per Serving):
- Calories 91
- Fat 4 g
- Carbohydrates 14.2 g
- Sugar 7.9 g
- Protein 2.5 g
- Cholesterol 0 mg

Flavorful Green Beans

Preparation Time: 5 minutes
Cooking Time: 10 minutes
Serve: 2

Ingredients:
- 2 cups green beans
- 1/2 tsp dried oregano
- 1/8 tsp red chili powder
- 1/8 tsp ground allspice
- 1/4 tsp ground cinnamon
- 2 tbsp olive oil
- 1/4 tsp ground coriander
- 1/4 tsp ground cumin
- 1/2 tsp salt

Directions:
1. Line multi-level air fryer basket with parchment paper.
2. Add all ingredients into the bowl and toss well.
3. Add green beans into the multi-level air fryer basket.
4. Place multi-level air fryer basket into the inner pot of the instant pot.
5. Secure pot with air fryer lid, select bake mode then cook at 370 F for 10 minutes. Stir halfway through.
6. Serve and enjoy.

Nutritional Value (Amount per Serving):
- Calories 158
- Fat 14.3 g
- Carbohydrates 8.6 g
- Sugar 1.6 g
- Protein 2.1 g
- Cholesterol 0 mg

Cheesy Cauliflower and Broccoli

Preparation Time: 10 minutes
Cooking Time: 20 minutes
Serve: 3

Ingredients:
- 2 cups cauliflower florets
- 2/3 cup Asiago cheese, shredded
- 2 cups broccoli florets
- 1/3 cup olive oil
- Pepper
- Salt

Directions:
1. Line multi-level air fryer basket with parchment paper.
2. Add cauliflower, cheese, broccoli, oil, pepper, and salt into the mixing bowl and toss well.
3. Add cauliflower and broccoli mixture into the multi-level air fryer basket.
4. Place multi-level air fryer basket into the inner pot of the instant pot.
5. Secure pot with air fryer lid, select bake mode then cook at 380 F for 20 minutes. Stir halfway through.
6. Serve and enjoy.

Nutritional Value (Amount per Serving):
- Calories 252
- Fat 24.5 g
- Carbohydrates 7.6 g
- Sugar 2.6 g
- Protein 4.6 g
- Cholesterol 6 mg

Broccoli Patties

Preparation Time: 10 minutes
Cooking Time: 20 minutes
Serve: 4
Ingredients:
- 2 cups broccoli florets, cooked & mashed
- 1 cup cheddar cheese, shredded
- 1/4 cup breadcrumbs
- 2 egg whites
- 1/8 tsp salt

Directions:
1. Line multi-level air fryer basket with parchment paper.
2. Add all ingredients into the mixing bowl and mix until well combined.
3. Make small patties from mixture and place into the multi-level air fryer basket.
4. Place multi-level air fryer basket into the inner pot of the instant pot.
5. Secure pot with air fryer lid, select bake mode then cook at 350 F for 20 minutes. Flip patties halfway through.
6. Serve and enjoy.

Nutritional Value (Amount per Serving):
- Calories 165
- Fat 9.9 g
- Carbohydrates 8.4 g
- Sugar 1.5 g
- Protein 11 g
- Cholesterol 30 mg

Tasty Jalapeno Poppers

Preparation Time: 10 minutes
Cooking Time: 15 minutes
Serve: 8
Ingredients:
- 4 jalapeno peppers, halved and remove seeds
- 1/2 cup cheddar cheese, shredded
- 4 tbsp pesto
- 1/4 cup cream cheese
- Pepper
- Salt

Directions:
1. Line multi-level air fryer basket with parchment paper.
2. In a bowl, mix together pesto, cheese, cream cheese, pepper, and salt.
3. Stuff cheese mixture into each jalapeno half and place jalapeno halves into the multi-level air fryer basket.
4. Place multi-level air fryer basket into the inner pot of the instant pot.
5. Secure pot with air fryer lid, select bake mode then cook at 380 F for 15 minutes.
6. Serve and enjoy.

Nutritional Value (Amount per Serving):
- Calories 91
- Fat 8.2 g
- Carbohydrates 1.3 g
- Sugar 0.8 g
- Protein 3.2 g
- Cholesterol 17 mg

Healthy Roasted Nuts

Preparation Time: 10 minutes
Cooking Time: 15 minutes
Serve: 6
Ingredients:
- 1 cup almonds
- 1 cup cashews
- 1 tbsp olive oil
- 1/4 tsp chili powder
- 1/2 tsp salt

Directions
1. Line multi-level air fryer basket with parchment paper.
2. Toss cashews, almonds, oil, chili powder, and salt into the bowl.
3. Add nuts into the multi-level air fryer basket.
4. Place multi-level air fryer basket into the inner pot of the instant pot.
5. Secure pot with air fryer lid, select bake mode then cook at 300 F for 15 minutes. Stir halfway through.
6. Serve and enjoy.

Nutritional Value (Amount per Serving):
- Calories 243
- Fat 20.9 g
- Carbohydrates 10.9 g
- Sugar 1.8 g
- Protein 6.9 g
- Cholesterol 0 mg

Zucchini Chips

Preparation Time: 10 minutes
Cooking Time: 30 minutes
Serve: 2
Ingredients:
- 2 medium zucchini, cut into 1/4-inch thick slices
- 1/2 cup Asiago cheese, grated
- 1/4 cup olive oil
- Pepper
- Salt

Directions:
1. Line multi-level air fryer basket with parchment paper.
2. In a bowl, toss zucchini slices with cheese, oil, pepper, and salt.
3. Arrange zucchini slices into the multi-level air fryer basket.
4. Place multi-level air fryer basket into the inner pot of the instant pot.

5. Secure pot with air fryer lid, select air fry mode then cook at 300 F for 30 minutes Flip zucchini slices halfway through.
6. Serve and enjoy.

Nutritional Value (Amount per Serving):
- Calories 272
- Fat 27.6 g
- Carbohydrates 6.6 g
- Sugar 3.4 g
- Protein 4.1 g
- Cholesterol 6 mg

Cream Cheese Stuff Mushrooms

Preparation Time: 10 minutes
Cooking Time: 5 minutes
Serve: 3

Ingredients:
- 10 baby mushrooms
- 1/4 tsp garlic powder
- 4 oz cream cheese
- 2 tbsp butter
- 3 bacon slices, cooked and crumbled
- 1/4 tsp onion powder
- Pepper
- Salt

Directions:
1. Line multi-level air fryer basket with parchment paper.
2. In a small bowl, mix together cream cheese, butter, onion powder, bacon, garlic powder, pepper, and salt.
3. Stuff cream cheese mixture into the mushrooms.
4. Place stuffed mushrooms into the multi-level air fryer basket.
5. Place multi-level air fryer basket into the inner pot of the instant pot.
6. Secure pot with air fryer lid, select bake mode then cook at 350 F for 5 minutes.
7. Serve and enjoy.

Nutritional Value (Amount per Serving):
- Calories 317
- Fat 29 g
- Carbohydrates 3.6 g
- Sugar 1.3 g
- Protein 11.9 g
- Cholesterol 83 mg

Savory Pecans

Preparation Time: 5 minutes
Cooking Time: 6 minutes
Serve: 6

Ingredients:
- 2 cups pecan halves
- 1/4 tsp chili powder
- 1 tbsp olive oil
- Salt

Directions:
1. Line multi-level air fryer basket with parchment paper.
2. Toss pecans with chili powder, oil, and salt.
3. Add pecans into the multi-level air fryer basket.
4. Place multi-level air fryer basket into the inner pot of the instant pot.
5. Secure pot with air fryer lid, select bake mode then cook at 380 F for 6 minutes.
6. Serve and enjoy.

Nutritional Value (Amount per Serving):
- Calories 160
- Fat 16.6 g
- Carbohydrates 2.9 g
- Sugar 0.7 g
- Protein 2.2 g
- Cholesterol 0 mg

Meatballs

Preparation Time: 10 minutes
Cooking Time: 25 minutes
Serve: 4

Ingredients:
- 1 lb ground turkey
- 1 jalapeno pepper, minced
- 1/2 tsp garlic powder
- 1/2 cup cilantro, chopped
- Salt

Directions:
1. Line multi-level air fryer basket with parchment paper.
2. Add all ingredients into the large bowl and mix until well combined.
3. Make small balls from mixture and place into the multi-level air fryer basket.
4. Place multi-level air fryer basket into the inner pot of the instant pot.
5. Secure pot with air fryer lid, select bake mode then cook at 380 F for 25 minutes. Flip halfway through.
6. Serve and enjoy.

Nutritional Value (Amount per Serving):
- Calories 224
- Fat 12.5 g
- Carbohydrates 0.5 g
- Sugar 0.2 g
- Protein 31.2 g
- Cholesterol 116 mg

Roasted Olives

Preparation Time: 10 minutes
Cooking Time: 5 minutes
Serve: 4

Ingredients:
- 1 cups olives
- 1/2 tsp dried fennel seeds
- 1/2 tsp dried oregano
- 2 tbsp olive oil
- Pepper

- Salt

Directions:
1. Line multi-level air fryer basket with parchment paper.
2. Add olives and remaining ingredients into the bowl and toss well.
3. Add olives into the multi-level air fryer basket.
4. Place multi-level air fryer basket into the inner pot of the instant pot.
5. Secure pot with air fryer lid, select air fry mode then cook at 300 F for 5 minutes. Stir halfway through.
6. Serve and enjoy.

Nutritional Value (Amount per Serving):
- Calories 100
- Fat 10.7 g
- Carbohydrates 2.4 g
- Sugar 0 g
- Protein 0.3 g
- Cholesterol 0 mg

Ranch Potato Wedges

Preparation Time: 10 minutes
Cooking Time: 30 minutes
Serve: 4

Ingredients:
- 2 potatoes, cut into wedges
- 1 tbsp ranch seasoning
- 2 tbsp olive oil

Directions:
1. Line multi-level air fryer basket with parchment paper.
2. Toss potato wedges with oil and ranch seasoning.
3. Add potato wedges into the multi-level air fryer basket.
4. Place multi-level air fryer basket into the inner pot of the instant pot.
5. Secure pot with air fryer lid, select bake mode then cook at 380 F for 30 minutes. Stir halfway through.
6. Serve and enjoy.

Nutritional Value (Amount per Serving):
- Calories 133
- Fat 7.1 g
- Carbohydrates 16.7 g
- Sugar 1.2 g
- Protein 1.8 g
- Cholesterol 0 mg

Easy Apple Chips

Preparation Time: 10 minutes
Cooking Time: 8 minutes
Serve: 4

Ingredients:
- 1 apple, sliced thinly
- 1/4 tsp cinnamon

Directions:
1. Line multi-level air fryer basket with parchment paper.
2. Season apple slices with cinnamon and arrange into the multi-level air fryer basket.
3. Place multi-level air fryer basket into the inner pot of the instant pot.
4. Secure pot with air fryer lid, select air fry mode then cook at 375 F for 8 minutes.
5. Serve and enjoy.

Nutritional Value (Amount per Serving):
- Calories 29
- Fat 0.1 g
- Carbohydrates 7.8 g
- Sugar 5.8 g
- Protein 0.2 g
- Cholesterol 0 mg

Beef Burger Patties

Preparation Time: 10 minutes
Cooking Time: 10 minutes
Serve: 4

Ingredients:
- 1 lb ground beef
- 1 tbsp garlic, minced
- 5 basil leaves, minced
- 8 mint leaves, minced
- 1 jalapeno pepper, minced
- 1/4 cup fresh parsley, chopped
- 1 tsp dried oregano
- 1 cup feta cheese, crumbled
- 1/4 tsp pepper
- 1/2 tsp kosher salt

Directions:
1. Line multi-level air fryer basket with parchment paper.
2. Add all ingredients into the mixing bowl and mix until well combined.
3. Make 4 equal shape patties from the meat mixture.
4. Place patties into the multi-level air fryer basket.
5. Place multi-level air fryer basket into the inner pot of the instant pot.
6. Secure pot with air fryer lid, select bake mode then cook at 380 F for 10 minutes.
7. Serve and enjoy.

Nutritional Value (Amount per Serving):
- Calories 327
- Fat 15.3 g
- Carbohydrates 4.9 g
- Sugar 1.7 g
- Protein 40.8 g
- Cholesterol 135 mg

Cheesy Zucchini Fries

Preparation Time: 10 minutes
Cooking Time: 10 minutes
Serve: 4

Ingredients:

- 2 zucchini, cut into fries shapes
- 1/2 cup breadcrumbs
- 1 egg, lightly beaten
- 1/2 tsp garlic powder
- 1 tsp Italian seasoning
- 1/2 cup Asiago cheese, grated
- Pepper
- Salt

Directions:
1. Line multi-level air fryer basket with parchment paper.
2. In a shallow dish, mix breadcrumbs, cheese, Italians seasoning, garlic powder, pepper, and salt.
3. In a shallow bowl, whisk the egg.
4. Dip zucchini fries into the egg and coat with breadcrumb mixture.
5. Place coated zucchini fries into the multi-level air fryer basket.
6. Place multi-level air fryer basket into the inner pot of the instant pot.
7. Secure pot with air fryer lid, select air fry mode then cook at 400 F for 10 minutes. Flip fries halfway through.
8. Serve and enjoy.

Nutritional Value (Amount per Serving):
- Calories 102
- Fat 3.3 g
- Carbohydrates 13.5 g
- Sugar 2.8 g
- Protein 5.3 g
- Cholesterol 45 mg

Delicious Zucchini Chips

Preparation Time: 10 minutes
Cooking Time: 30 minutes
Serve: 2
Ingredients:
- 2 zucchini, cut into 1/4-inch thick slices
- 1/2 tsp garlic powder
- 1/2 cup cheddar cheese, grated
- 1 tbsp rosemary, chopped
- 1/4 tsp oregano
- 1/4 cup olive oil
- Pepper
- Salt

Directions:
1. Line multi-level air fryer basket with parchment paper.
2. In a mixing bowl, toss zucchini slices with remaining ingredients.
3. Arrange zucchini slices into the multi-level air fryer basket.
4. Place multi-level air fryer basket into the inner pot of the instant pot.
5. Secure pot with air fryer lid, select air fry mode then cook at 300 F for 30 minutes. Flip halfway through.
6. Serve and enjoy.

Nutritional Value (Amount per Serving):
- Calories 370
- Fat 35.2 g
- Carbohydrates 8.7 g
- Sugar 3.7 g
- Protein 9.6 g
- Cholesterol 30 mg

Turkey Stuffed Poblanos

Preparation Time: 10 minutes
Cooking Time: 15 minutes
Serve: 6
Ingredients:
- 3 poblano peppers, cut in half & remove seeds
- 1 1/2 cup artichoke dip
- 1 cup turkey, cooked and chopped
- 2 oz mozzarella cheese, grated

Directions:
1. Line multi-level air fryer basket with parchment paper.
2. In a small bowl, mix turkey, artichoke dip, and half cheese.
3. Stuff turkey mixture into the poblano peppers.
4. Place stuffed poblano peppers into the multi-level air fryer basket. Top with remaining cheese.
5. Place multi-level air fryer basket into the inner pot of the instant pot.
6. Secure pot with air fryer lid, select air fry mode then cook at 350 F for 15 minutes.
7. Serve and enjoy.

Nutritional Value (Amount per Serving):
- Calories 275
- Fat 18.9 g
- Carbohydrates 12.5 g
- Sugar 3.2 g
- Protein 18 g
- Cholesterol 73 mg

Easy Ranch Zucchini Chips

Preparation Time: 10 minutes
Cooking Time: 15 minutes
Serve: 2
Ingredients:
- 1 egg
- 2 zucchini, cut into thin slices
- 1 tsp ranch seasoning
- Pepper
- Salt

Directions:
1. Line multi-level air fryer basket with parchment paper.
2. Brush zucchini slices with egg and sprinkle with ranch seasoning, pepper, and salt.
3. Arrange zucchini slices into the multi-level air fryer basket.
4. Place multi-level air fryer basket into the inner pot of the instant pot.

5. Secure pot with air fryer lid, select air fry mode then cook at 380 F for 15 minutes. Flip zucchini slices after 10 minutes.
6. Serve and enjoy.

Nutritional Value (Amount per Serving):
- Calories 63
- Fat 2.5 g
- Carbohydrates 6.8 g
- Sugar 3.6 g
- Protein 5.2 g
- Cholesterol 82 mg

Healthy Beetroot Chips

Preparation Time: 10 minutes
Cooking Time: 15 minutes
Serve: 4

Ingredients:
- 1 beetroot, wash, peeled, and thinly sliced
- 1 tsp olive oil
- Pepper
- Salt

Directions:
1. Line multi-level air fryer basket with parchment paper.
2. Brush beetroot slices with oil and season with pepper and salt.
3. Arrange beetroot slices into the multi-level air fryer basket.
4. Place multi-level air fryer basket into the inner pot of the instant pot.
5. Secure pot with air fryer lid, select air fry mode then cook at 300 F for 15 minutes. Flip beetroot slices after 10 minutes.
6. Serve and enjoy.

Nutritional Value (Amount per Serving):
- Calories 19
- Fat 1.2 g
- Carbohydrates 2.1 g
- Sugar 1.7 g
- Protein 0.4 g
- Cholesterol 0 mg

Meatballs

Preparation Time: 10 minutes
Cooking Time: 10 minutes
Serve: 6

Ingredients:
- 2 lbs ground turkey
- 1/4 cup fresh parsley, chopped
- 1/2 cup breadcrumbs
- 1/2 cup ricotta cheese
- 2 eggs, lightly beaten
- 1 tsp pepper
- 2 tsp salt

Directions:
1. Line multi-level air fryer basket with parchment paper.
2. Add all ingredients into the large bowl and mix until well combined.
3. Make meatballs from mixture and place into the multi-level air fryer basket.
4. Place multi-level air fryer basket into the inner pot of the instant pot.
5. Secure pot with air fryer lid, select air fry mode then cook at 380 F for 10 minutes.
6. Serve and enjoy.

Nutritional Value (Amount per Serving):
- Calories 382
- Fat 20.2 g
- Carbohydrates 8 g
- Sugar 0.8 g
- Protein 46.9 g
- Cholesterol 215 mg

Air Fry Vegetables

Preparation Time: 10 minutes
Cooking Time: 18 minutes
Serve: 4

Ingredients:
- 1 cup broccoli florets
- 1 cup cauliflower, cut into florets
- 1 tbsp olive oil
- 1 cup carrots, sliced
- 1/4 tsp garlic powder
- Pepper
- Salt

Directions:
1. Line multi-level air fryer basket with parchment paper.
2. Add all ingredients into the bowl and toss well.
3. Add vegetables into the multi-level air fryer basket.
4. Place multi-level air fryer basket into the inner pot of the instant pot.
5. Secure pot with air fryer lid, select air fry mode then cook at 380 F for 18 minutes. Stir halfway through.
6. Serve and enjoy.

Nutritional Value (Amount per Serving):
- Calories 56
- Fat 3.6 g
- Carbohydrates 5.7 g
- Sugar 2.4 g
- Protein 1.4 g
- Cholesterol 0 mg

Meatballs

Preparation Time: 10 minutes
Cooking Time: 25 minutes
Serve: 6

Ingredients:
- 1 egg
- 1 lb ground chicken
- 1 garlic clove, minced

- 1/2 tsp ground cumin
- 1/2 tsp dried oregano
- 1 tsp mint, chopped
- 1/4 cup breadcrumbs
- 1/4 cup fresh parsley, chopped
- 1/4 onion, minced
- 1/2 tsp salt

Directions:
1. Line multi-level air fryer basket with parchment paper.
2. Add all ingredients into the large bowl and mix until well combined.
3. Make meatballs from mixture and place into the multi-level air fryer basket.
4. Place multi-level air fryer basket into the inner pot of the instant pot.
5. Secure pot with air fryer lid, select air fry mode then cook at 375 F for 25 minutes. Flip meatballs halfway through.
6. Serve and enjoy.

Nutritional Value (Amount per Serving):
- Calories 177
- Fat 6.6 g
- Carbohydrates 4.3 g
- Sugar 0.6 g
- Protein 23.6 g
- Cholesterol 95 mg

Meatballs

Preparation Time: 10 minutes
Cooking Time: 15 minutes
Serve: 8
Ingredients:
- 4 oz ground sausage meat
- 3 tbsp breadcrumbs
- 2 garlic cloves, minced
- 1 small onion, chopped
- 1/4 tsp garlic powder
- 1/4 tsp onion powder
- Pepper
- Salt

Directions:
1. Line multi-level air fryer basket with parchment paper.
2. Add all ingredients into the mixing bowl and mix until well combined.
3. Make meatballs from mixture and place into the multi-level air fryer basket.
4. Place multi-level air fryer basket into the inner pot of the instant pot.
5. Secure pot with air fryer lid, select air fry mode then cook at 360 F for 15 minutes.
6. Serve and enjoy.

Nutritional Value (Amount per Serving):
- Calories 52
- Fat 2.3 g
- Carbohydrates 5.5 g
- Sugar 0.8 g
- Protein 2.3 g
- Cholesterol 5 mg

Eggplant Fries

Preparation Time: 10 minutes
Cooking Time: 8 minutes
Serve: 2
Ingredients:
- 1 eggplant, sliced
- 1 tsp olive oil
- Pepper
- Salt

Directions:
1. Line multi-level air fryer basket with parchment paper.
2. Brush eggplant slices with oil and season with pepper and salt.
3. Add eggplant slices into the multi-level air fryer basket.
4. Place multi-level air fryer basket into the inner pot of the instant pot.
5. Secure pot with air fryer lid, select air fry mode then cook at 400 F for 8 minutes. Flip after 5 minutes.
6. Serve and enjoy.

Nutritional Value (Amount per Serving):
- Calories 77
- Fat 2.7 g
- Carbohydrates 13.5 g
- Sugar 6.9 g
- Protein 2.3 g
- Cholesterol 0 mg

Radish Chips

Preparation Time: 10 minutes
Cooking Time: 12 minutes
Serve: 2
Ingredients:
- 1/2 lb radishes, sliced thinly
- 1/4 tsp chili powder
- 1/2 tbsp olive oil
- Pepper
- Salt

Directions:
1. Line multi-level air fryer basket with parchment paper.
2. Brush slices radishes with oil and season with chili powder, pepper, and salt.
3. Arrange sliced radishes into the multi-level air fryer basket.
4. Place multi-level air fryer basket into the inner pot of the instant pot.
5. Secure pot with air fryer lid, select air fry mode then cook at 380 F for 12 minutes.
6. Serve and enjoy.

Nutritional Value (Amount per Serving):
- Calories 49
- Fat 3.7 g
- Carbohydrates 4.1 g
- Sugar 2.1 g

- Protein 0.8 g
- Cholesterol 0 mg

Cajun Zucchini Chips

Preparation Time: 10 minutes
Cooking Time: 16 minutes
Serve: 2
Ingredients:
- 1 zucchini, cut into 1/8-inch thick slices
- 1 tbsp olive oil
- 1 tsp Cajun seasoning
- Pepper
- Salt

Directions:
1. Line multi-level air fryer basket with parchment paper.
2. Brush zucchini slices with oil and season with cajun seasoning, pepper, and salt.
3. Arrange zucchini slices into the multi-level air fryer basket.
4. Place multi-level air fryer basket into the inner pot of the instant pot.
5. Secure pot with air fryer lid, select air fry mode then cook at 370 F for 16 minutes. Flip zucchini slices halfway through.
6. Serve and enjoy.

Nutritional Value (Amount per Serving):
- Calories 76
- Fat 7.2 g
- Carbohydrates 3.3 g
- Sugar 1.7 g
- Protein 1.2 g
- Cholesterol 0 mg

Spicy Okra

Preparation Time: 10 minutes
Cooking Time: 12 minutes
Serve: 2
Ingredients:
- 1/2 lb okra, trimmed and sliced
- 1 tsp olive oil
- 1/2 tsp chili powder
- 1/8 tsp red chili flakes
- 1/8 tsp paprika
- 1/8 tsp pepper
- 1/4 tsp salt

Directions:
1. Line multi-level air fryer basket with parchment paper.
2. Add all ingredients into the bowl and toss well.
3. Add okra into the multi-level air fryer basket.
4. Place multi-level air fryer basket into the inner pot of the instant pot.
5. Secure pot with air fryer lid, select air fry mode then cook at 350 F for 12 minutes. Stir halfway through.
6. Serve and enjoy.

Nutritional Value (Amount per Serving):
- Calories 68
- Fat 2.7 g
- Carbohydrates 9 g
- Sugar 1.7 g
- Protein 2.3 g
- Cholesterol 0 mg

Tasty Cajun Potato Wedges

Preparation Time: 10 minutes
Cooking Time: 25 minutes
Serve: 2
Ingredients:
- 2 potatoes, cut into wedges
- 1 tbsp olive oil
- 1/2 tbsp Cajun spice
- Pepper
- Salt

Directions:
1. Line multi-level air fryer basket with parchment paper.
2. Toss potato wedges with oil, cajun spice, pepper, and salt.
3. Add potato wedges into the multi-level air fryer basket.
4. Place multi-level air fryer basket into the inner pot of the instant pot.
5. Secure pot with air fryer lid, select air fry mode then cook at 375 F for 25 minutes. Stir halfway through.
6. Serve and enjoy.

Nutritional Value (Amount per Serving):
- Calories 207
- Fat 7.2 g
- Carbohydrates 33.5 g
- Sugar 2.5 g
- Protein 3.6 g
- Cholesterol 0 mg

Spicy Baby Potatoes

Preparation Time: 10 minutes
Cooking Time: 20 minutes
Serve: 4
Ingredients:
- 1 lb baby potatoes
- 2 tbsp olive oil
- 1/4 tsp paprika
- 1/4 cup hot sauce
- Pepper
- Salt

Directions:
1. Line multi-level air fryer basket with parchment paper.
2. In a bowl, toss baby potatoes with oil, paprika, hot sauce, pepper, and salt.
3. Add baby potatoes into the multi-level air fryer basket.

4. Place multi-level air fryer basket into the inner pot of the instant pot.
5. Secure pot with air fryer lid, select air fry mode then cook at 375 F for 20 minutes. Stir halfway through.
6. Serve and enjoy.

Nutritional Value (Amount per Serving):
- Calories 128
- Fat 7.2 g
- Carbohydrates 14.5 g
- Sugar 0.2 g
- Protein 3 g
- Cholesterol 0 mg

Tasty Potato Chips

Preparation Time: 10 minutes
Cooking Time: 30 minutes
Serve: 2

Ingredients:
- 1 medium potato, thinly sliced
- 2 tsp olive oil
- 1/8 tsp pepper
- 1/2 tsp oregano
- 1/4 tsp chili powder
- 1/8 tsp thyme
- 1/8 tsp rosemary
- Salt

Directions:
1. Line multi-level air fryer basket with parchment paper.
2. Add potato slices and remaining ingredients into the bowl and toss well.
3. Arrange potato slices into the multi-level air fryer basket.
4. Place multi-level air fryer basket into the inner pot of the instant pot.
5. Secure pot with air fryer lid, select air fry mode then cook at 400 F for 30 minutes. Flip halfway through.
6. Serve and enjoy.

Nutritional Value (Amount per Serving):
- Calories 125
- Fat 4.9 g
- Carbohydrates 19.2 g
- Sugar 0.9 g
- Protein 2.3 g
- Cholesterol 0 mg

Roasted Nuts

Preparation Time: 10 minutes
Cooking Time: 15 minutes
Serve: 6

Ingredients:
- 1/2 cup cashew nuts
- 1 cup almonds
- 1 tbsp olive oil
- 1 cup peanuts
- 1/4 tsp chili powder
- 1/2 tsp salt

Directions
1. Line multi-level air fryer basket with parchment paper.
2. Add all ingredients into the bowl and toss well.
3. Add nuts into the multi-level air fryer basket.
4. Place multi-level air fryer basket into the inner pot of the instant pot.
5. Secure pot with air fryer lid, select air fry mode then cook at 320 F for 15 minutes. Stir after 10 minutes.
6. Serve and enjoy.

Nutritional Value (Amount per Serving):
- Calories 315
- Fat 27.5 g
- Carbohydrates 11.1 g
- Sugar 2.2 g
- Protein 11.4 g
- Cholesterol 0 mg

Healthy Kale Chips

Preparation Time: 10 minutes
Cooking Time: 3 minutes
Serve: 2

Ingredients:
- 1 head kale, tear into 1 1/2-inch piece
- 1 tbsp olive oil

Directions
1. Line multi-level air fryer basket with parchment paper.
2. Rub kale pieces with oil and place into the multi-level air fryer basket.
3. Place multi-level air fryer basket into the inner pot of the instant pot.
4. Secure pot with air fryer lid, select air fry mode then cook at 400 F for 3 minutes.
5. Serve and enjoy.

Nutritional Value (Amount per Serving):
- Calories 77
- Fat 7 g
- Carbohydrates 3.5 g
- Sugar 0 g
- Protein 1 g
- Cholesterol 0 mg

Crispy Onion Rings

Preparation Time: 10 minutes
Cooking Time: 8 minutes
Serve: 2

Ingredients:
- 1 egg, lightly beaten
- 1 onion, sliced into rings
- 1/2 cup breadcrumbs
- 1/4 tsp chili powder
- Pepper
- Salt

Directions

1. Line multi-level air fryer basket with parchment paper.
2. Add egg in a small bowl and whisk well.
3. In a shallow dish, mix breadcrumbs, chili powder, pepper, and salt.
4. Dip onion slice in egg and coat with breadcrumbs.
5. Place coated onion slices into the multi-level air fryer basket.
6. Place multi-level air fryer basket into the inner pot of the instant pot.
7. Secure pot with air fryer lid, select air fry mode then cook at 350 F for 8 minutes.
8. Serve and enjoy.

Nutritional Value (Amount per Serving):
- Calories 161
- Fat 3.7 g
- Carbohydrates 25 g
- Sugar 4.2 g
- Protein 7 g
- Cholesterol 82 mg

Tasty BBQ Chickpeas

Preparation Time: 10 minutes
Cooking Time: 12 minutes
Serve: 4
Ingredients:
- 14 oz can chickpeas, drained and pat dry
- 1 tsp brown sugar
- 1 1/2 tsp paprika
- 1/4 tsp pepper
- 1 tbsp olive oil
- 1/2 tsp dry mustard
- 1/2 tsp garlic powder
- 1/2 tsp celery salt

Directions:
1. Line multi-level air fryer basket with parchment paper.
2. Add chickpeas into the bowl and toss with remaining ingredients.
3. Add chickpeas into the multi-level air fryer basket.
4. Place multi-level air fryer basket into the inner pot of the instant pot.
5. Secure pot with air fryer lid, select air fry mode then cook at 375 F for 12 minutes. Stir halfway through.
6. Serve and enjoy.

Nutritional Value (Amount per Serving):
- Calories 157
- Fat 4.9 g
- Carbohydrates 24.1 g
- Sugar 0.9 g
- Protein 5.2 g
- Cholesterol 0 mg

Vegetable Fritters

Preparation Time: 10 minutes
Cooking Time: 15 minutes
Serve: 2
Ingredients:
- 1 egg, lightly beaten
- 1 1/2 cups frozen vegetable, steam & mashed
- 1/2 tbsp breadcrumbs
- 1/4 cup cheddar cheese, shredded
- Pepper
- Salt

Directions:
1. Line multi-level air fryer basket with parchment paper.
2. Add all ingredients into the mixing bowl and mix until well combined.
3. Make small patties from mixture and place into the multi-level air fryer basket.
4. Place multi-level air fryer basket into the inner pot of the instant pot.
5. Secure pot with air fryer lid, select air fry mode then cook at 390 F for 15 minutes. Flip halfway through.
6. Serve and enjoy.

Nutritional Value (Amount per Serving):
- Calories 184
- Fat 7.2 g
- Carbohydrates 19.5 g
- Sugar 4.6 g
- Protein 10.4 g
- Cholesterol 97 mg

Cheesy Carrot Fries

Preparation Time: 10 minutes
Cooking Time: 15 minutes
Serve: 4
Ingredients:
- 4 carrots, peeled and cut into fries
- 2 tbsp olive oil
- 2 tbsp Asiago cheese, grated
- Pepper
- Salt

Directions:
1. Line multi-level air fryer basket with parchment paper.
2. Add carrots and remaining ingredients into the bowl and toss well.
3. Add carrot fries into the multi-level air fryer basket.
4. Place multi-level air fryer basket into the inner pot of the instant pot.
5. Secure pot with air fryer lid, select air fry mode then cook at 350 F for 15 minutes. Stir halfway through.
6. Serve and enjoy.

Nutritional Value (Amount per Serving):
- Calories 135
- Fat 11 g
- Carbohydrates 6 g
- Sugar 3 g
- Protein 4 g

- Cholesterol 13 mg

Stuffed Mushrooms

Preparation Time: 10 minutes
Cooking Time: 30 minutes
Serve: 4
Ingredients:
- 20 mushrooms, clean & remove stems
- 2 oz cream cheese, softened
- 1/2 cup cheddar cheese, shredded
- 1 cup chicken, cooked & chopped
- 1/2 tsp garlic, crushed
- 1/8 cup hot sauce
- 1/4 cup mayonnaise
- Pepper
- Salt

Directions:
1. Line multi-level air fryer basket with parchment paper.
2. Add mushrooms into the multi-level air fryer basket.
3. Place multi-level air fryer basket into the inner pot of the instant pot.
4. Secure pot with air fryer lid, select bake mode then cook at 380 F for 15 minutes.
5. Remove mushrooms from the air fryer basket and let it cool completely.
6. In a bowl, mix together chicken, 3/4 cup cheese, cream cheese, mayonnaise, hot sauce, garlic, pepper, and salt.
7. Stuff chicken mixture into each mushroom and top with remaining cheese.
8. Place stuffed mushrooms into the multi-level air fryer basket.
9. Secure pot with air fryer lid, select bake mode then cook at 380 F for 15 minutes.
10. Serve and enjoy.

Nutritional Value (Amount per Serving):
- Calories 237
- Fat 15.9 g
- Carbohydrates 7.3 g
- Sugar 2.7 g
- Protein 17.8 g
- Cholesterol 61 mg

Stuffed Sweet Peppers

Preparation Time: 10 minutes
Cooking Time: 12 minutes
Serve: 6
Ingredients:
- 3 mini sweet peppers, cut in half & remove seeds
- 1/4 tsp garlic powder
- 1 tbsp green onions, sliced
- 2 oz cream cheese
- 1/2 tsp soy sauce
- 1/4 cup cheddar cheese, shredded
- 2 bacon slices, cooked and chopped

Directions:
1. Line multi-level air fryer basket with parchment paper.
2. In a small bowl, mix cream cheese, green onions, garlic powder, bacon slices, cheddar cheese, and soy sauce until well combined.
3. Stuff cream cheese mixture into each pepper half.
4. Place stuff peppers into the multi-level air fryer basket.
5. Place multi-level air fryer basket into the inner pot of the instant pot.
6. Secure pot with air fryer lid, select air fry mode then cook at 400 F for 12 minutes.
7. Serve and enjoy.

Nutritional Value (Amount per Serving):
- Calories 106
- Fat 7.7 g
- Carbohydrates 5.1 g
- Sugar 3.1 g
- Protein 4.9 g
- Cholesterol 22 mg

Easy Cauliflower Popcorn

Preparation Time: 10 minutes
Cooking Time: 30 minutes
Serve: 6
Ingredients:
- 1 medium cauliflower head, cut into florets
- 2 tbsp olive oil
- 3/4 cup breadcrumbs
- 1/4 tsp chili powder
- Pepper
- Salt

Directions:
1. Line multi-level air fryer basket with parchment paper.
2. Add cauliflower florets and remaining ingredients into the mixing bowl and toss well.
3. Add cauliflower florets into the multi-level air fryer basket.
4. Place multi-level air fryer basket into the inner pot of the instant pot.
5. Secure pot with air fryer lid, select air fry mode then cook at 400 F for 30 minutes. Flip halfway through.
6. Serve and enjoy.

Nutritional Value (Amount per Serving):
- Calories 118
- Fat 5.5 g
- Carbohydrates 14.9 g
- Sugar 3.2 g
- Protein 3.7 g
- Cholesterol 0 mg

Cheesy Cauliflower Bites

Preparation Time: 10 minutes
Cooking Time: 15 minutes
Serve: 6

Ingredients:
- 5 eggs whites
- 1/2 cup cauliflower rice
- 1 cup mozzarella cheese, shredded
- Pepper
- Salt

Directions:
1. Line multi-level air fryer basket with parchment paper.
2. Add all ingredients into the bowl and mix until well combined.
3. Pour mixture into mini silicone muffin molds.
4. Place silicone muffin molds into the multi-level air fryer basket.
5. Place multi-level air fryer basket into the inner pot of the instant pot.
6. Secure pot with air fryer lid, select air fry mode then cook at 400 F for 15 minutes.
7. Serve and enjoy.

Nutritional Value (Amount per Serving):
- Calories 64
- Fat 2.3 g
- Carbohydrates 4.9 g
- Sugar 0.2 g
- Protein 5 g
- Cholesterol 3 mg

Easy Cinnamon Cashews

Preparation Time: 10 minutes
Cooking Time: 15 minutes
Serve: 4

Ingredients:
- 1 cup cashews
- 2 tbsp cinnamon

Directions:
1. Line multi-level air fryer basket with parchment paper.
2. Soak cashews into the water overnight. Drain well and pat dry.
3. Season cashews with cinnamon and place into the multi-level air fryer basket.
4. Place multi-level air fryer basket into the inner pot of the instant pot.
5. Secure pot with air fryer lid, select bake mode then cook at 350 F for 15 minutes.
6. Serve and enjoy.

Nutritional Value (Amount per Serving):
- Calories 205
- Fat 15.9 g
- Carbohydrates 13.9 g
- Sugar 1.8 g
- Protein 5.4 g
- Cholesterol 0 mg

Simple Crisp Bacon Slices

Preparation Time: 5 minutes
Cooking Time: 10 minutes
Serve: 5

Ingredients:
- 5 bacon slices

Directions:
1. Line multi-level air fryer basket with parchment paper.
2. Place bacon slices into the multi-level air fryer basket.
3. Place multi-level air fryer basket into the inner pot of the instant pot.
4. Secure pot with air fryer lid, select air fry mode then cook at 400 F for 10 minutes.
5. Serve and enjoy.

Nutritional Value (Amount per Serving):
- Calories 103
- Fat 7.9 g
- Carbohydrates 0.3 g
- Sugar 0 g
- Protein 7 g
- Cholesterol 21 mg

Flavors Jalapeno Poppers

Preparation Time: 10 minutes
Cooking Time: 13 minutes
Serve: 4

Ingredients:
- 4 jalapeno peppers, slice in half and deseeded
- 2 tbsp salsa
- 4 oz goat cheese, crumbled
- 1/4 tsp chili powder
- Pepper
- Salt

Directions:
1. Line multi-level air fryer basket with parchment paper.
2. In a small bowl, mix together cheese, salsa, chili powder, pepper, and salt.
3. Stuff cheese mixture into each jalapeno halves and place it into the multi-level air fryer basket.
4. Place multi-level air fryer basket into the inner pot of the instant pot.
5. Secure pot with air fryer lid, select air fry mode then cook at 350 F for 13 minutes.
6. Serve and enjoy.

Nutritional Value (Amount per Serving):
- Calories 137
- Fat 10.3 g
- Carbohydrates 2.3 g
- Sugar 1.3 g
- Protein 9 g
- Cholesterol 30 mg

Paprika Eggplant Chips

Preparation Time: 5 minutes
Cooking Time: 20 minutes
Serve: 4

Ingredients:
- 1 eggplant, cut into 1-inch slices

- 1 tsp paprika
- 2 tbsp olive oil
- 1/8 tsp cayenne

Directions:
1. Line multi-level air fryer basket with parchment paper.
2. Add all ingredients into the mixing bowl and toss well.
3. Arrange eggplant slices into the multi-level air fryer basket.
4. Place multi-level air fryer basket into the inner pot of the instant pot.
5. Secure pot with air fryer lid, select air fry mode then cook at 375 F for 20 minutes. Flip halfway through.
6. Serve and enjoy.

Nutritional Value (Amount per Serving):
- Calories 90
- Fat 7.3 g
- Carbohydrates 7.1 g
- Sugar 3.5 g
- Protein 1.2 g
- Cholesterol 0 mg

Blue Cheese Jalapeno Poppers

Preparation Time: 10 minutes
Cooking Time: 20 minutes
Serve: 5

Ingredients:
- 5 jalapeno peppers, halved and remove seeds
- 1/2 tsp garlic powder
- 5 oz blue cheese
- 4 oz cream cheese, softened
- 3 oz bacon, cooked and crumbled

Directions:
1. Line multi-level air fryer basket with parchment paper.
2. In a bowl, mix together cream cheese, bacon, blue cheese, and garlic powder.
3. Stuff cheese mixture into each jalapeno half and place it into the multi-level air fryer basket.
4. Place multi-level air fryer basket into the inner pot of the instant pot.
5. Secure pot with air fryer lid, select bake mode then cook at 350 F for 20 minutes.
6. Serve and enjoy.

Nutritional Value (Amount per Serving):
- Calories 278
- Fat 23.4 g
- Carbohydrates 2.7 g
- Sugar 0.7 g
- Protein 14.3 g
- Cholesterol 65 mg

Chapter 8: Dehydrate

Dehydrated Brussels Sprouts

Preparation Time: 10 minutes
Cooking Time: 8 hours
Serve: 4
Ingredients:
- 1 lb Brussels sprouts, cut the root and separate leaves
- 2 tbsp nutritional yeast
- 1/2 cup cashews
- 1 bell peppers
- 1 fresh lemon juice
- 1/4 cup water
- 1/2 tsp sea salt

Directions:
1. Line multi-level air fryer basket with parchment paper.
2. Add Brussels sprouts into the bowl and set aside.
3. Add remaining ingredients into the blender and blend until smooth.
4. Pour blended mixture over sprouts and toss well.
5. Arrange Brussels sprouts into the multi-level air fryer basket.
6. Place multi-level air fryer basket into the inner pot of the instant pot.
7. Secure pot with air fryer lid, select dehydrate mode then cook at 125 F for 8 hours.

Nutritional Value (Amount per Serving):
- Calories 177
- Fat 8.8 g
- Carbohydrates 20.7 g
- Sugar 5.1 g
- Protein 9.2 g
- Cholesterol 0 mg

Dehydrated Zucchini Chips

Preparation Time: 10 minutes
Cooking Time: 6 hours
Serve: 2
Ingredients:
- 1 zucchini, cut into 1/4-inch slices
- 1/2 tsp olive oil
- 1/8 tsp cayenne pepper
- Salt

Directions:
1. Line multi-level air fryer basket with parchment paper.
2. Add all ingredients into the bowl and toss well.
3. Arrange zucchini slices into the multi-level air fryer basket.
4. Place multi-level air fryer basket into the inner pot of the instant pot.
5. Secure pot with air fryer lid, select dehydrate mode then cook at 135 F for 6 hours.

Nutritional Value (Amount per Serving):
- Calories 26
- Fat 1.4 g
- Carbohydrates 3.3 g
- Sugar 1.7 g
- Protein 1.2 g
- Cholesterol 0 mg

Dehydrated Eggplant Slices

Preparation Time: 10 minutes
Cooking Time: 4 hours
Serve: 4
Ingredients:
- 1 eggplant, cut into 1/4-inch thick slices
- 1 tsp paprika

Directions:
1. Line multi-level air fryer basket with parchment paper.
2. Arrange eggplant slices into the multi-level air fryer basket. Sprinkle with paprika.
3. Place multi-level air fryer basket into the inner pot of the instant pot.
4. Secure pot with air fryer lid, select dehydrate mode then cook at 145 F for 4 hours.

Nutritional Value (Amount per Serving):
- Calories 30
- Fat 0.3 g
- Carbohydrates 7 g
- Sugar 3.5 g
- Protein 1.2 g
- Cholesterol 0 mg

Dehydrated Zucchini Chips

Preparation Time: 10 minutes
Cooking Time: 8 hours
Serve: 4
Ingredients:
- 2 cups zucchini, sliced thinly
- 1 tbsp vinegar
- 1 tbsp olive oil
- 1 tsp sea salt

Directions:
1. Line multi-level air fryer basket with parchment paper.
2. Add zucchini slices, vinegar, oil, and salt into the bowl and toss well.
3. Arrange zucchini slices into the multi-level air fryer basket.
4. Place multi-level air fryer basket into the inner pot of the instant pot.
5. Secure pot with air fryer lid, select dehydrate mode then cook at 135 F for 8 hours.

Nutritional Value (Amount per Serving):
- Calories 40
- Fat 3.6 g
- Carbohydrates 1.9 g
- Sugar 1 g

- Protein 0.7 g
- Cholesterol 0 mg

Dehydrated Carrots

Preparation Time: 10 minutes
Cooking Time: 8 hours
Serve: 2
Ingredients:
- 1 1/2 cups shredded carrots
- 1/2 tbsp sugar
- 1 tbsp coconut oil, melted
- 1/4 tsp ground cinnamon
- 1/4 tsp sea salt

Directions:
1. Line multi-level air fryer basket with parchment paper.
2. Add shredded carrots, sugar, oil, cinnamon, and salt into the bowl and toss well.
3. Spread shredded carrots into the multi-level air fryer basket.
4. Place multi-level air fryer basket into the inner pot of the instant pot.
5. Secure pot with air fryer lid, select dehydrate mode then cook at 125 F for 8 hours.

Nutritional Value (Amount per Serving):
- Calories 104
- Fat 6.8 g
- Carbohydrates 11.3 g
- Sugar 7.1 g
- Protein 0.7 g
- Cholesterol 0 mg

Dehydrated Cauliflower Popcorn

Preparation Time: 10 minutes
Cooking Time: 8 hours
Serve: 4
Ingredients:
- 3 cups cauliflower florets
- 1 tbsp nutritional yeast
- 1 tbsp olive oil
- 1 tsp chili powder
- 1 tsp ground cumin
- Salt

Directions:
1. Line multi-level air fryer basket with parchment paper.
2. Add all ingredients into the bowl and toss well.
3. Place cauliflower florets into the multi-level air fryer basket.
4. Place multi-level air fryer basket into the inner pot of the instant pot.
5. Secure pot with air fryer lid, select dehydrate mode then cook at 115 F for 8 hours.

Nutritional Value (Amount per Serving):
- Calories 62
- Fat 4 g
- Carbohydrates 5.7 g
- Sugar 1.9 g
- Protein 2.8 g
- Cholesterol 0 mg

Dehydrated Broccoli Chips

Preparation Time: 10 minutes
Cooking Time: 8 hours
Serve: 3
Ingredients:
- 1/2 lb broccoli florets
- 2 tbsp hemp seeds
- 1 tbsp nutritional yeast
- 1/2 tsp onion powder
- 1/4 cup vegetable broth

Directions:
1. Line multi-level air fryer basket with parchment paper.
2. Add broccoli florets in a bowl and set aside.
3. Add remaining ingredients into the blender and blend until smooth.
4. Pour blended mixture over broccoli and toss well.
5. Place broccoli florets into the multi-level air fryer basket.
6. Place multi-level air fryer basket into the inner pot of the instant pot.
7. Secure pot with air fryer lid, select dehydrate mode then cook at 115 F for 8 hours.

Nutritional Value (Amount per Serving):
- Calories 42
- Fat 0.5 g
- Carbohydrates 7 g
- Sugar 1.5 g
- Protein 4.1 g
- Cholesterol 0 mg

Dehydrated Squash Chips

Preparation Time: 10 minutes
Cooking Time: 10 hours
Serve: 4
Ingredients:
- 1 yellow squash, cut into 1/8-inch thick slices
- 2 tsp olive oil
- 2 tbsp vinegar
- Salt

Directions:
1. Line multi-level air fryer basket with parchment paper.
2. Add all ingredients into the bowl and toss well.
3. Arrange squash slices into the multi-level air fryer basket.
4. Place multi-level air fryer basket into the inner pot of the instant pot.
5. Secure pot with air fryer lid, select dehydrate mode then cook at 115 F for 10 hours.

Nutritional Value (Amount per Serving):
- Calories 29

- Fat 2.4 g
- Carbohydrates 1.7 g
- Sugar 0.9 g
- Protein 0.6 g
- Cholesterol 0 mg

Dehydrated Sweet Potato Chips

Preparation Time: 10 minutes
Cooking Time: 6 hours
Serve: 2
Ingredients:
- 1 sweet potato, peel and sliced thinly
- 1/2 tsp coconut oil, melted
- 1/8 tsp ground cinnamon
- Seal salt

Directions:
1. Line multi-level air fryer basket with parchment paper.
2. Add all ingredients into the bowl and toss well.
3. Arrange sweet potato slices into the multi-level air fryer basket.
4. Place multi-level air fryer basket into the inner pot of the instant pot.
5. Secure pot with air fryer lid, select dehydrate mode then cook at 125 F for 6 hours.

Nutritional Value (Amount per Serving):
- Calories 134
- Fat 2.8 g
- Carbohydrates 25 g
- Sugar 1.4 g
- Protein 2.7 g
- Cholesterol 0 mg

Dehydrated Bell Peppers

Preparation Time: 10 minutes
Cooking Time: 12 hours
Serve: 2
Ingredients:
- 2 bell peppers, cut into 1/2-inch pieces

Directions:
1. Line multi-level air fryer basket with parchment paper.
2. Arrange bell peppers pieces into the multi-level air fryer basket.
3. Place multi-level air fryer basket into the inner pot of the instant pot.
4. Secure pot with air fryer lid, select dehydrate mode then cook at 135 F for 12 minutes.

Nutritional Value (Amount per Serving):
- Calories 38
- Fat 0.3 g
- Carbohydrates 9 g
- Sugar 6 g
- Protein 1.2 g
- Cholesterol 0 mg

Dehydrated Kale Chips

Preparation Time: 10 minutes
Cooking Time: 3 hours
Serve: 2
Ingredients:
- 1 kale heads, cut into pieces
- 1/2 tbsp fresh lemon juice
- 1 1/2 tbsp nutritional yeast
- 1 tbsp olive oil
- 1/2 tsp garlic powder
- 1/2 tsp sea salt

Directions:
1. Line multi-level air fryer basket with parchment paper.
2. Add kale and remaining ingredients into the bowl and mix well.
3. Arrange kale into the multi-level air fryer basket.
4. Place multi-level air fryer basket into the inner pot of the instant pot.
5. Secure pot with air fryer lid, select dehydrate mode then cook at 145 F for 3 hours.

Nutritional Value (Amount per Serving):
- Calories 111
- Fat 7.5 g
- Carbohydrates 8.5 g
- Sugar 0.3 g
- Protein 4.9 g
- Cholesterol 0 mg

Dehydrated Kiwi

Preparation Time: 10 minutes
Cooking Time: 6 hours
Serve: 3
Ingredients:
- 3 kiwis, peeled and cut into 1/4-inch thick slices
- 1 tbsp lemon juice

Directions:
1. Line multi-level air fryer basket with parchment paper.
2. Brush kiwi slices with lemon juice and arrange into the multi-level air fryer basket.
3. Place multi-level air fryer basket into the inner pot of the instant pot.
4. Secure pot with air fryer lid, select dehydrate mode then cook at 135 F for 6 hours.

Nutritional Value (Amount per Serving):
- Calories 48
- Fat 0.4 g
- Carbohydrates 11.3 g
- Sugar 6.9 g
- Protein 0.9 g
- Cholesterol 0 mg

Dehydrated Pecans

Preparation Time: 10 minutes
Cooking Time: 12 hours
Serve: 4
Ingredients:

- 1 cup pecan halves, soaked in water overnight
- 1/8 tsp nutmeg
- 1/2 tsp cinnamon
- 1/2 cup maple syrup

Directions:
1. Line multi-level air fryer basket with parchment paper.
2. Add all ingredients into the bowl and toss well.
3. Arrange pecans into the multi-level air fryer basket.
4. Place multi-level air fryer basket into the inner pot of the instant pot.
5. Secure pot with air fryer lid, select dehydrate mode then cook at 105 F for 12 hours.

Nutritional Value (Amount per Serving):
- Calories 208
- Fat 10.8 g
- Carbohydrates 28.8 g
- Sugar 24 g
- Protein 1.6 g
- Cholesterol 0 mg

Dehydrated Raspberries

Preparation Time: 10 minutes
Cooking Time: 12 hours
Serve: 2

Ingredients:
- 2 cups raspberries, wash and dry
- 2 tbsp lemon juice

Directions:
1. Line multi-level air fryer basket with parchment paper.
2. Add raspberries and lemon juice in a bowl and toss well.
3. Arrange raspberries into the multi-level air fryer basket.
4. Place multi-level air fryer basket into the inner pot of the instant pot.
5. Secure pot with air fryer lid, select dehydrate mode then cook at 135 F for 12 hours.

Nutritional Value (Amount per Serving):
- Calories 68
- Fat 0.9 g
- Carbohydrates 15 g
- Sugar 5.8 g
- Protein 1.6 g
- Cholesterol 0 mg

Dehydrated Almonds

Preparation Time: 10 minutes
Cooking Time: 12 hours
Serve: 2

Ingredients:
- 1 cups almonds, soak in water for overnight
- 1/2 tbsp fresh rosemary, chopped
- 1/2 tsp chili powder
- 1/2 tbsp olive oil
- Kosher salt

Directions:
1. Line multi-level air fryer basket with parchment paper.
2. Add all ingredients into the bowl and toss well.
3. Arrange almonds into the multi-level air fryer basket.
4. Place multi-level air fryer basket into the inner pot of the instant pot.
5. Secure pot with air fryer lid, select dehydrate mode then cook at 125 F for 12 hours.

Nutritional Value (Amount per Serving):
- Calories 310
- Fat 27.5 g
- Carbohydrates 11.1 g
- Sugar 2.1 g
- Protein 10.2 g
- Cholesterol 0 mg

Dehydrated Strawberries

Preparation Time: 10 minutes
Cooking Time: 6 hours
Serve: 2

Ingredients:
- 1 cup strawberries, sliced 1/4-inch thick

Directions:
1. Line multi-level air fryer basket with parchment paper.
2. Arrange strawberry slices into the multi-level air fryer basket.
3. Place multi-level air fryer basket into the inner pot of the instant pot.
4. Secure pot with air fryer lid, select dehydrate mode then cook at 135 F for 6 hours.

Nutritional Value (Amount per Serving):
- Calories 23
- Fat 0.2 g
- Carbohydrates 5.5 g
- Sugar 3.5 g
- Protein 0.5 g
- Cholesterol 0 mg

Dehydrated Pineapple Slices

Preparation Time: 10 minutes
Cooking Time: 8 hours
Serve: 6

Ingredients:
- 6 pineapple slices, 1/8-inch thick

Directions:
1. Line multi-level air fryer basket with parchment paper.
2. Arrange pineapple slices into the multi-level air fryer basket.
3. Place multi-level air fryer basket into the inner pot of the instant pot.
4. Secure pot with air fryer lid, select dehydrate mode then cook at 125 F for 8 hours.

Nutritional Value (Amount per Serving):

- Calories 82
- Fat 0.2 g
- Carbohydrates 21.7 g
- Sugar 16.3 g
- Protein 0.9 g
- Cholesterol 0 mg

Dehydrated Green Apple Slices

Preparation Time: 10 minutes
Cooking Time: 6 hours
Serve: 2
Ingredients:
- 2 green apples, cored and sliced 1/8-inch thick
- 1/2 lemon juice

Directions:
1. Line multi-level air fryer basket with parchment paper.
2. Add apple slices and lime juice in a bowl and toss well.
3. Arrange apple slices into the multi-level air fryer basket.
4. Place multi-level air fryer basket into the inner pot of the instant pot.
5. Secure pot with air fryer lid, select dehydrate mode then cook at 145 F for 6 hours.

Nutritional Value (Amount per Serving):
- Calories 119
- Fat 0.5 g
- Carbohydrates 31.1 g
- Sugar 23.5 g
- Protein 0.7 g
- Cholesterol 0 mg

Dehydrated Mango

Preparation Time: 10 minutes
Cooking Time: 6 hours
Serve: 2
Ingredients:
- 1 mango, peel, & cut into 1/4-inch thick slices

Directions:
1. Line multi-level air fryer basket with parchment paper.
2. Arrange mango slices into the multi-level air fryer basket.
3. Place multi-level air fryer basket into the inner pot of the instant pot.
4. Secure pot with air fryer lid, select dehydrate mode then cook at 135 F for 6 hours.

Nutritional Value (Amount per Serving):
- Calories 101
- Fat 0.6 g
- Carbohydrates 25.2 g
- Sugar 23 g
- Protein 1.4 g
- Cholesterol 0 mg

Dehydrated Apple Chips

Preparation Time: 10 minutes
Cooking Time: 8 hours
Serve: 2
Ingredients:
- 2 apples, cored, sliced 1/8-inch thick
- 1 tbsp lemon juice
- 1 tbsp vinegar
- 1/2 tsp ground cinnamon
- 1 cup of water

Directions:
1. Line multi-level air fryer basket with parchment paper.
2. In a bowl, add water, lemon juice, and vinegar and mix well. Add apple slices and let sit for 5 minutes.
3. Remove apple slices from water and pat dry.
4. Arrange apple slices into the multi-level air fryer basket.
5. Place multi-level air fryer basket into the inner pot of the instant pot.
6. Secure pot with air fryer lid, select dehydrate mode then cook at 135 F for 8 hours.

Nutritional Value (Amount per Serving):
- Calories 121
- Fat 0.5 g
- Carbohydrates 31.5 g
- Sugar 23.4 g
- Protein 0.7 g
- Cholesterol 0 mg

Dehydrated Spicy Almonds

Preparation Time: 10 minutes
Cooking Time: 12 hours
Serve: 4
Ingredients:
- 1 cup almonds, soaked in water for overnight, drain & pat dry
- 1/2 tbsp olive oil
- 1/2 tsp red chili powder
- 1/8 tsp paprika

Directions:
1. Line multi-level air fryer basket with parchment paper.
2. Toss almonds with oil, chili powder, and paprika.
3. Spread almonds into the multi-level air fryer basket.
4. Place multi-level air fryer basket into the inner pot of the instant pot.
5. Secure pot with air fryer lid, select dehydrate mode then cook at 125 F for 12 hours.

Nutritional Value (Amount per Serving):
- Calories 154
- Fat 13.7 g
- Carbohydrates 5.3 g
- Sugar 1 g
- Protein 5.1 g

- Cholesterol 0 mg

Dehydrated Peach

Preparation Time: 10 minutes
Cooking Time: 6 hours
Serve: 2
Ingredients:
- 2 peaches, cut and remove pits and sliced
- 1/4 cup lemon juice

Directions:
1. Line multi-level air fryer basket with parchment paper.
2. Add lemon juice and peach slices into the bowl and toss well.
3. Arrange peach slices into the multi-level air fryer basket.
4. Place multi-level air fryer basket into the inner pot of the instant pot.
5. Secure pot with air fryer lid, select dehydrate mode then cook at 135 F for 6 hours.

Nutritional Value (Amount per Serving):
- Calories 66
- Fat 0.6 g
- Carbohydrates 14.6 g
- Sugar 14.6 g
- Protein 1.6 g
- Cholesterol 0 mg

Dehydrated Bananas

Preparation Time: 10 minutes
Cooking Time: 6 hours
Serve: 2
Ingredients:
- 2 bananas, cut into 1/8-inch thick slices
- 1/2 cup fresh lemon juice

Directions:
1. Line multi-level air fryer basket with parchment paper.
2. Add sliced bananas and lemon juice in a bowl and toss well.
3. Arrange banana slices into the multi-level air fryer basket.
4. Place multi-level air fryer basket into the inner pot of the instant pot.
5. Secure pot with air fryer lid, select dehydrate mode then cook at 135 F for 6 hours.

Nutritional Value (Amount per Serving):
- Calories 120
- Fat 0.9 g
- Carbohydrates 28.2 g
- Sugar 15.7 g
- Protein 1.8 g
- Cholesterol 0 mg

Dehydrated Mango

Preparation Time: 10 minutes
Cooking Time: 6 hours
Serve: 3
Ingredients:
- 2 mangoes, Peel & cut into 1/4-inch thick slices
- 2 tbsp lemon juice
- 1/2 tbsp honey

Directions:
1. Line multi-level air fryer basket with parchment paper.
2. In a bowl, mix together lemon juice and honey and set aside. Add mango slices and coat well.
3. Arrange mango slices into the multi-level air fryer basket.
4. Place multi-level air fryer basket into the inner pot of the instant pot.
5. Secure pot with air fryer lid, select dehydrate mode then cook at 135 F for 6 hours.

Nutritional Value (Amount per Serving):
- Calories 147
- Fat 0.9 g
- Carbohydrates 36.7 g
- Sugar 33.7 g
- Protein 1.9 g
- Cholesterol 0 mg

Dehydrated Pork Jerky

Preparation Time: 10 minutes
Cooking Time: 4 hours
Serve: 3
Ingredients:
- 1/2 lb pork loin, cut into thin slices
- 1/2 tsp sesame oil
- 1/2 tbsp chili sauce
- 1/2 tbsp brown sugar
- 1/2 tbsp Worcestershire sauce
- 1/4 tsp onion powder
- 1/4 tsp garlic powder
- 2 tbsp soy sauce
- 1/2 tsp black pepper
- Salt

Directions:
1. Line multi-level air fryer basket with parchment paper.
2. Add all ingredients except meat slices into the bowl and mix well.
3. Add sliced meat in the bowl and mix well.
4. Cover the bowl and place it in the refrigerator overnight.
5. Arrange marinated meat slices into the multi-level air fryer basket.
6. Place multi-level air fryer basket into the inner pot of the instant pot.
7. Secure pot with air fryer lid, select dehydrate mode then cook at 160 F for 4 hours.

Nutritional Value (Amount per Serving):
- Calories 206
- Fat 11.3 g
- Carbohydrates 3.4 g
- Sugar 2.3 g
- Protein 21.4 g
- Cholesterol 60 mg

Dehydrated Eggplant

Preparation Time: 10 minutes
Cooking Time: 4 hours
Serve: 2
Ingredients:
- 1 eggplant, cut into 1/4-inch thick slices

Directions:
1. Line multi-level air fryer basket with parchment paper.
2. Arrange eggplant slices into the multi-level air fryer basket.
3. Place multi-level air fryer basket into the inner pot of the instant pot.
4. Secure pot with air fryer lid, select dehydrate mode then cook at 145 F for 4 hours.

Nutritional Value (Amount per Serving):
- Calories 57
- Fat 0.4 g
- Carbohydrates 13.5 g
- Sugar 6.9 g
- Protein 2.2 g
- Cholesterol 0 mg

Dehydrated Turkey Jerky

Preparation Time: 10 minutes
Cooking Time: 4 hours
Serve: 2
Ingredients:
- 1/2 lb turkey meat, cut into thin slices
- 1 tsp brown sugar
- 2 tbsp Worcestershire sauce
- 1/8 tsp Tabasco sauce
- 1 tbsp soy sauce
- 1/2 tbsp liquid smoke
- 1 tsp garlic powder
- 1/2 tbsp onion powder
- 1/4 tsp salt

Directions:
1. Line multi-level air fryer basket with parchment paper.
2. Add all ingredients except meat in the zip-lock bag and mix until well combined.
3. Add meat slices to the bag, seal bag, and place in the refrigerator overnight.
4. Arrange marinated meat slices into the multi-level air fryer basket.
5. Place multi-level air fryer basket into the inner pot of the instant pot.
6. Secure pot with air fryer lid, select dehydrate mode then cook at 160 F for 4 hours.

Nutritional Value (Amount per Serving):
- Calories 228
- Fat 5.7 g
- Carbohydrates 7.5 g
- Sugar 5.6 g
- Protein 34.1 g
- Cholesterol 86 mg

Dehydrated Cucumber Slices

Preparation Time: 10 minutes
Cooking Time: 12 hours
Serve: 2
Ingredients:
- 1 cucumber, sliced
- Pepper
- Salt

Directions:
1. Line multi-level air fryer basket with parchment paper.
2. Arrange cucumber slices into the multi-level air fryer basket.
3. Place multi-level air fryer basket into the inner pot of the instant pot.
4. Secure pot with air fryer lid, select dehydrate mode then cook at 135 F for 12 hours.

Nutritional Value (Amount per Serving):
- Calories 23
- Fat 0.2 g
- Carbohydrates 5.5 g
- Sugar 2.5 g
- Protein 1 g
- Cholesterol 0 mg

Dehydrated Beet

Preparation Time: 10 minutes
Cooking Time: 10 hours
Serve: 2
Ingredients:
- 1 beet, sliced thinly

Directions:
1. Line multi-level air fryer basket with parchment paper.
2. Arrange beet slices into the multi-level air fryer basket.
3. Place multi-level air fryer basket into the inner pot of the instant pot.
4. Secure pot with air fryer lid, select dehydrate mode then cook at 135 F for 10 hours.

Nutritional Value (Amount per Serving):
- Calories 22
- Fat 0.1 g
- Carbohydrates 5 g
- Sugar 4 g
- Protein 0.8 g
- Cholesterol 0 mg

Dehydrated Tomato

Preparation Time: 10 minutes
Cooking Time: 6 hours
Serve: 2
Ingredients:
- 2 tomatoes, sliced thinly
- Pepper
- Salt

Directions:

1. Line multi-level air fryer basket with parchment paper.
2. Arrange tomato slices into the multi-level air fryer basket.
3. Place multi-level air fryer basket into the inner pot of the instant pot.
4. Secure pot with air fryer lid, select dehydrate mode then cook at 135 F for 6 hours.

Nutritional Value (Amount per Serving):
- Calories 22
- Fat 0.3 g
- Carbohydrates 4.8 g
- Sugar 3.2 g
- Protein 1.1 g
- Cholesterol 0 mg

Dehydrated Beef Jerky

Preparation Time: 10 minutes
Cooking Time: 6 hours
Serve: 3

Ingredients:
- 1/2 lb flank steak, cut into thin slices
- 1/2 tbsp red pepper flakes
- 1/2 tbsp ranch seasoning
- 2 tbsp Worcestershire sauce
- 1/8 tsp cayenne pepper
- 1/2 tsp liquid smoke
- 1 tbsp soy sauce

Directions:
1. Line multi-level air fryer basket with parchment paper.
2. Add all ingredients into the large bowl and mix well, cover and place in the refrigerator overnight.
3. Arrange marinated meat slices into the multi-level air fryer basket.
4. Place multi-level air fryer basket into the inner pot of the instant pot.
5. Secure pot with air fryer lid, select dehydrate mode then cook at 145 F for 6 minutes.

Nutritional Value (Amount per Serving):
- Calories 168
- Fat 6.5 g
- Carbohydrates 3 g
- Sugar 2.2 g
- Protein 21.5 g
- Cholesterol 42 mg

Dehydrated Flank Steak Jerky

Preparation Time: 10 minutes
Cooking Time: 4 hours
Serve: 4

Ingredients:
- 1 lb flank steak, cut into 1/4-inch thick slices
- 2 tbsp coconut amino
- 1 tbsp garlic powder

Directions:
1. Line multi-level air fryer basket with parchment paper.
2. Add all ingredients into the zip-lock bag, seal bag, and place in the refrigerator overnight.
3. Remove meat slices from marinade and place it into the multi-level air fryer basket.
4. Place multi-level air fryer basket into the inner pot of the instant pot.
5. Secure pot with air fryer lid, select dehydrate mode then cook at 145 F for 4 hours.

Nutritional Value (Amount per Serving):
- Calories 227
- Fat 9.5 g
- Carbohydrates 3 g
- Sugar 0.5 g
- Protein 31.9 g
- Cholesterol 62 mg

Dehydrated Green Beans

Preparation Time: 10 minutes
Cooking Time: 6 hours
Serve: 2

Ingredients:
- 1/2 lb green beans
- Salt

Directions:
1. Line multi-level air fryer basket with parchment paper.
2. Arrange green beans into the multi-level air fryer basket. Season with salt.
3. Place multi-level air fryer basket into the inner pot of the instant pot.
4. Secure pot with air fryer lid, select dehydrate mode then cook at 125 F for 6 hours.

Nutritional Value (Amount per Serving):
- Calories 35
- Fat 0.1 g
- Carbohydrates 8.1 g
- Sugar 1.6 g
- Protein 2.1 g
- Cholesterol 0 mg

Dehydrated Parsnips

Preparation Time: 10 minutes
Cooking Time: 6 hours
Serve: 3

Ingredients:
- 2 parsnips, peel & thinly sliced
- Salt

Directions:
1. Line multi-level air fryer basket with parchment paper.
2. Arrange parsnips slices into the multi-level air fryer basket. Season with salt.
3. Place multi-level air fryer basket into the inner pot of the instant pot.
4. Secure pot with air fryer lid, select dehydrate mode then cook at 115 F for 6 minutes.

Nutritional Value (Amount per Serving):

- Calories 67
- Fat 0.3 g
- Carbohydrates 16 g
- Sugar 4.3 g
- Protein 1.1 g
- Cholesterol 0 mg

Dehydrated Salmon Jerky

Preparation Time: 10 minutes
Cooking Time: 4 hours
Serve: 2
Ingredients:
- 1 lb salmon, sliced in strips
- 1 tbsp black pepper
- 1/2 cup brown sugar
- 1/2 cup soy sauce
- 1/2 orange juice
- 1 1/2 tsp black pepper
- 2 tbsp liquid smoke
- 1 1/2 tbsp smoked sea salt

Directions:
1. Line multi-level air fryer basket with parchment paper.
2. Add all ingredients into the zip-lock bag, seal bag, and place in the refrigerator overnight.
3. Arrange marinated salmon slices into the multi-level air fryer basket.
4. Place multi-level air fryer basket into the inner pot of the instant pot.
5. Secure pot with air fryer lid, select dehydrate mode then cook at 160 F for 4 minutes.

Nutritional Value (Amount per Serving):
- Calories 493
- Fat 14.2 g
- Carbohydrates 45.7 g
- Sugar 38.1 g
- Protein 48.7 g
- Cholesterol 100 mg

Dehydrated Carrot

Preparation Time: 10 minutes
Cooking Time: 8 hours
Serve: 2
Ingredients:
- 2 carrots, peel & thinly sliced
- Salt

Directions:
1. Line multi-level air fryer basket with parchment paper.
2. Arrange carrot slices into the multi-level air fryer basket. Season with salt.
3. Place multi-level air fryer basket into the inner pot of the instant pot.
4. Secure pot with air fryer lid, select dehydrate mode then cook at 115 F for 8 hours.

Nutritional Value (Amount per Serving):
- Calories 25
- Fat 0 g
- Carbohydrates 6 g
- Sugar 3 g
- Protein 0.5 g
- Cholesterol 0 mg

Dehydrated Chicken Jerky

Preparation Time: 10 minutes
Cooking Time: 4 hours
Serve: 2
Ingredients:
- 1/2 lb chicken tenders, boneless, skinless and cut into 1/4-inch strips
- 1/4 tsp garlic powder
- 1/2 tsp lemon juice
- 1/4 cup soy sauce
- 1/8 tsp ground ginger
- 1/8 tsp black pepper

Directions:
1. Line multi-level air fryer basket with parchment paper.
2. Add all ingredients into the zip-lock bag, seal bag, and place in the refrigerator for 1 hour.
3. Arrange marinated meat slices into the multi-level air fryer basket.
4. Place multi-level air fryer basket into the inner pot of the instant pot.
5. Secure pot with air fryer lid, select dehydrate mode then cook at 145 F for 4 hours.

Nutritional Value (Amount per Serving):
- Calories 235
- Fat 8.4 g
- Carbohydrates 2.9 g
- Sugar 0.7 g
- Protein 34.9 g
- Cholesterol 101 mg

Dehydrated Dragon Fruit

Preparation Time: 10 minutes
Cooking Time: 6 hours
Serve: 2
Ingredients:
- 1 dragon fruit, peel & cut into 1/4-inch thick slices

Directions:
1. Line multi-level air fryer basket with parchment paper.
2. Arrange dragon fruit slices into the multi-level air fryer basket.
3. Place multi-level air fryer basket into the inner pot of the instant pot.
4. Secure pot with air fryer lid, select dehydrate mode then cook at 115 F for 6 hours.

Nutritional Value (Amount per Serving):
- Calories 23
- Fat 0 g
- Carbohydrates 6 g
- Sugar 6 g
- Protein 0 g

Dehydrated Asian Salmon Jerky

Preparation Time: 10 minutes
Cooking Time: 3 hours
Serve: 3
Ingredients:
- 1/2 lb salmon, cut into 1/4-inch slices
- 1 tbsp fresh lemon juice
- 1/2 tbsp molasses
- 1/4 cup soy sauce
- 1/4 tsp liquid smoke
- 1/2 tsp black pepper

Directions:
1. Line multi-level air fryer basket with parchment paper.
2. Add all ingredients into the zip-lock bag, seal bag, and place in the refrigerator overnight.
3. Arrange marinated salmon slices into the multi-level air fryer basket.
4. Place multi-level air fryer basket into the inner pot of the instant pot.
5. Secure pot with air fryer lid, select dehydrate mode then cook at 145 F for 3 hours.

Nutritional Value (Amount per Serving):
- Calories 123
- Fat 4.7 g
- Carbohydrates 4.5 g
- Sugar 2.3 g
- Protein 16.1 g
- Cholesterol 33 mg

Dehydrated Orange

Preparation Time: 10 minutes
Cooking Time: 6 hours
Serve: 2
Ingredients:
- 2 oranges, peel & cut into slices

Directions:
1. Line multi-level air fryer basket with parchment paper.
2. Arrange orange slices into the multi-level air fryer basket.
3. Place multi-level air fryer basket into the inner pot of the instant pot.
4. Secure pot with air fryer lid, select dehydrate mode then cook at 135 F for 6 hours.

Nutritional Value (Amount per Serving):
- Calories 86
- Fat 0.2 g
- Carbohydrates 21.6 g
- Sugar 17.2 g
- Protein 1.7 g
- Cholesterol 0 mg

Dehydrated Mexican Pork Jerky

Preparation Time: 10 minutes
Cooking Time: 4 hours
Serve: 2
Ingredients:
- 1/2 lb pork lean meat, sliced thinly
- 1/4 tsp garlic powder
- 1/2 tsp chili powder
- 1/2 tsp paprika
- 1/4 tsp oregano
- 1/8 tsp black pepper
- 1/2 tsp salt

Directions:
1. Line multi-level air fryer basket with parchment paper.
2. Add all ingredients into the zip-lock bag, seal bag, and place in the refrigerator overnight.
3. Arrange marinated meat slices into the multi-level air fryer basket.
4. Place multi-level air fryer basket into the inner pot of the instant pot.
5. Secure pot with air fryer lid, select dehydrate mode then cook at 160 F for 4 hours.

Nutritional Value (Amount per Serving):
- Calories 266
- Fat 13.9 g
- Carbohydrates 1.1 g
- Sugar 0.2 g
- Protein 32.5 g
- Cholesterol 101 mg

Dehydrated Lamb Jerky

Preparation Time: 10 minutes
Cooking Time: 3 hours
Serve: 3
Ingredients:
- 1 lb lamb, boneless & cut into thin strips
- 1/2 tsp onion powder
- 1 1/2 tbsp Worcestershire sauce
- 2 tbsp soy sauce
- 1/4 tsp black pepper
- 1/2 tbsp oregano
- 1/2 tsp garlic powder

Directions:
1. Line multi-level air fryer basket with parchment paper.
2. Add all ingredients into the zip-lock bag, seal bag, and place in the refrigerator overnight.
3. Arrange marinated meat slices into the multi-level air fryer basket.
4. Place multi-level air fryer basket into the inner pot of the instant pot.
5. Secure pot with air fryer lid, select dehydrate mode then cook at 145 F for 3 hours.

Nutritional Value (Amount per Serving):
- Calories 300
- Fat 11.2 g
- Carbohydrates 3.6 g
- Sugar 2 g
- Protein 43.4 g
- Cholesterol 136 mg

Dehydrated Teriyaki Beef Jerky

Preparation Time: 10 minutes
Cooking Time: 3 hours
Serve: 3
Ingredients:
- 1/2 lbs beef bottom round thin meat
- 1 tbsp Worcestershire sauce
- 1/2 tsp liquid smoke
- 1/4 cup teriyaki sauce
- 1/2 tsp onion powder
- 1/2 tsp garlic, minced
- 1/2 tsp red pepper flakes
- 2 tbsp soy sauce

Directions:
1. Line multi-level air fryer basket with parchment paper.
2. Cut meat into the thin slices.
3. Add all ingredients into the zip-lock bag, seal bag, and place in the refrigerator overnight.
4. Arrange marinated meat slices into the multi-level air fryer basket.
5. Place multi-level air fryer basket into the inner pot of the instant pot.
6. Secure pot with air fryer lid, select dehydrate mode then cook at 160 F for 3 hours.

Nutritional Value (Amount per Serving):
- Calories 169
- Fat 5 g
- Carbohydrates 6.2 g
- Sugar 4.7 g
- Protein 23.2 g
- Cholesterol 67 mg

Dehydrated Spicy Beef Jerky

Preparation Time: 10 minutes
Cooking Time: 3 hours
Serve: 4
Ingredients:
- 1 lb flank steak, trimmed fat and sliced into thin strips
- 1 tsp black pepper
- 1/2 tbsp brown sugar
- 5 tbsp soy sauce
- 5 tbsp Worcestershire sauce
- 1/2 tsp red pepper flakes
- 1/2 tsp liquid smoke
- 1/2 tsp garlic powder
- 1/2 tsp onion powder

Directions:
1. Line multi-level air fryer basket with parchment paper.
2. Add all ingredients into the zip-lock bag, seal bag, and place in the refrigerator overnight.
3. Arrange marinated meat slices into the multi-level air fryer basket.
4. Place multi-level air fryer basket into the inner pot of the instant pot.
5. Secure pot with air fryer lid, select dehydrate mode then cook at 160 F for 3 hours.

Nutritional Value (Amount per Serving):
- Calories 258
- Fat 9.5 g
- Carbohydrates 7.3 g
- Sugar 5.4 g
- Protein 33 g
- Cholesterol 62 mg

Dehydrated Tofu Jerky

Preparation Time: 10 minutes
Cooking Time: 4 hours
Serve: 4
Ingredients:
- 1 block tofu, pressed
- 1 tbsp sriracha
- 3 drops liquid smoke
- 1 tbsp Worcestershire sauce

Directions:
1. Line multi-level air fryer basket with parchment paper.
2. Cut tofu in half then cut into the slices.
3. Add all ingredients into the zip-lock bag, seal bag, and place in the refrigerator overnight.
4. Arrange tofu slices into the multi-level air fryer basket.
5. Place multi-level air fryer basket into the inner pot of the instant pot.
6. Secure pot with air fryer lid, select dehydrate mode then cook at 145 F for 4 hours.

Nutritional Value (Amount per Serving):
- Calories 23
- Fat 1 g
- Carbohydrates 1.9 g
- Sugar 0.9 g
- Protein 1.9 g
- Cholesterol 0 mg

Dehydrated Kiwi

Preparation Time: 10 minutes
Cooking Time: 12 hours
Serve: 4
Ingredients:
- 2 kiwis, peeled & cut into 1/4-inch thick slices

Directions:
1. Line multi-level air fryer basket with parchment paper.
2. Arrange kiwi slices into the multi-level air fryer basket.
3. Place multi-level air fryer basket into the inner pot of the instant pot.
4. Secure pot with air fryer lid, select dehydrate mode then cook at 135 F for 12 hours.

Nutritional Value (Amount per Serving):
- Calories 23
- Fat 0.2 g
- Carbohydrates 5.6 g

- Sugar 3.4 g
- Protein 0.4 g
- Cholesterol 0 mg

Dehydrated Asian Beef Jerky

Preparation Time: 10 minutes
Cooking Time: 4 hours
Serve: 4
Ingredients:
- 1 lb London broil, sliced thinly
- 1/2 tsp onion powder
- 1 1/2 tbsp brown sugar
- 1 1/2 tbsp soy sauce
- 1/2 tsp sesame oil
- 1/4 tsp garlic powder

Directions:
1. Line multi-level air fryer basket with parchment paper.
2. Add all ingredients into the zip-lock bag, seal bag, and place in the refrigerator overnight.
3. Arrange marinated meat slices into the multi-level air fryer basket.
4. Place multi-level air fryer basket into the inner pot of the instant pot.
5. Secure pot with air fryer lid, select dehydrate mode then cook at 160 F for 4 hours.

Nutritional Value (Amount per Serving):
- Calories 66
- Fat 2.3 g
- Carbohydrates 4.7 g
- Sugar 3.5 g
- Protein 6.7 g
- Cholesterol 0 mg

Dehydrated Chickpeas

Preparation Time: 10 minutes
Cooking Time: 10 hours
Serve: 4
Ingredients:
- 10 oz can chickpeas, drained and rinsed

Directions:
1. Line multi-level air fryer basket with parchment paper.
2. Spread chickpeas into the multi-level air fryer basket.
3. Place multi-level air fryer basket into the inner pot of the instant pot.
4. Secure pot with air fryer lid, select dehydrate mode then cook at 135 F for 10 hours.

Nutritional Value (Amount per Serving):
- Calories 84
- Fat 0.8 g
- Carbohydrates 16 g
- Sugar 0 g
- Protein 3.5 g
- Cholesterol 0 mg

Dehydrated Pineapple Pieces

Preparation Time: 10 minutes
Cooking Time: 12 hours
Serve: 2
Ingredients:
- 1 cup pineapple chunks

Directions:
1. Line multi-level air fryer basket with parchment paper.
2. Arrange pineapple chunks into the multi-level air fryer basket.
3. Place multi-level air fryer basket into the inner pot of the instant pot.
4. Secure pot with air fryer lid, select dehydrate mode then cook at 135 F for 12 hours.

Nutritional Value (Amount per Serving):
- Calories 41
- Fat 0.1 g
- Carbohydrates 10.8 g
- Sugar 8.1 g
- Protein 0.4 g
- Cholesterol 0 mg

Dehydrated Summer Squash

Preparation Time: 10 minutes
Cooking Time: 10 hours
Serve: 2
Ingredients:
- 1 yellow summer squash, sliced thinly

Directions:
1. Line multi-level air fryer basket with parchment paper.
2. Arrange squash slices into the multi-level air fryer basket.
3. Place multi-level air fryer basket into the inner pot of the instant pot.
4. Secure pot with air fryer lid, select dehydrate mode then cook at 115 F for 10 hours.

Nutritional Value (Amount per Serving):
- Calories 10
- Fat 0 g
- Carbohydrates 2 g
- Sugar 0.5 g
- Protein 0.5 g
- Cholesterol 0 mg

Dehydrated Eggplant Bacon

Preparation Time: 10 minutes
Cooking Time: 4 hours
Serve: 4
Ingredients:
- 1 medium eggplant, cut into the 1/4-inch thick slices
- 1 1/2 tsp smoked paprika
- 1/4 tsp onion powder
- 1/4 tsp garlic powder

Directions:
1. Line multi-level air fryer basket with parchment paper.

2. Toss eggplant slices with onion powder, garlic powder, and paprika in a bowl.
3. Arrange eggplant slices into the multi-level air fryer basket.
4. Place multi-level air fryer basket into the inner pot of the instant pot.
5. Secure pot with air fryer lid, select dehydrate mode then cook at 145 F for 4 hours.

Nutritional Value (Amount per Serving):
- Calories 32
- Fat 0.3 g
- Carbohydrates 7.4 g
- Sugar 3.6 g
- Protein 1.3 g
- Cholesterol 0 mg

Dehydrated Shredded Carrots

Preparation Time: 10 minutes
Cooking Time: 10 hours
Serve: 4

Ingredients:
- 10 oz shredded carrots

Directions:
1. Line multi-level air fryer basket with parchment paper.
2. Spread shredded carrots into the multi-level air fryer basket.
3. Place multi-level air fryer basket into the inner pot of the instant pot.
4. Secure pot with air fryer lid, select dehydrate mode then cook at 125 F for 10 hours.

Nutritional Value (Amount per Serving):
- Calories 29
- Fat 0 g
- Carbohydrates 7 g
- Sugar 3.5 g
- Protein 0.6 g
- Cholesterol 0 mg

Dehydrated Tomatoes

Preparation Time: 10 minutes
Cooking Time: 6 hours
Serve: 2

Ingredients:
- 1 cup cherry tomatoes, cut in half
- 1/2 tbsp olive oil
- 1/2 tsp Italian seasoning
- 1/4 tsp salt

Directions:
1. Line multi-level air fryer basket with parchment paper.
2. In a bowl, toss tomatoes with Italian seasoning, oil, and salt.
3. Arrange tomatoes cut side up into the multi-level air fryer basket.
4. Place multi-level air fryer basket into the inner pot of the instant pot.
5. Secure pot with air fryer lid, select dehydrate mode then cook at 135 F for 6 hours.

Nutritional Value (Amount per Serving):
- Calories 50
- Fat 4 g
- Carbohydrates 3.6 g
- Sugar 2.5 g
- Protein 0.8 g
- Cholesterol 1 mg

Dehydrated Okra

Preparation Time: 10 minutes
Cooking Time: 12 hours
Serve: 2

Ingredients:
- 5 pods okra, slice into rounds

Directions:
1. Line multi-level air fryer basket with parchment paper.
2. Arrange okra slices into the multi-level air fryer basket.
3. Place multi-level air fryer basket into the inner pot of the instant pot.
4. Secure pot with air fryer lid, select dehydrate mode then cook at 130 F for 12 hours.

Nutritional Value (Amount per Serving):
- Calories 45
- Fat 0.5 g
- Carbohydrates 9 g
- Sugar 4.8 g
- Protein 3.8 g
- Cholesterol 0 mg

Dehydrated Pear

Preparation Time: 10 minutes
Cooking Time: 4 hours
Serve: 2

Ingredients:
- 1 pear, cut into 1/4-inch thick slices

Directions:
1. Line multi-level air fryer basket with parchment paper.
2. Arrange pear slices into the multi-level air fryer basket.
3. Place multi-level air fryer basket into the inner pot of the instant pot.
4. Secure pot with air fryer lid, select dehydrate mode then cook at 160 F for 4 hours.

Nutritional Value (Amount per Serving):
- Calories 40
- Fat 0.1 g
- Carbohydrates 10.6 g
- Sugar 6.8 g
- Protein 0.3 g
- Cholesterol 0 mg

Dehydrated Lemon

Preparation Time: 10 minutes
Cooking Time: 10 hours
Serve: 4

Ingredients:
- 3 lemons, cut into 1/4-inch thick slices

Directions:
1. Line multi-level air fryer basket with parchment paper.
2. Arrange lemon slices into the multi-level air fryer basket.
3. Place multi-level air fryer basket into the inner pot of the instant pot.
4. Secure pot with air fryer lid, select dehydrate mode then cook at 125 F for 10 hours.

Nutritional Value (Amount per Serving):
- Calories 13
- Fat 0.1 g
- Carbohydrates 4.1 g
- Sugar 1.1 g
- Protein 0.5 g
- Cholesterol 0 mg

Dehydrated Mushroom

Preparation Time: 10 minutes
Cooking Time: 4 hours
Serve: 4

Ingredients:
- 1 cup mushrooms, clean and cut into 1/8-inch thick slices

Directions:
1. Line multi-level air fryer basket with parchment paper.
2. Arrange mushroom slices into the multi-level air fryer basket.
3. Place multi-level air fryer basket into the inner pot of the instant pot.
4. Secure pot with air fryer lid, select dehydrate mode then cook at 160 F for 4 hours.

Nutritional Value (Amount per Serving):
- Calories 4
- Fat 0.1 g
- Carbohydrates 0.6 g
- Sugar 0.3 g
- Protein 0.6 g
- Cholesterol 0 mg

Dehydrated Snap Peas

Preparation Time: 10 minutes
Cooking Time: 4 hours
Serve: 2

Ingredients:
- 1 cups snap peas

Directions:
1. Line multi-level air fryer basket with parchment paper.
2. Arrange snap peas into the multi-level air fryer basket.
3. Place multi-level air fryer basket into the inner pot of the instant pot.
4. Secure pot with air fryer lid, select dehydrate mode then cook at 135 F for 4 hours.

Nutritional Value (Amount per Serving):
- Calories 59
- Fat 0.3 g
- Carbohydrates 10.5 g
- Sugar 4.1 g
- Protein 3.9 g
- Cholesterol 0 mg

Dehydrated Avocado

Preparation Time: 10 minutes
Cooking Time: 5 hours
Serve: 2

Ingredients:
- 2 avocados, halved and pitted
- 1/2 lemon juice
- 1/4 tsp sea salt

Directions:
1. Line multi-level air fryer basket with parchment paper.
2. Cut avocado into the slices.
3. Drizzle lemon juice over avocado slices.
4. Arrange avocado slices into the multi-level air fryer basket. Season with salt.
5. Place multi-level air fryer basket into the inner pot of the instant pot.
6. Secure pot with air fryer lid, select dehydrate mode then cook at 160 F for 5 hours.

Nutritional Value (Amount per Serving):
- Calories 413
- Fat 39.3 g
- Carbohydrates 17.5 g
- Sugar 1.3 g
- Protein 3.9 g
- Cholesterol 0 mg

Dehydrated Parsnips Chips

Preparation Time: 10 minutes
Cooking Time: 5 hours
Serve: 2

Ingredients:
- 2 parsnips, peel and thinly sliced
- 1 tsp fresh lemon juice
- Salt

Directions:
1. Line multi-level air fryer basket with parchment paper.
2. In a bowl, add parsnips, lemon juice, and salt and toss well.
3. Arrange parsnips slices into the multi-level air fryer basket.
4. Place multi-level air fryer basket into the inner pot of the instant pot.
5. Secure pot with air fryer lid, select dehydrate mode then cook at 115 F for 5 hours.

Nutritional Value (Amount per Serving):
- Calories 100
- Fat 0.4 g
- Carbohydrates 24 g
- Sugar 6.4 g
- Protein 1.6 g
- Cholesterol 0 mg

Chapter 9: Desserts

Greek Blueberry Muffins

Preparation Time: 10 minutes
Cooking Time: 30 minutes
Serve: 12
Ingredients:
- 3 eggs
- 2 tsp baking powder
- 1/4 cup Swerve
- 2 1/2 cups almond flour
- 1 tsp vanilla
- 5 oz plain yogurt
- 1/2 cup fresh blueberries

Directions:
1. In a bowl, whisk together yogurt, vanilla, eggs, and salt until smooth.
2. Add almond flour, baking powder, and swerve and mix until smooth.
3. Add blueberries and stir well.
4. Pour batter into the 12 greased silicone muffin molds.
5. Place the dehydrating tray in the air fryer basket.
6. Place 6 silicone muffin molds onto the dehydrating tray.
7. Place multi-level air fryer basket into the inner pot of the instant pot.
8. Secure pot with air fryer lid, select bake mode then cook at 325 F for 30 minutes.
9. Cook remaining muffins.
10. Serve and enjoy.

Nutritional Value (Amount per Serving):
- Calories 63
- Fat 4.2 g
- Carbohydrates 3.5 g
- Sugar 1.8 g
- Protein 3.4 g
- Cholesterol 42 mg

Delicious Lemon Cupcake

Preparation Time: 10 minutes
Cooking Time: 15 minutes
Serve: 12
Ingredients:
- 2 eggs
- 1 fresh lemon juice
- 1 tsp baking powder
- 1 tbsp lemon zest
- 1/3 cup butter, melted
- 1/2 cup yogurt
- 1/4 cup coconut flour
- 1 cup almond flour
- 1/3 cup swerve

Directions:
1. Add all ingredients into the mixing bowl and mix until well combined.
2. Pour batter into the 12 greased silicone muffin molds.
3. Place the dehydrating tray in the air fryer basket.
4. Place 6 silicone muffin molds onto the dehydrating tray.
5. Place multi-level air fryer basket into the inner pot of the instant pot.
6. Secure pot with air fryer lid, select bake mode then cook at 350 F for 15 minutes.
7. Cook remaining cupcakes.
8. Serve and enjoy.

Nutritional Value (Amount per Serving):
- Calories 79
- Fat 7.2 g
- Carbohydrates 1.9 g
- Sugar 1 g
- Protein 2.1 g
- Cholesterol 41 mg

Choco Peanut Butter Muffins

Preparation Time: 10 minutes
Cooking Time: 20 minutes
Serve: 12
Ingredients:
- 1/2 cup maple syrup
- 1/2 cup cocoa powder
- 1 cup applesauce
- 1 cup peanut butter
- 1 tsp baking soda
- 1 tsp vanilla

Directions:
1. Add all ingredients into the blender and blend until smooth.
2. Pour batter into the 12 greased silicone muffin molds.
3. Place the dehydrating tray in the air fryer basket.
4. Place 6 silicone muffin molds onto the dehydrating tray.
5. Place multi-level air fryer basket into the inner pot of the instant pot.
6. Secure pot with air fryer lid, select bake mode then cook at 320 F for 20 minutes.
7. Cook remaining muffins.
8. Serve and enjoy.

Nutritional Value (Amount per Serving):
- Calories 178
- Fat 11.3 g
- Carbohydrates 17.3 g
- Sugar 12 g
- Protein 6.1 g
- Cholesterol 0 mg

Baked Apple Slices

Preparation Time: 10 minutes
Cooking Time: 25 minutes

Serve: 6
Ingredients:
- 2 apples, peel, core, and slice
- 1 tsp cinnamon
- 2 tbsp butter
- 1/4 cup of sugar
- 1/4 cup brown sugar
- 1/4 tsp salt

Directions:
1. Line multi-level air fryer basket with parchment paper.
2. Add all ingredients into the zip-lock bag, seal bag, and shake well.
3. Add apple slices into the multi-level air fryer basket.
4. Place multi-level air fryer basket into the inner pot of the instant pot.
5. Secure pot with air fryer lid, select bake mode then cook at 350 F for 25 minutes.
6. Serve and enjoy.

Nutritional Value (Amount per Serving):
- Calories 128
- Fat 4 g
- Carbohydrates 24.8 g
- Sugar 21.9 g
- Protein 0.3 g
- Cholesterol 10 mg

Chocolate Brownies Muffins

Preparation Time: 10 minutes
Cooking Time: 20 minutes
Serve: 12
Ingredients:
- 1 1/3 cups all-purpose flour
- 1/2 cup water
- 1/2 tsp vanilla
- 1/3 cup cocoa powder
- 1/2 cup butter, melted
- 1 cup of sugar
- 1/2 tsp baking powder
- 1/2 tsp salt

Directions:
1. In a large bowl, mix together flour, cocoa powder, sugar, baking powder, and salt.
2. In a small bowl, whisk together melted butter, water, and vanilla.
3. Pour oil mixture into the flour mixture and mix until well combined.
4. Pour batter into the 12 greased silicone muffin molds.
5. Place the dehydrating tray in the air fryer basket.
6. Place 6 silicone muffin molds onto the dehydrating tray.
7. Place multi-level air fryer basket into the inner pot of the instant pot.
8. Secure pot with air fryer lid, select bake mode then cook at 350 F for 20 minutes.
9. Cook remaining muffins.
10. Serve and enjoy.

Nutritional Value (Amount per Serving):
- Calories 187
- Fat 8.1 g
- Carbohydrates 28.7 g
- Sugar 16.8 g
- Protein 1.9 g
- Cholesterol 20 mg

Low-Carb Chocolate Muffins

Preparation Time: 10 minutes
Cooking Time: 15 minutes
Serve: 8
Ingredients:
- 3 eggs
- 1 cup almond flour
- 1/3 cup butter, melted
- 1/3 cup cocoa powder
- 1 tbsp gelatin
- 1/2 cup Swerve

Directions:
1. Add all ingredients into the bowl and stir until just combined.
2. Pour batter into the 8 greased silicone muffin molds.
3. Place the dehydrating tray in the air fryer basket.
4. Place 6 silicone muffin molds onto the dehydrating tray.
5. Place multi-level air fryer basket into the inner pot of the instant pot.
6. Secure pot with air fryer lid, select bake mode then cook at 350 F for 15 minutes.
7. Cook remaining muffins.
8. Serve and enjoy.

Nutritional Value (Amount per Serving):
- Calories 119
- Fat 11.5 g
- Carbohydrates 2.9 g
- Sugar 0.3 g
- Protein 3.6 g
- Cholesterol 82 mg

Moist Lemon Muffins

Preparation Time: 10 minutes
Cooking Time: 15 minutes
Serve: 6
Ingredients:
- 1 egg
- 1 cup flour
- 1/2 tsp vanilla
- 1/2 cup milk
- 2 tbsp canola oil
- 1/4 tsp baking soda
- 3/4 tsp baking powder
- 1 tsp lemon zest, grated
- 1/2 cup sugar
- 1/2 tsp salt

Directions:
1. In a bowl, whisk egg, vanilla, milk, oil, and sugar until creamy.
2. Add remaining ingredients and stir until just combined.
3. Pour batter into the 6 greased silicone muffin molds.
4. Place the dehydrating tray in the air fryer basket.
5. Place 6 silicone muffin molds onto the dehydrating tray.
6. Place multi-level air fryer basket into the inner pot of the instant pot.
7. Secure pot with air fryer lid, select bake mode then cook at 350 F for 15 minutes.
8. Serve and enjoy.

Nutritional Value (Amount per Serving):
- Calories 202
- Fat 6 g
- Carbohydrates 34 g
- Sugar 17.8 g
- Protein 3.8 g
- Cholesterol 34 mg

Healthy Carrot Muffins

Preparation Time: 10 minutes
Cooking Time: 20 minutes
Serve: 6

Ingredients:
- 1 egg
- 1 cup all-purpose flour
- 1/4 cup granulated sugar
- 1/2 tbsp canola oil
- 1 1/2 tsp baking powder
- 1/4 tsp nutmeg
- 1 tsp cinnamon
- 1/4 cup applesauce
- 3/4 cup grated carrots
- 1 tsp vanilla
- 1/4 cup light brown sugar
- 1/4 tsp salt

Directions:
1. Add all ingredients into the bowl and mix until well combined.
2. Pour batter into the 6 greased silicone muffin molds.
3. Place the dehydrating tray in the air fryer basket.
4. Place 6 silicone muffin molds onto the dehydrating tray.
5. Place multi-level air fryer basket into the inner pot of the instant pot.
6. Secure pot with air fryer lid, select bake mode then cook at 350 F for 20 minutes.
7. Serve and enjoy.

Nutritional Value (Amount per Serving):
- Calories 165
- Fat 2.2 g
- Carbohydrates 33.7 g
- Sugar 16.2 g
- Protein 3.2 g
- Cholesterol 27 mg

Baked Peaches

Preparation Time: 10 minutes
Cooking Time: 30 minutes
Serve: 4

Ingredients:
- 4 freestone peaches, cut in half and remove stones
- 2 tbsp sugar
- 8 tsp brown sugar
- 1 tsp cinnamon
- 4 tbsp butter, cut into pieces

Directions:
1. Line multi-level air fryer basket with parchment paper.
2. Place peach halves in a multi-level air fryer basket and top each half with 1 tsp brown sugar.
3. Place butter pieces on top of each peach half.
4. Mix together cinnamon and sugar and sprinkle over peaches.
5. Place multi-level air fryer basket into the inner pot of the instant pot.
6. Secure pot with air fryer lid, select bake mode then cook at 375 F for 30 minutes.
7. Serve and enjoy.

Nutritional Value (Amount per Serving):
- Calories 199
- Fat 11.5 g
- Carbohydrates 7.3 g
- Sugar 21.8 g
- Protein 1.2 g
- Cholesterol 31 mg

Delicious Banana Walnut Muffins

Preparation Time: 10 minutes
Cooking Time: 10 minutes
Serve: 4

Ingredients:
- 4 tbsp flour
- 1/4 cup banana, mashed
- 1/4 cup oats
- 1 tbsp walnuts, chopped
- 1/2 tsp baking powder
- 1/4 cup powdered sugar
- 1/4 cup butter

Directions:
1. In a bowl, mix together mashed banana, walnuts, sugar, and butter.
2. In another bowl, mix together flour, baking powder, and oats.
3. Add flour mixture to the banana mixture and mix well.
4. Pour batter into the 4 greased silicone muffin molds.

5. Place the dehydrating tray in the air fryer basket.
6. Place 4 silicone muffin molds onto the dehydrating tray.
7. Place multi-level air fryer basket into the inner pot of the instant pot.
8. Secure pot with air fryer lid, select air fry mode then cook at 320 F for 10 minutes.
9. Serve and enjoy.

Nutritional Value (Amount per Serving):
- Calories 200
- Fat 13.1 g
- Carbohydrates 19.5 g
- Sugar 8.6 g
- Protein 2.2 g
- Cholesterol 31 mg

Chocolate Lava Cake

Preparation Time: 10 minutes
Cooking Time: 8 minutes
Serve: 2

Ingredients:
- 1 egg
- 2 tbsp erythritol
- 2 tbsp water
- 2 tbsp cocoa powder
- 1/8 tsp vanilla
- 1/2 tsp baking powder
- 1 tbsp butter, melted
- 1 tbsp flax meal
- 1/8 tsp stevia

Directions:
1. Add all ingredients to the bowl and whisk well.
2. Pour batter into the 2 greased ramekins.
3. Place the dehydrating tray in the air fryer basket.
4. Place ramekins onto the dehydrating tray.
5. Place multi-level air fryer basket into the inner pot of the instant pot.
6. Secure pot with air fryer lid, select air fry mode then cook at 350 F for 8 minutes
7. Serve and enjoy.

Nutritional Value (Amount per Serving):
- Calories 111
- Fat 9.9 g
- Carbohydrates 19.8 g
- Sugar 15.3 g
- Protein 4.6 g
- Cholesterol 97 mg

Yummy Nutella Sandwich

Preparation Time: 10 minutes
Cooking Time: 7 minutes
Serve: 2

Ingredients:
- 4 bread slices
- 1 banana, cut into slices
- 1 tbsp butter, softened
- 1/4 cup Nutella

Directions:
1. Line multi-level air fryer basket with parchment paper.
2. Spread butter on one side of each bread slices and place butter side down.
3. Spread Nutella on another side of each bread slices.
4. Place banana slices on 2 bread slices and top with remaining bread slices.
5. Place sandwiches into the multi-level air fryer basket.
6. Place multi-level air fryer basket into the inner pot of the instant pot.
7. Secure pot with air fryer lid, select air fry mode then cook at 370 F for 7 minutes. Flip sandwiches after 5 minutes.
8. Serve and enjoy.

Nutritional Value (Amount per Serving):
- Calories 176
- Fat 7.9 g
- Carbohydrates 25.5 g
- Sugar 10.5 g
- Protein 2.3 g
- Cholesterol 15 mg

Sweet Pineapple Wedges

Preparation Time: 10 minutes
Cooking Time: 10 minutes
Serve: 2

Ingredients:
- 1/2 small pineapple, peeled, cored, and cut into wedges
- 1/4 cup brown sugar
- 1 1/2 tbsp butter, melted

Directions:
1. Line multi-level air fryer basket with parchment paper.
2. Brush pineapple wedges with butter and sprinkle with brown sugar.
3. Place pineapple wedges into the multi-level air fryer basket.
4. Place multi-level air fryer basket into the inner pot of the instant pot.
5. Secure pot with air fryer lid, select air fry mode then cook at 400 F for 10 minutes.
6. Serve and enjoy.

Nutritional Value (Amount per Serving):
- Calories 166
- Fat 8.7 g
- Carbohydrates 23.2 g
- Sugar 21.7 g
- Protein 0.3 g
- Cholesterol 23 mg

Quick Choco Mug Cake

Preparation Time: 10 minutes
Cooking Time: 10 minutes

Serve: 2
Ingredients:
- 1/2 cup self-raising flour
- 6 tsp butter, melted
- 6 tbsp milk
- 2 tbsp cocoa powder
- 10 tbsp caster sugar

Directions:
1. Add all ingredients to the bowl and mix until well combined.
2. Pour mixture into the 2 greased ramekins.
3. Place the dehydrating tray in the air fryer basket.
4. Place ramekins onto the dehydrating tray.
5. Place multi-level air fryer basket into the inner pot of the instant pot.
6. Secure pot with air fryer lid, select air fry mode then cook at 390 F for 10 minutes.
7. Serve and enjoy.

Nutritional Value (Amount per Serving):
- Calories 475
- Fat 13.4 g
- Carbohydrates 89.1 g
- Sugar 62.3 g
- Protein 5.8 g
- Cholesterol 34 mg

Cinnamon Pineapple Slices

Preparation Time: 10 minutes
Cooking Time: 20 minutes
Serve: 4
Ingredients:
- 4 pineapple slices
- 1/2 cup brown sugar
- 1 tsp cinnamon

Directions:
1. Line multi-level air fryer basket with parchment paper.
2. Add cinnamon, pineapple slices, and brown sugar in a zip-lock bag, seal bag, and place in the refrigerator for 30 minutes.
3. Place pineapple slices into the multi-level air fryer basket.
4. Place multi-level air fryer basket into the inner pot of the instant pot.
5. Secure pot with air fryer lid, select air fry mode then cook at 350 F for 20 minutes. Flip halfway through.
6. Serve and enjoy.

Nutritional Value (Amount per Serving):
- Calories 152
- Fat 0.2 g
- Carbohydrates 39.9 g
- Sugar 33.9 g
- Protein 0.9 g
- Cholesterol 0 mg

Coconut Sunbutter Brownie Bites

Preparation Time: 10 minutes
Cooking Time: 10 minutes
Serve: 4
Ingredients:
- 1 egg, lightly beaten
- 1/2 tsp vanilla
- 1/4 cup maple syrup
- 1/2 cup sunbutter
- 2 tbsp coconut flour
- 2 tbsp cocoa powder

Directions:
1. In a bowl, combine together sunbutter, egg, vanilla, and maple syrup.
2. Add coconut flour and cocoa powder and stir to combine.
3. Pour batter into the 4 greased silicone muffin molds.
4. Place the dehydrating tray in the air fryer basket.
5. Place 4 silicone muffin molds onto the dehydrating tray.
6. Place multi-level air fryer basket into the inner pot of the instant pot.
7. Secure pot with air fryer lid, select bake mode then cook at 350 F for 10 minutes.
8. Serve and enjoy.

Nutritional Value (Amount per Serving):
- Calories 192
- Fat 5.6 g
- Carbohydrates 31.3 g
- Sugar 14.9 g
- Protein 4.7 g
- Cholesterol 41 mg

Zucchini Coconut Muffins

Preparation Time: 10 minutes
Cooking Time: 20 minutes
Serve: 6
Ingredients:
- 2 eggs, lightly beaten
- 1 medium zucchini, shredded and squeeze out all liquid
- 1/4 cup milk
- 1/4 cup maple syrup
- 1 cup sunbutter
- 1/4 cup coconut flour
- 1/2 cup cocoa powder

Directions:
1. In a large bowl, combine together sunbutter, milk, eggs, and maple syrup.
2. Add coconut flour, zucchini, and cocoa powder and stir to combine.
3. Pour batter into the 6 greased silicone muffin molds.
4. Place the dehydrating tray in the air fryer basket.
5. Place 6 silicone muffin molds onto the dehydrating tray.
6. Place multi-level air fryer basket into the inner pot of the instant pot.

7. Secure pot with air fryer lid, select bake mode then cook at 350 F for 20 minutes.
8. Serve and enjoy.

Nutritional Value (Amount per Serving):
- Calories 351
- Fat 24.1 g
- Carbohydrates 24.1 g
- Sugar 13.1 g
- Protein 13.3 g
- Cholesterol 55 mg

Easy Chocolate Cookies

Preparation Time: 10 minutes
Cooking Time: 10 minutes
Serve: 5

Ingredients:
- 1 tbsp chocolate protein powder
- 1/2 cup almond flour
- 1/2 cup sunflower seed butter

Directions:
1. Line multi-level air fryer basket with parchment paper.
2. In a large bowl, add all ingredients and mix until combined.
3. Make small balls from mixture and place into the multi-level air fryer basket.
4. Place multi-level air fryer basket into the inner pot of the instant pot.
5. Secure pot with air fryer lid, select air fry mode then cook at 350 F for 10 minutes.
6. Serve and enjoy.

Nutritional Value (Amount per Serving):
- Calories 234
- Fat 18.1 g
- Carbohydrates 10.2 g
- Sugar 0.8 g
- Protein 11.4 g
- Cholesterol 8 mg

Healthy Nut Cookies

Preparation Time: 15 minutes
Cooking Time: 20 minutes
Serve: 8

Ingredients:
- 1/2 cup pecans
- 1/4 cup Swerve
- 2 1/2 coconut flour
- 1/2 cup almond flour
- 1/4 cup butter
- 1/2 tsp vanilla
- 1 tsp gelatin

Directions:
1. Line multi-level air fryer basket with parchment paper.
2. Add butter, vanilla, gelatin, swerve, coconut flour, and almond flour into the food processor and process until crumbs form.
3. Add pecans and process until chopped.
4. Make 8 cookies from the prepared mixture and place it into the multi-level air fryer basket.
5. Place multi-level air fryer basket into the inner pot of the instant pot.
6. Secure pot with air fryer lid, select bake mode then cook at 350 F for 20 minutes.
7. Serve and enjoy.

Nutritional Value (Amount per Serving):
- Calories 106
- Fat 9.8 g
- Carbohydrates 3.6 g
- Sugar 0.5 g
- Protein 2.1 g
- Cholesterol 15 mg

Peanut Butter Cookies

Preparation Time: 10 minutes
Cooking Time: 15 minutes
Serve: 16

Ingredients:
- 1 egg
- 1 cup peanut butter
- 1 tsp vanilla
- 1/2 cup Swerve

Directions:
1. Line multi-level air fryer basket with parchment paper.
2. Add all ingredients into the large bowl and mix until well combined.
3. Make cookies from mixture and place half of the cookies into the multi-level air fryer basket.
4. Place multi-level air fryer basket into the inner pot of the instant pot.
5. Secure pot with air fryer lid, select bake mode then cook at 350 F for 15 minutes.
6. Cook remaining cookies.
7. Serve and enjoy.

Nutritional Value (Amount per Serving):
- Calories 100
- Fat 8.4 g
- Carbohydrates 3.3 g
- Sugar 1.6 g
- Protein 4.4 g
- Cholesterol 10 mg

Pumpkin Cookies

Preparation Time: 10 minutes
Cooking Time: 20 minutes
Serve: 24

Ingredients:
- 1 egg
- 1/2 cup pumpkin puree
- 2 cups almond flour
- 1/2 tsp baking powder
- 1/2 tsp pumpkin pie spice
- 1 tsp vanilla
- 1/2 cup butter
- 1 tsp liquid stevia

Directions:
1. Line multi-level air fryer basket with parchment paper.
2. Add all ingredients into the large bowl and mix until well combined.
3. Make cookies from the mixture and place 6 cookies into the multi-level air fryer basket.
4. Place multi-level air fryer basket into the inner pot of the instant pot.
5. Secure pot with air fryer lid, select bake mode then cook at 300 F for 20 minutes.
6. Cook remaining cookies.
7. Serve and enjoy.

Nutritional Value (Amount per Serving):
- Calories 52
- Fat 5.2 g
- Carbohydrates 1 g
- Sugar 0.3 g
- Protein 0.8 g
- Cholesterol 17 mg

Hazelnut Cookies

Preparation Time: 10 minutes
Cooking Time: 10 minutes
Serve: 6

Ingredients:
- 3 tbsp butter, softened
- 2 1/2 tbsp erythritol
- 1/4 cup almond flour
- 6 tbsp hazelnut flour
- 10 drops liquid stevia

Directions:
1. Line multi-level air fryer basket with parchment paper.
2. Add all ingredients into the large bowl and mix until well combined.
3. Make small balls from mixture and place into the multi-level air fryer basket.
4. Place multi-level air fryer basket into the inner pot of the instant pot.
5. Secure pot with air fryer lid, select bake mode then cook at 350 F for 10 minutes.
6. Serve and enjoy.

Nutritional Value (Amount per Serving):
- Calories 103
- Fat 10.6 g
- Carbohydrates 7.8 g
- Sugar 6.5 g
- Protein 1.3 g
- Cholesterol 15 mg

Delicious Gingersnap Cookies

Preparation Time: 10 minutes
Cooking Time: 10 minutes
Serve: 6

Ingredients:
- 1 egg
- 1/2 tsp ground ginger
- 1 tsp baking powder
- 3/4 cup erythritol
- 2/4 cup butter, melted
- 1 1/2 cups almond flour
- 1/2 tsp vanilla
- 1/8 tsp ground cloves
- 1/4 tsp ground nutmeg
- 1/4 tsp ground cinnamon
- Pinch of salt

Directions:
1. Line multi-level air fryer basket with parchment paper.
2. Add all ingredients into the large bowl and mix until well combined.
3. Cover mixture and place in the fridge for 30 minutes.
4. Make cookies from mixture and place into the multi-level air fryer basket.
5. Place multi-level air fryer basket into the inner pot of the instant pot.
6. Secure pot with air fryer lid, select bake mode then cook at 350 F for 10-15 minutes.
7. Serve and enjoy.

Nutritional Value (Amount per Serving):
- Calories 189
- Fat 19.6 g
- Carbohydrates 32.3 g
- Sugar 30.4 g
- Protein 2.6 g
- Cholesterol 68 mg

Almond Cookies

Preparation Time: 10 minutes
Cooking Time: 10 minutes
Serve: 5

Ingredients:
- 1/2 cup almond flour
- 2 tbsp butter, softened
- 1/2 tsp vanilla
- 2 tbsp erythritol
- Pinch of salt

Directions:
1. Line multi-level air fryer basket with parchment paper.
2. Add all ingredients into the large bowl and mix until well combined.
3. Make cookies from mixture and place into the multi-level air fryer basket.
4. Place multi-level air fryer basket into the inner pot of the instant pot.
5. Secure pot with air fryer lid, select bake mode then cook at 350 F for 10 minutes.
6. Serve and enjoy.

Nutritional Value (Amount per Serving):
- Calories 58
- Fat 6 g
- Carbohydrates 6.7 g
- Sugar 6.2 g
- Protein 0.7 g
- Cholesterol 12 mg

Cranberry Orange Cupcakes

Preparation Time: 10 minutes
Cooking Time: 20 minutes
Serve: 8
Ingredients:
- 4 eggs
- 1 tsp orange zest
- 2 tsp mixed spice
- 2 tsp cinnamon
- 1/4 cup erythritol
- 1 cup butter, softened
- 2/3 cup dried cranberries
- 1 1/2 cups almond flour
- 1 tsp vanilla

Directions:
1. In a bowl, add sweetener and melted butter and beat until fluffy.
2. Add cinnamon, vanilla, and mixed spice and stir well.
3. Add egg one by one and stir until well combined.
4. Add almond flour, orange zest, and cranberries and mix until well combined.
5. Pour batter into the 8 greased silicone muffin molds.
6. Place the dehydrating tray in the air fryer basket.
7. Place 6 silicone muffin molds onto the dehydrating tray.
8. Place multi-level air fryer basket into the inner pot of the instant pot.
9. Secure pot with air fryer lid, select bake mode then cook at 350 F for 20 minutes.
10. Cook remaining cupcakes.
11. Serve and enjoy.

Nutritional Value (Amount per Serving):
- Calories 273
- Fat 27.9 g
- Carbohydrates 10.3 g
- Sugar 8.3 g
- Protein 4.2 g
- Cholesterol 143 mg

Vanilla Butter Cupcakes

Preparation Time: 10 minutes
Cooking Time: 35 minutes
Serve: 12
Ingredients:
- 5 eggs
- 1 cup Swerve
- 4 oz cream cheese, softened
- 1 tsp vanilla
- 1 tsp orange extract
- 1 tsp baking powder
- 6 oz almond flour
- 1/2 cup butter, softened

Directions:
1. Add all ingredients into the mixing bowl and whisk until batter is fluffy.
2. Pour batter into the 12 greased silicone muffin molds.
3. Place the dehydrating tray in the air fryer basket.
4. Place 6 silicone muffin molds onto the dehydrating tray.
5. Place multi-level air fryer basket into the inner pot of the instant pot.
6. Secure pot with air fryer lid, select bake mode then cook at 350 F for 35 minutes.
7. Cook remaining cupcakes.
8. Serve and enjoy.

Nutritional Value (Amount per Serving):
- Calories 210
- Fat 19.8 g
- Carbohydrates 3.9 g
- Sugar 0.8 g
- Protein 6.1 g
- Cholesterol 99 mg

Choco Chip Pumpkin Muffins

Preparation Time: 10 minutes
Cooking Time: 30 minutes
Serve: 12
Ingredients:
- 2 eggs
- 2 cups all-purpose flour
- 1/2 cup chocolate chips
- 1 cup can pumpkin
- 1 tsp baking soda
- 1/2 cup olive oil
- 1 tsp pumpkin pie spice
- 1/2 cup maple syrup

Directions:
1. In a large bowl, mix together pumpkin pie spice, flour, baking soda, and salt.
2. In a separate bowl, whisk together eggs, pumpkin puree, oil, and maple syrup.
3. Slowly add dry mixture to the wet mixture and mix well.
4. Add chocolate chips and fold well.
5. Pour batter into the 12 greased silicone muffin molds.
6. Place the dehydrating tray in the air fryer basket.
7. Place 6 silicone muffin molds onto the dehydrating tray.
8. Place multi-level air fryer basket into the inner pot of the instant pot.
9. Secure pot with air fryer lid, select bake mode then cook at 350 F for 30 minutes.
10. Cook remaining muffins.
11. Serve and enjoy.

Nutritional Value (Amount per Serving):
- Calories 237
- Fat 11.5 g
- Carbohydrates 30.7 g

- Sugar 12.2 g
- Protein 3.8 g
- Cholesterol 29 mg

Brownies Cupcake

Preparation Time: 10 minutes
Cooking Time: 30 minutes
Serve: 12
Ingredients:
- 3 large eggs
- 2 tsp vanilla
- 1/2 cup brown sugar
- 1 1/2 cup granulated sugar
- 4 oz dark chocolate, chopped
- 3/4 cup butter
- 1 1/2 cups chocolate chunk
- 1 cup all-purpose flour
- 1 cup of cocoa powder
- 1 tsp salt

Directions:
1. Add 2 oz dark chocolate and butter in a microwave-safe bowl and microwave for 30 seconds. Stir well.
2. Transfer chocolate and butter mixture in a bowl and whisk until smooth.
3. Add eggs, vanilla, and sugar and whisk well.
4. Add cocoa powder, chocolate chunks, flour, remaining dark chocolate, and salt and fold well.
5. Pour batter into the 12 greased silicone muffin molds.
6. Place the dehydrating tray in the air fryer basket.
7. Place 6 silicone muffin molds onto the dehydrating tray.
8. Place multi-level air fryer basket into the inner pot of the instant pot.
9. Secure pot with air fryer lid, select bake mode then cook at 350 F for 30 minutes.
10. Cook remaining cupcakes.
11. Serve and enjoy.

Nutritional Value (Amount per Serving):
- Calories 362
- Fat 17.6 g
- Carbohydrates 51.6 g
- Sugar 36.1 g
- Protein 5 g
- Cholesterol 80 mg

Chocolate Banana Muffins

Preparation Time: 10 minutes
Cooking Time: 20 minutes
Serve: 4
Ingredients:
- 1/2 cup almond butter
- 1 cup bananas
- 2 tbsp cocoa powder
- 1 scoop protein powder

Directions:
1. Add all ingredients into the blender and blend until smooth.
2. Pour batter into the 4 greased silicone muffin molds.
3. Place the dehydrating tray in the air fryer basket.
4. Place 4 silicone muffin molds onto the dehydrating tray.
5. Place multi-level air fryer basket into the inner pot of the instant pot.
6. Secure pot with air fryer lid, select bake mode then cook at 350 F for 20 minutes.
7. Serve and enjoy.

Nutritional Value (Amount per Serving):
- Calories 82
- Fat 2.1 g
- Carbohydrates 11.4 g
- Sugar 5 g
- Protein 6.9 g
- Cholesterol 16 mg

Lemon Cinnamon Apple Slices

Preparation Time: 10 minutes
Cooking Time: 20 minutes
Serve: 6
Ingredients:
- 5 large sweet apples, cut into 1/4-inch thick slices
- 2 tbsp fresh lemon juice
- 2 tsp cinnamon

Directions:
1. Line multi-level air fryer basket with parchment paper.
2. Add all ingredients to the bowl and toss well.
3. Transfer apple slices into the multi-level air fryer basket.
4. Place multi-level air fryer basket into the inner pot of the instant pot.
5. Secure pot with air fryer lid, select bake mode then cook at 350 F for 20 minutes.
6. Serve and enjoy.

Nutritional Value (Amount per Serving):
- Calories 100
- Fat 0.4 g
- Carbohydrates 26.4 g
- Sugar 19.5 g
- Protein 0.6 g
- Cholesterol 0 mg

Strawberry Muffins

Preparation Time: 10 minutes
Cooking Time: 20 minutes
Serve: 12
Ingredients:
- 3 eggs
- 2/3 cup strawberries, diced
- 1/3 cup heavy cream
- 1 tsp vanilla

- 2 1/2 cups almond flour
- 1/2 cup Swerve
- 5 tbsp butter, melted
- 1 tsp cinnamon
- 2 tsp baking powder
- 1/4 tsp Himalayan salt

Directions:
1. In a bowl, beat together butter and swerve. Add eggs, cream, and vanilla and beat until frothy.
2. Sift together flour, baking powder, cinnamon, and salt.
3. Add almond flour mixture to the wet ingredients and mix until combined.
4. Add strawberries and fold well.
5. Pour batter into the 12 greased silicone muffin molds.
6. Place the dehydrating tray in the air fryer basket.
7. Place 6 silicone muffin molds onto the dehydrating tray.
8. Place multi-level air fryer basket into the inner pot of the instant pot.
9. Secure pot with air fryer lid, select bake mode then cook at 350 F for 20 minutes.
10. Cook remaining muffins.
11. Serve and enjoy.

Nutritional Value (Amount per Serving):
- Calories 108
- Fat 10.1 g
- Carbohydrates 2.7 g
- Sugar 0.7 g
- Protein 2.8 g
- Cholesterol 58 mg

Cream Cheese Muffins

Preparation Time: 10 minutes
Cooking Time: 20 minutes
Serve: 5

Ingredients:
- 1 egg
- 4 oz cream cheese
- 1/2 tsp ground cinnamon
- 1/2 tsp vanilla
- 1/4 cup Swerve

Directions:
1. In a bowl, mix together cream cheese, vanilla, Swerve, and eggs until soft.
2. Pour batter into the 5 greased silicone muffin molds. Sprinkle cinnamon on top.
3. Place the dehydrating tray in the air fryer basket.
4. Place 5 silicone muffin molds onto the dehydrating tray.
5. Place multi-level air fryer basket into the inner pot of the instant pot.
6. Secure pot with air fryer lid, select bake mode then cook at 350 F for 20 minutes.
7. Serve and enjoy.

Nutritional Value (Amount per Serving):
- Calories 94
- Fat 8.8 g
- Carbohydrates 1 g
- Sugar 0.2 g
- Protein 2.8 g
- Cholesterol 58 mg

Easy Lemon Cheese Muffins

Preparation Time: 10 minutes
Cooking Time: 14 minutes
Serve: 12

Ingredients:
- 3 eggs
- 1 tsp lemon extract
- 1/4 cup heavy cream
- 4 true lemon packets
- 2 tbsp poppy seeds
- 1 tsp baking powder
- 1/3 cup Swerve
- 1/4 cup coconut oil
- 1/4 cup ricotta cheese
- 1 cup almond flour

Directions:
1. Add all ingredients into the large mixing bowl and beat until fluffy.
2. Pour batter into the 12 greased silicone muffin molds.
3. Place the dehydrating tray in the air fryer basket.
4. Place 6 silicone muffin molds onto the dehydrating tray.
5. Place multi-level air fryer basket into the inner pot of the instant pot.
6. Secure pot with air fryer lid, select bake mode then cook at 320 F for 14 minutes.
7. Cook remaining muffins.
8. Serve and enjoy.

Nutritional Value (Amount per Serving):
- Calories 93
- Fat 8.8 g
- Carbohydrates 1.6 g
- Sugar 0.4 g
- Protein 2.8 g
- Cholesterol 46 mg

Chocolate Walnut Cupcakes

Preparation Time: 10 minutes
Cooking Time: 35 minutes
Serve: 6

Ingredients:
- 2 eggs
- 1 tsp vanilla
- 1/4 cup cocoa powder
- 1/2 cup butter, melted
- 1/2 cup walnuts, chopped
- 1/4 cup all-purpose flour
- 1 cup brown sugar
- Pinch of salt

Directions:
1. In a bowl, whisk together butter, cocoa powder, eggs, and vanilla.
2. Stir in walnuts, flour, sugar, and salt.
3. Pour batter into the 6 greased silicone muffin molds.
4. Place the dehydrating tray in the air fryer basket.
5. Place 6 silicone muffin molds onto the dehydrating tray.
6. Place multi-level air fryer basket into the inner pot of the instant pot.
7. Secure pot with air fryer lid, select bake mode then cook at 320 F for 35 minutes.
8. Serve and enjoy.

Nutritional Value (Amount per Serving):
- Calories 342
- Fat 23.5 g
- Carbohydrates 30.9 g
- Sugar 23.8 g
- Protein 5.7 g
- Cholesterol 95 mg

Cinnamon Cranberry Cupcakes

Preparation Time: 10 minutes
Cooking Time: 30 minutes
Serve: 6

Ingredients:
- 2 eggs
- 1/4 tsp cinnamon
- 1 tsp baking powder
- 1/2 cup cranberries
- 1 tsp vanilla
- 1/4 cup sour cream
- 1/4 cup Swerve
- 1 1/2 cups almond flour

Directions:
1. In a bowl, beat sour cream, vanilla, and eggs.
2. Add remaining ingredients except for cranberries and beat until smooth.
3. Add cranberries and fold well.
4. Pour batter into the 6 greased silicone muffin molds.
5. Place the dehydrating tray in the air fryer basket.
6. Place 6 silicone muffin molds onto the dehydrating tray.
7. Place multi-level air fryer basket into the inner pot of the instant pot.
8. Secure pot with air fryer lid, select bake mode then cook at 325 F for 25-30 minutes.
9. Serve and enjoy.

Nutritional Value (Amount per Serving):
- Calories 90
- Fat 7 g
- Carbohydrates 3.5 g
- Sugar 0.8 g
- Protein 3.7 g
- Cholesterol 59 mg

Simple Blueberry Cupcakes

Preparation Time: 10 minutes
Cooking Time: 45 minutes
Serve: 12

Ingredients:
- 1 egg
- 2 cups all-purpose flour
- 2 tsp baking powder
- 1/3 cup sugar
- 2 cups blueberries
- 1/2 cup butter, melted
- 1/2 cup milk
- Pinch of salt

Directions:
1. In a large bowl, mix together all-purpose flour, baking powder, sugar, and salt.
2. In a separate bowl, whisk egg, butter, and milk.
3. Add flour mixture into the egg mixture and mix until well combined.
4. Pour batter into the 12 greased silicone muffin molds.
5. Place the dehydrating tray in the air fryer basket.
6. Place 6 silicone muffin molds onto the dehydrating tray.
7. Place multi-level air fryer basket into the inner pot of the instant pot.
8. Secure pot with air fryer lid, select bake mode then cook at 350 F for 45 minutes.
9. Cook remaining cupcakes.
10. Serve and enjoy.

Nutritional Value (Amount per Serving):
- Calories 189
- Fat 8.5 g
- Carbohydrates 25.9 g
- Sugar 8.5 g
- Protein 3.2 g
- Cholesterol 35 mg

Chocolate Chip Cookies

Preparation Time: 10 minutes
Cooking Time: 10 minutes
Serve: 6

Ingredients:
- 1 tbsp egg, beaten
- 1/4 tsp vanilla
- 2 tbsp granulated sugar
- 2 tbsp brown sugar
- 2 tbsp butter.
- 1/4 cup chocolate chips
- 1/4 tsp baking soda
- 1/4 cup all-purpose flour

Directions:
1. Line multi-level air fryer basket with parchment paper.
2. In a bowl, cream together butter, sugar, and brown sugar using a fork.

3. Add baking soda, flour, vanilla, and egg and mix until well combined.
4. Add chocolate chips and fold well.
5. Make small cookies from mixture and place into the multi-level air fryer basket.
6. Place multi-level air fryer basket into the inner pot of the instant pot.
7. Secure pot with air fryer lid, select bake mode then cook at 375 F for 10 minutes.
8. Serve and enjoy.

Nutritional Value (Amount per Serving):
- Calories 121
- Fat 6.2 g
- Carbohydrates 15.1 g
- Sugar 10.6 g
- Protein 1.4 g
- Cholesterol 21 mg

Cinnamon Pumpkin Pie

Preparation Time: 10 minutes
Cooking Time: 25 minutes
Serve: 2

Ingredients:
- 1/2 cup can pumpkin puree
- 1 tsp cornstarch
- 1/4 cup granulated sugar
- 2 tbsp milk
- 3 tbsp heavy cream
- 1/2 tsp vanilla
- 1/2 tsp ground cinnamon

Directions:
1. In a saucepan, whisk together pumpkin puree, cinnamon, cornstarch, sugar, milk, and heavy cream. Bring to boil.
2. Boil pumpkin mixture until thickens, about 2 minutes.
3. Remove saucepan from heat. Add vanilla and stir well.
4. Pour mixture into the 2 greased ramekins.
5. Place the dehydrating tray in the air fryer basket.
6. Place 2 ramekins onto the dehydrating tray.
7. Place multi-level air fryer basket into the inner pot of the instant pot.
8. Secure pot with air fryer lid, select bake mode then cook at 350 F for 25 minutes.
9. Serve and enjoy.

Nutritional Value (Amount per Serving):
- Calories 199
- Fat 8.7 g
- Carbohydrates 30.7 g
- Sugar 26.9 g
- Protein 1.2 g
- Cholesterol 32 mg

Easy Nutella Cupcakes

Preparation Time: 10 minutes
Cooking Time: 30 minutes
Serve: 12

Ingredients:
- 2 eggs
- 1/2 cup all-purpose flour
- 1 1/2 cup Nutella

Directions:
1. Add all ingredients into the mixing bowl and mix until well combined.
2. Pour batter into the 12 greased silicone muffin molds.
3. Place the dehydrating tray in the air fryer basket.
4. Place 6 silicone muffin molds onto the dehydrating tray.
5. Place multi-level air fryer basket into the inner pot of the instant pot.
6. Secure pot with air fryer lid, select bake mode then cook at 350 F for 30 minutes.
7. Cook remaining cupcakes.
8. Serve and enjoy.

Nutritional Value (Amount per Serving):
- Calories 54
- Fat 2.2 g
- Carbohydrates 6.9 g
- Sugar 2.6 g
- Protein 1.7 g
- Cholesterol 27 mg

Flour-Less Banana Muffins

Preparation Time: 10 minutes
Cooking Time: 20 minutes
Serve: 4

Ingredients:
- 1 cup overripe bananas
- 1/2 cup almond butter, melted
- 1 scoop protein powder
- 2 tbsp cocoa powder

Directions:
1. Add all ingredients into the blender and blend until smooth.
2. Pour batter into the 4 greased silicone muffin molds.
3. Place the dehydrating tray in the air fryer basket.
4. Place 4 silicone muffin molds onto the dehydrating tray.
5. Place multi-level air fryer basket into the inner pot of the instant pot.
6. Secure pot with air fryer lid, select bake mode then cook at 350 F for 20 minutes.
7. Serve and enjoy.

Nutritional Value (Amount per Serving):
- Calories 82
- Fat 2.1 g
- Carbohydrates 11.4 g
- Sugar 5 g
- Protein 6.9 g
- Cholesterol 16 mg

Fudgy Brownie Bites

Preparation Time: 10 minutes
Cooking Time: 45 minutes
Serve: 8
Ingredients:
- 3 eggs
- 2/3 cup all-purpose flour
- 2 tsp vanilla
- 2 cups granulated sugar
- 1 cup butter, melted
- 1 tsp vanilla
- 3/4 tsp baking powder
- 2/3 cup cocoa powder
- 3/4 tsp salt

Directions:
1. In a large bowl, whisk sugar, butter, and vanilla. Add eggs and whisk well.
2. In a separate bowl, mix together flour, baking powder, cocoa powder, and salt.
3. Add flour mixture into the sugar mixture and stir until well combined.
4. Pour batter into the 8 greased silicone muffin molds.
5. Place the dehydrating tray in the air fryer basket.
6. Place 6 silicone muffin molds onto the dehydrating tray.
7. Place multi-level air fryer basket into the inner pot of the instant pot.
8. Secure pot with air fryer lid, select bake mode then cook at 350 F for 45 minutes.
9. Cook remaining brownie bites.
10. Serve and enjoy.

Nutritional Value (Amount per Serving):
- Calories 473
- Fat 25.7 g
- Carbohydrates 62.5 g
- Sugar 50.5 g
- Protein 4.7 g
- Cholesterol 122 mg

Butter Cookies

Preparation Time: 10 minutes
Cooking Time: 10 minutes
Serve: 36
Ingredients:
- 1 egg
- 2 cups flour
- 2 tsp baking soda
- 1 1/4 cups brown sugar
- 1 1/2 sticks butter
- ½ tsp vanilla
- 1/2 tsp salt

Directions:
1. Line multi-level air fryer basket with parchment paper.
2. In a bowl, mix together flour, baking soda, and salt.
3. In a another bowl, beat butter, vanilla, and sugar using a hand mixer until smooth. Add egg and beat well.
4. Slowly add flour mixture and beat until just mixed.
5. Make cookies from the mixture.
6. Place 8 cookies into the multi-level air fryer basket.
7. Place multi-level air fryer basket into the inner pot of the instant pot.
8. Secure pot with air fryer lid, select bake mode then cook at 375 F for 10 minutes.
9. Cook remaining cookies.
10. Serve and enjoy.

Nutritional Value (Amount per Serving):
- Calories 80
- Fat 4 g
- Carbohydrates 10.3 g
- Sugar 4.9 g
- Protein 0.9 g
- Cholesterol 15 mg

Blonde Brownie Bites

Preparation Time: 10 minutes
Cooking Time: 20 minutes
Serve: 16
Ingredients:
- 2 eggs
- 1 1/4 cup brown sugar
- 1 cup butter, melted
- 2 cups flour
- 2 tsp baking powder
- 2 tsp vanilla
- 1/2 tsp salt

Directions:
1. In a medium bowl, mix together butter and brown sugar.
2. Add eggs and vanilla and mix well.
3. Add flour, baking powder, and salt and mix until just combined.
4. Pour batter into the 16 greased silicone muffin molds.
5. Place the dehydrating tray in the air fryer basket.
6. Place 6 silicone muffin molds onto the dehydrating tray.
7. Place multi-level air fryer basket into the inner pot of the instant pot.
8. Secure pot with air fryer lid, select bake mode then cook at 350 F for 20 minutes.
9. Cook remaining brownie bites.
10. Serve and enjoy.

Nutritional Value (Amount per Serving):
- Calories 212
- Fat 12.2 g
- Carbohydrates 23.5 g
- Sugar 11.2 g
- Protein 2.4 g
- Cholesterol 51 mg

Choco Chip Brownie Bites

Preparation Time: 10 minutes
Cooking Time: 20 minutes
Serve: 2
Ingredients:
- 1 egg
- 1/2 cup sugar
- 1 tbsp cocoa powder
- 1/2 cup semisweet chocolate chips
- 1/4 cup butter
- 1/4 cup all-purpose flour
- 1 tsp vanilla
- 1/4 tsp salt

Directions:
1. Melt butter and chocolate chips in a saucepan.
2. Remove saucepan from heat and whisk in sugar, cocoa powder, and salt.
3. Whisk in vanilla and egg. Add flour and stir well.
4. Pour batter into the 2 greased ramekins.
5. Place the dehydrating tray in the air fryer basket.
6. Place 2 ramekins onto the dehydrating tray.
7. Place multi-level air fryer basket into the inner pot of the instant pot.
8. Secure pot with air fryer lid, select bake mode then cook at 350 F for 20 minutes.
9. Serve and enjoy.

Nutritional Value (Amount per Serving):
- Calories 631
- Fat 34.7 g
- Carbohydrates 83.9 g
- Sugar 66.6 g
- Protein 7.1 g
- Cholesterol 143 mg

Chocolate Almond Butter Muffins

Preparation Time: 10 minutes
Cooking Time: 20 minutes
Serve: 12
Ingredients:
- 1 cup almond butter
- 1 cup applesauce
- 1/2 cup maple syrup
- 1/2 cup dark cocoa powder
- 1 tsp baking soda
- 1 tsp vanilla

Directions:
1. Add all ingredients into the blender and blend until smooth.
2. Pour batter into the 12 greased silicone muffin molds.
3. Place the dehydrating tray in the air fryer basket.
4. Place 6 silicone muffin molds onto the dehydrating tray.
5. Place multi-level air fryer basket into the inner pot of the instant pot.
6. Secure pot with air fryer lid, select bake mode then cook at 350 F for 20 minutes.
7. Cook remaining muffins.
8. Serve and enjoy.

Nutritional Value (Amount per Serving):
- Calories 61
- Fat 1.2 g
- Carbohydrates 13.9 g
- Sugar 10 g
- Protein 1.1 g
- Cholesterol 0 mg

Coffee Cupcakes

Preparation Time: 10 minutes
Cooking Time: 35 minutes
Serve: 12
Ingredients:
- 2 eggs
- 1 tbsp baking powder
- 2 1/2 cups almond flour
- 1 cup sour cream
- 1/2 cup Swerve
- 1/2 cup butter, softened
- 1/4 tsp nutmeg
- 1/2 tsp xanthan gum
- 1/2 tsp baking soda

Directions:
1. In a mixing bowl, beat butter and sweetener until smooth. Add eggs and beat well.
2. Add sour cream and mix well. Add nutmeg, xanthan gum, baking soda, baking powder, and almond flour and blend well.
3. Pour batter into the 12 greased silicone muffin molds.
4. Place the dehydrating tray in the air fryer basket.
5. Place 6 silicone muffin molds onto the dehydrating tray.
6. Place multi-level air fryer basket into the inner pot of the instant pot.
7. Secure pot with air fryer lid, select bake mode then cook at 350 F for 35 minutes.
8. Cook remaining cupcakes.
9. Serve and enjoy.

Nutritional Value (Amount per Serving):
- Calories 154
- Fat 15.4 g
- Carbohydrates 2.8 g
- Sugar 0.3 g
- Protein 2.9 g
- Cholesterol 56 mg

Zucchini Muffins

Preparation Time: 10 minutes
Cooking Time: 25 minutes
Serve: 8
Ingredients:

- 6 eggs
- 1 cup zucchini, grated
- 3/4 cup almond flour
- 1/4 tsp ground nutmeg
- 1/2 tsp baking soda
- 4 drops liquid stevia
- 1/4 cup Swerve
- 1/3 cup butter, melted

Directions:
1. Add all ingredients except zucchini in a bowl and mix well.
2. Add zucchini and stir well.
3. Pour batter into the 8 greased silicone muffin molds.
4. Place the dehydrating tray in the air fryer basket.
5. Place 6 silicone muffin molds onto the dehydrating tray.
6. Place multi-level air fryer basket into the inner pot of the instant pot.
7. Secure pot with air fryer lid, select bake mode then cook at 350 F for 25 minutes.
8. Cook remaining muffins.
9. Serve and enjoy.

Nutritional Value (Amount per Serving):
- Calories 133
- Fat 12.3 g
- Carbohydrates 1.4 g
- Sugar 0.6 g
- Protein 5 g
- Cholesterol 143 mg

Walnut Cookies

Preparation Time: 10 minutes
Cooking Time: 18 minutes
Serve: 18
Ingredients:
- 1 egg
- 2 cups almond flour
- 3/4 tsp ground cardamom
- 2 tbsp coconut flour
- 1 cup walnuts, finely chopped
- 1/2 cup Swerve
- 1 tsp vanilla
- 1/2 cup butter, softened
- Pinch of salt

Directions:
1. Line multi-level air fryer basket with parchment paper.
2. In a mixing bowl, whisk together almond flour, cardamom, coconut flour, and walnuts.
3. In a separate bowl, beat butter and sweetener until fluffy. Add egg and vanilla and beat for 1 minute.
4. Add almond mixture and beat until dough forms.
5. Make cookies from the mixture and place half cookies into the multi-level air fryer basket.
6. Place multi-level air fryer basket into the inner pot of the instant pot.
7. Secure pot with air fryer lid, select bake mode then cook at 325 F for 18 minutes.
8. Cook remaining cookies.
9. Serve and enjoy.

Nutritional Value (Amount per Serving):
- Calories 117
- Fat 11.2 g
- Carbohydrates 2.4 g
- Sugar 0.4 g
- Protein 2.9 g
- Cholesterol 23 mg

Cappuccino Muffins

Preparation Time: 10 minutes
Cooking Time: 25 minutes
Serve: 6
Ingredients:
- 2 eggs
- 1/2 tsp espresso powder
- 1/2 tsp cinnamon
- 1 tsp baking powder
- 1/8 cup coconut flour
- 1/4 cup sour cream
- 1/4 cup Swerve
- 1 cup almond flour
- 1/2 tsp vanilla
- 1/8 tsp salt

Directions:
1. Add sour cream, vanilla, espresso powder, and eggs in a blender and blend until smooth.
2. Add almond flour, cinnamon, baking powder, coconut flour, sweetener, and salt and blend to combine.
3. Pour batter into the 6 greased silicone muffin molds.
4. Place the dehydrating tray in the air fryer basket.
5. Place 6 silicone muffin molds onto the dehydrating tray.
6. Place multi-level air fryer basket into the inner pot of the instant pot.
7. Secure pot with air fryer lid, select bake mode then cook at 350 F for 25 minutes.
8. Serve and enjoy.

Nutritional Value (Amount per Serving):
- Calories 72
- Fat 5.8 g
- Carbohydrates 2.4 g
- Sugar 0.4 g
- Protein 3.2 g
- Cholesterol 59 mg

Chocolate Macaroon

Preparation Time: 10 minutes
Cooking Time: 20 minutes
Serve: 10
Ingredients:

- 1 egg
- 1/8 cup coconut oil
- 1/4 tsp baking powder
- 1/8 cup cocoa powder
- 1 1/2 tbsp coconut flour
- 1/2 cup almond flour
- 2 1/2 tbsp shredded coconut
- 2 1/2 erythritol
- 1/2 tsp vanilla
- Pinch of salt

Directions:
1. Line multi-level air fryer basket with parchment paper.
2. Add all ingredients into the bowl and mix until well combined.
3. Make small balls from mixture and place into the multi-level air fryer basket.
4. Place multi-level air fryer basket into the inner pot of the instant pot.
5. Secure pot with air fryer lid, select bake mode then cook at 350 F for 15-20 minutes.
6. Serve and enjoy.

Nutritional Value (Amount per Serving):
- Calories 50
- Fat 4.5 g
- Carbohydrates 3.2 g
- Sugar 1.5 g
- Protein 1.2 g
- Cholesterol 16 mg

Chapter 10: 30-Day Meal Plan

Day 1
Breakfast- Delicious Breakfast Potatoes
Lunch- Juicy Chicken Breasts
Dinner-Juicy & Tender Pork Chops
Day 2
Breakfast- Breakfast French Toast Sticks
Lunch- Quick & Healthy Salmon
Dinner-Dijon Maple Pork Chops
Day 3
Breakfast- Classic Cheese Sandwich
Lunch- Easy & Tasty Parmesan Chicken
Dinner-Simple Spiced Pork Chops
Day 4
Breakfast- Breakfast Potato Hash
Lunch- Crispy White Fish Fillets
Dinner-Quick & Simple Pork Chops
Day 5
Breakfast-Egg Stuffed Peppers
Lunch- Delicious Lemon Chicken
Dinner-Pork Chops with Sauce
Day 6
Breakfast- Baked Oatmeal
Lunch- Perfect Air Fryer Salmon
Dinner-Perfect Air Fry Pork Chops
Day 7
Breakfast- Healthy Banana Muffins
Lunch- Flavorful Chicken Breast
Dinner-Herb Seasoned Pork Chops
Day 8
Breakfast- Healthy Quinoa Egg Muffins
Lunch- Simple Garlic Butter Salmon
Dinner-Delicious Mini Meatloaf
Day 9
Breakfast- Broccoli Breakfast Muffins
Lunch- Perfect Air Fry Chicken Breast
Dinner-Tasty & Juicy Steak
Day 10
Breakfast- Italian Egg Muffins
Lunch- Herbed Salmon
Dinner-Air Fry Steak Bites
Day 11
Breakfast- Spinach Ham Egg Muffins
Lunch- Chicken with Vegetables
Dinner-Steak Bites with Potatoes
Day 12
Breakfast- Pumpkin Pie Muffins
Lunch- Air Fryer Cod
Dinner-Beef with Veggies
Day 13
Breakfast- Broccoli Bacon Egg Muffins
Lunch- Perfect Chicken Thighs
Dinner-Juicy & Tender Lamb Chops
Day 14
Breakfast- Delicious Frittata Muffins
Lunch- Honey Glazed Fish Fillets
Dinner-Herb Pork Chops
Day 15
Breakfast- Kale Egg Muffins
Lunch- Spicy Hassel-back Chicken
Dinner-Classic Lamb Chops

Day 16
Breakfast- Delicious Breakfast Potatoes
Lunch- Juicy Chicken Breasts
Dinner-Juicy & Tender Pork Chops
Day 17
Breakfast- Breakfast French Toast Sticks
Lunch- Quick & Healthy Salmon
Dinner-Dijon Maple Pork Chops
Day 18
Breakfast- Classic Cheese Sandwich
Lunch- Easy & Tasty Parmesan Chicken
Dinner-Simple Spiced Pork Chops
Day 19
Breakfast- Breakfast Potato Hash
Lunch- Crispy White Fish Fillets
Dinner-Quick & Simple Pork Chops
Day 20
Breakfast-Egg Stuffed Peppers
Lunch- Delicious Lemon Chicken
Dinner-Pork Chops with Sauce
Day 21
Breakfast- Baked Oatmeal
Lunch- Perfect Air Fryer Salmon
Dinner-Perfect Air Fry Pork Chops
Day 22
Breakfast- Healthy Banana Muffins
Lunch- Flavorful Chicken Breast
Dinner-Herb Seasoned Pork Chops
Day 23
Breakfast- Healthy Quinoa Egg Muffins
Lunch- Simple Garlic Butter Salmon
Dinner-Delicious Mini Meatloaf
Day 24
Breakfast- Broccoli Breakfast Muffins
Lunch- Perfect Air Fry Chicken Breast
Dinner-Tasty & Juicy Steak
Day 25
Breakfast- Italian Egg Muffins
Lunch- Herbed Salmon
Dinner-Air Fry Steak Bites
Day 26
Breakfast- Spinach Ham Egg Muffins
Lunch- Chicken with Vegetables
Dinner-Steak Bites with Potatoes
Day 27
Breakfast- Pumpkin Pie Muffins
Lunch- Air Fryer Cod
Dinner-Beef with Veggies
Day 28
Breakfast- Broccoli Bacon Egg Muffins
Lunch- Perfect Chicken Thighs
Dinner-Juicy & Tender Lamb Chops
Day 29
Breakfast- Delicious Frittata Muffins
Lunch- Honey Glazed Fish Fillets
Dinner-Herb Pork Chops
Day 30
Breakfast- Kale Egg Muffins
Lunch- Spicy Hassel-back Chicken
Dinner-Classic Lamb Chops

Appendix : Recipes Index

A
- Air Fried Okra 80
- Air Fry Bell Peppers 79
- Air Fry Chicken Livers 33
- Air Fry Corn 75
- Air Fry Green Beans 80
- Air Fry Mix Vegetables 86
- Air Fry Nuts 92
- Air Fry Scallops 67
- Air Fry Steak Bites 46
- Air Fry Tilapia 68
- Air Fry Vegetables 100
- Air Fryer Cod 59
- Almond Cookies 128
- Almond Flour Breakfast Biscuits 12
- Asian Chicken Breast 32
- Asian Chicken Thighs 34
- Asian Pork Ribs 43

B
- Bagel Seasoned Brussels Sprouts 85
- Bagel Seasoned Fish Fillets 71
- Baked Apple Slices 122
- Baked Fish Fillet with Pepper 64
- Baked Halibut Fillets 72
- Baked Oatmeal 13
- Baked Peaches 124
- Baked Pork Chops 45
- Balsamic Vegetables 90
- Basil Mahi Mahi 72
- Basil Pork Loin 55
- Beef Burger Patties 98
- Beef Skewers 48
- Beef with Veggies 47
- Beef Zucchini Burgers 51
- Best Baked Chicken Drumsticks 35
- Blackened Fish Fillets 72
- Blonde Brownie Bites 134
- Blue Cheese Jalapeno Poppers 107
- Blueberry Breakfast Muffins 24
- Breaded Cod 60
- Breakfast Bagels 11
- Breakfast French Toast Sticks 10
- Breakfast Potato Hash 12
- Breakfast Quiche Cups 23
- Breakfast Sausage Balls 15
- Breakfast Sausage Balls 19
- Breakfast Sausage Patties 18
- Broccoli & Brussels Sprouts 87
- Broccoli Bacon Egg Muffins 17
- Broccoli Breakfast Muffins 14
- Broccoli Fritters 78
- Broccoli Patties 96
- Brownies Cupcake 130
- Butter Cookies 134

C
- Cajun Chicken Breasts 39
- Cajun Fish Fillets 66
- Cajun Pork Chops 55
- Cajun Sausage 12
- Cajun Shrimp 62
- Cajun Zucchini Chips 102
- Cappuccino Muffins 136
- Cauliflower Hummus 91
- Cauliflower Tomato Roast 78
- Cheddar Cheese Sausage Biscuits 15
- Cheddar Kale Egg Cups 20
- Cheese Cracker Crust Pork Chops 52
- Cheese Crust Salmon 71
- Cheese Garlic Chicken Wings 26
- Cheese Garlic Shrimp 65
- Cheese Herb Cod 65
- Cheese Mustard Pork Chops 42
- Cheese Paprika Cod 72
- Cheesy Baked Tilapia 70
- Cheesy Beef Patties 53
- Cheesy Carrot Fries 104
- Cheesy Cauliflower and Broccoli 95
- Cheesy Cauliflower Bites 105
- Cheesy Egg Muffins 14
- Cheesy Veggie Fritters 74
- Cheesy Zucchini Eggplant 88
- Cheesy Zucchini Fries 98
- Chicken with Vegetables 28
- Chickpea Zucchini Patties 83
- Chili Honey Salmon 64
- Chili Lime Sweet Potatoes 82
- Choco Chip Brownie Bites 135
- Choco Chip Pumpkin Muffins 129
- Choco Peanut Butter Muffins 122
- Chocolate Almond Butter Muffins 135
- Chocolate Banana Muffins 130
- Chocolate Brownies Muffins 123
- Chocolate Chip Cookies 132
- Chocolate Lava Cake 125
- Chocolate Macaroon 136
- Chocolate Walnut Cupcakes 131
- Cinnamon Butternut Squash 89
- Cinnamon Cranberry Cupcakes 132
- Cinnamon Lamb Chops 52
- Cinnamon Pineapple Slices 126
- Cinnamon Pumpkin Pie 133
- Cinnamon Sweet Potato Muffins 21
- Citrusy Salmon 69
- Classic Cheese Sandwich 10
- Classic Lamb Chops 50
- Coconut Sunbutter Brownie Bites 126
- Coffee Cupcakes 135
- Cranberry Orange Cupcakes 129
- Cream Cheese Muffins 131
- Cream Cheese Stuff Mushrooms 97
- Cripsy Pork Belly Bites 44
- Crispy Chicken Drumsticks 31
- Crispy Crusted Pork Chops 43
- Crispy Green Beans 81
- Crispy Onion Rings 103
- Crispy Pork Chops 52
- Crispy Tofu 92
- Crispy White Fish Fillets 57

Crunchy Chickpeas 91
Crunchy Pork Belly Crack 44

D

Dehydrated Almonds 111
Dehydrated Apple Chips 112
Dehydrated Asian Beef Jerky 119
Dehydrated Asian Salmon Jerky 117
Dehydrated Avocado 121
Dehydrated Bananas 113
Dehydrated Beef Jerky 115
Dehydrated Beet 114
Dehydrated Bell Peppers 110
Dehydrated Broccoli Chips 109
Dehydrated Brussels Sprouts 108
Dehydrated Carrot 116
Dehydrated Carrots 109
Dehydrated Cauliflower Popcorn 109
Dehydrated Chicken Jerky 116
Dehydrated Chickpeas 119
Dehydrated Cucumber Slices 114
Dehydrated Dragon Fruit 116
Dehydrated Eggplant 114
Dehydrated Eggplant Bacon 119
Dehydrated Eggplant Slices 108
Dehydrated Flank Steak Jerky 115
Dehydrated Green Apple Slices 112
Dehydrated Green Beans 115
Dehydrated Kale Chips 110
Dehydrated Kiwi 110
Dehydrated Kiwi 118
Dehydrated Lamb Jerky 117
Dehydrated Lemon 120
Dehydrated Mango 112
Dehydrated Mango 113
Dehydrated Mexican Pork Jerky 117
Dehydrated Mushroom 121
Dehydrated Okra 120
Dehydrated Orange 117
Dehydrated Parsnips 115
Dehydrated Parsnips Chips 121
Dehydrated Peach 113
Dehydrated Pear 120
Dehydrated Pecans 110
Dehydrated Pineapple Pieces 119
Dehydrated Pineapple Slices 111
Dehydrated Pork Jerky 113
Dehydrated Raspberries 111
Dehydrated Salmon Jerky 116
Dehydrated Shredded Carrots 120
Dehydrated Snap Peas 121
Dehydrated Spicy Almonds 112
Dehydrated Spicy Beef Jerky 118
Dehydrated Squash Chips 109
Dehydrated Strawberries 111
Dehydrated Summer Squash 119
Dehydrated Sweet Potato Chips 110
Dehydrated Teriyaki Beef Jerky 118
Dehydrated Tofu Jerky 118
Dehydrated Tomato 114
Dehydrated Tomatoes 120
Dehydrated Turkey Jerky 114
Dehydrated Zucchini Chips 108
Dehydrated Zucchini Chips 108
Delicious & Moist Pork Chops 43
Delicious Air Fry Prawns 65
Delicious Bagel Chicken Tenders 29
Delicious Banana Muffins 24
Delicious Banana Walnut Muffins 124
Delicious Beef Kebabs 54
Delicious Blackened Shrimp 66
Delicious Breakfast Potatoes 10
Delicious Crab Cakes 58
Delicious Fish Sticks 70
Delicious Frittata Muffins 18
Delicious Gingersnap Cookies 128
Delicious Jalapeno Poppers 94
Delicious Lemon Chicken 27
Delicious Lemon Cupcake 122
Delicious Lemon Pepper Chicken Thighs 33
Delicious Lemon Pepper Shrimp 61
Delicious Mini Meatloaf 45
Delicious Sriracha Chicken Wings 38
Delicious Tuna Patties 63
Delicious Turkey Nuggets 38
Delicious Zucchini Chips 99
Dijon Crab Cakes 60
Dijon Maple Pork Chops 40

E

Easy & Tasty Parmesan Chicken 26
Easy Apple Chips 98
Easy BBQ Chicken Legs 30
Easy Beef Patties 48
Easy Breakfast Biscuits 10
Easy Cauliflower Popcorn 105
Easy Chicken Nuggets 37
Easy Chocolate Cookies 127
Easy Cinnamon Cashews 106
Easy Green Beans 86
Easy Lemon Cheese Muffins 131
Easy Lemon Garlic Shrimp 70
Easy Mustard Pork Chops 56
Easy Nutella Cupcakes 133
Easy Ranch Chicken Wings 36
Easy Ranch Zucchini Chips 99
Easy Roasted Broccoli 79
Easy Shrimp Scampi 69
Easy Tuna Cakes 57
Easy Turkey Patties 38
Egg Stuffed Peppers 13
Eggplant Fries 101
Flavorful Chicken & Potatoes 39
Flavorful Chicken Breast 27
Flavorful Green Beans 95
Flavorful Marinated Fish Fillets 64
Flavorful Okra 86
Flavorful Ranch Potatoes 77
Flavors Beef Strips 56
Flavors Chicken Wings 37
Flavors Jalapeno Poppers 106
Flavors Rosemary Thyme Lamb Chops 50

Flour-Less Banana Muffins 133
Fudgy Brownie Bites 133

G

Garlic Tomato Shrimp 62
Garlicky Baby Potatoes 80
Ginger Garlic Chicken Thighs 32
Ginger Garlic Chicken Thighs 39
Greek Blueberry Muffins 122
Greek Fish Fillets 65
Greek Ribeye Steak 44
Green Beans & Potatoes 85

H

Hazelnut Cookies 128
Healthy Air Fry Mushrooms 82
Healthy Artichoke Hearts 89
Healthy Banana Muffins 13
Healthy Beetroot Chips 100
Healthy Carrot Muffins 124
Healthy Chicken Drumsticks 30
Healthy Chicken Vegetable Patties 36
Healthy Coconut Shrimp 58
Healthy Egg Stuffed Avocado 13
Healthy Kale Chips 103
Healthy Kale Muffins 23
Healthy Nut Cookies 127
Healthy Oatmeal Cups 22
Healthy Pork Patties 49
Healthy Quinoa Egg Muffins 14
Healthy Ratatouille 89
Healthy Roasted Asparagus 78
Healthy Roasted Nuts 96
Healthy Root Vegetables 90
Healthy Salmon Patties 60
Herb Mushrooms 74
Herb Pork Chops 50
Herb Seasoned Pork Chops 42
Herbed Salmon 59
Homemade Breakfast Sausage 16
Honey Cinnamon Potato Bites 92
Honey Dijon Chicken 35
Honey Garlic Pork Chops 54
Honey Ginger Pork Shoulder 55
Honey Glazed Fish Fillets 60

I

Italian Egg Muffins 16

J

Jalapeno Cheese Biscuits 15
Jerk Chicken 37
Juicy & Tender Lamb Chops 50
Juicy & Tender Pork Chops 40
Juicy Chicken Breasts 26
Juicy Ranch Pork Chops 42
Juicy Turkey Legs 34

K

Kale Egg Muffins 20

L

Lemon Cinnamon Apple Slices 130
Lemon Garlic Brussels Sprouts 74
Lemon Pepper Chicken Breasts 31
Lemon Pepper Tilapia 63

Low-Carb Chocolate Muffins 123

M

Maple Chickpeas 94
Marinated Pork Chops 44
Marinated Steak Fajitas 47
Meatballs 100
Meatballs 100
Meatballs 101
Meatballs 34
Meatballs 46
Meatballs 48
Meatballs 49
Meatballs 49
Meatballs 51
Meatballs 52
Meatballs 53
Meatballs 53
Meatballs 54
Meatballs 97
Mediterranean Fish Fillet 69
Mesquite Seasoned Pork Chops 40
Mexican Chicken 31
Mexican Steak Fajitas 46
Miso White Fish Fillets 68
Moist Lemon Muffins 123

O

Oat Cinnamon Muffins 23
Oats Raspberry Muffins 20
Old Bay Seasoned Cauliflower Florets 84
Old Bay Shrimp 61
Onion Pork Chops 51

P

Paprika Eggplant Chips 106
Parmesan Chicken Tenders 29
Parmesan Shrimp 57
Peanut Butter Cookies 127
Pecan Crust Halibut Fillets 71
Perfect Air Fry Chicken Breast 28
Perfect Air Fry Pork Chops 42
Perfect Air Fryer Salmon 58
Perfect Baked Pork Chops 45
Perfect Broccoli Tater Tots 21
Perfect Chicken Thighs 28
Perfect Egg Bites 11
Perfect Juicy Chicken Drumsticks 31
Perfectly Tender Chicken Breast 30
Pesto Fish Fillets 69
Pizza Egg Muffins 17
Pork Belly Strips 55
Pork Chops with Sauce 41
Pork Sausage Balls 41
Pork Tenderloin 54
Potato Beans & Mushrooms 88
Potato Patties 74
Pumpkin Cookies 127
Pumpkin Pie Muffins 17

Q

Quick & Healthy Salmon 57
Quick & Simple Pork Chops 41
Quick BBQ Chicken Breast 30

Quick Choco Mug Cake 125
Quick Taco Shrimp 58

R

Radish Chips 101
Ranch Chicken Wings 32
Ranch Potato Wedges 98
Roasted Asparagus 76
Roasted Brussels Sprouts 84
Roasted Carrots & Potatoes 77
Roasted Carrots 87
Roasted Cauliflower & Pepper 79
Roasted Cauliflower 76
Roasted Mushrooms & Cauliflower 78
Roasted Nuts 103
Roasted Olives 97
Roasted Potatoes 76
Roasted Squash 88
Roasted Sweet Potatoes 22
Roasted Vegetables 90
Rosemary Basil Salmon 64
Rosemary Chicken Breasts 38
Rosemary Garlic Shrimp 62
Rosemary Potatoes 83

S

Savory Pecans 97
Shrimp Fajitas 61
Shrimp with Pepper & Zucchini 61
Shrimp with Sausage & Peppers 62
Shrimp with Vegetables 67
Simple & Healthy Asparagus 86
Simple & Quick Chicken Tenders 27
Simple Air Fry Cabbage 85
Simple Blueberry Cupcakes 132
Simple Crisp Bacon Slices 106
Simple Crisp Tofu 75
Simple Garlic Butter Salmon 59
Simple Spiced Pork Chops 40
Smoked Paprika Salmon 68
Soft Sweet Potato Rolls 15
Spicy & Easy Chicken Drumsticks 33
Spicy Baby Potatoes 102
Spicy Brussels Sprouts 77
Spicy Brussels Sprouts 81
Spicy Cashew Nuts 91
Spicy Cauliflower Florets 81
Spicy Chicken Wings 37
Spicy Hassel Back Chicken 29
Spicy Lemon Pepper Shrimp 63
Spicy Okra 102
Spicy Potato Fries 94
Spicy Scallops 67
Spicy Sweet Potato Fries 75
Spicy Walnuts 92
Spinach Ham Egg Muffins 16
Steak & Mushrooms 45
Steak Bites with Potatoes 47
Strawberry Muffins 130

Stuffed Mushrooms 105
Stuffed Peppers 87
Stuffed Sweet Peppers 105
Sweet Pineapple Wedges 125
Sweet Potato Chickpea Breakfast Hash 21
Sweet Potato Quinoa Patties 93
Sweet Potatoes & Brussels Sprouts 81

T

Tasty & Juicy Steak 46
Tasty BBQ Chickpeas 104
Tasty Breakfast Cookies 19
Tasty Butternut Squash 82
Tasty Cajun Chicken Thighs 35
Tasty Cajun Potato Wedges 102
Tasty Carrot Fries 93
Tasty Chicken Fajitas 28
Tasty Chicken Fritters 36
Tasty Crab Patties 68
Tasty Eggplant Cubes 80
Tasty Green Beans 89
Tasty Hassel Back Potatoes 91
Tasty Herb Mushrooms 84
Tasty Jalapeno Poppers 96
Tasty Pecan Pie Muffins 20
Tasty Pesto Scallops 71
Tasty Pork Riblets 49
Tasty Potato Chips 103
Tasty Potato Wedges 94
Tasty Roasted Olives 93
Tasty Tater Tots 12
Tasty Tuna Patties 66
Tender & Juicy Chicken Tenders 26
Tofu Bites 83
Tomato Pepper Egg Cups 25
Tomato Spinach Egg Muffins 24
Turkey Patties 18
Turkey Patties 35
Turkey Skewers 34
Turkey Stuffed Poblanos 99

V

Vanilla Butter Cupcakes 129
Vegetable Breakfast Hash 22
Vegetable Fritters 104
Vegetable Skewers 95

W

Walnut Cookies 136
White Fish Fillets 67

Y

Yummy Nutella Sandwich 125

Z

Zucchini & Squash 85
Zucchini Breakfast Cakes 19
Zucchini Cheese Burger 76
Zucchini Cheese Patties 83
Zucchini Chips 96
Zucchini Coconut Muffins 126
Zucchini Muffins 135

www.ingramcontent.com/pod-product-compliance
Lightning Source LLC
Chambersburg PA
CBHW081114080526
44587CB00021B/3585